A
DESCRIPTIVE CATALOGUE

OF THE

MUSICAL INSTRUMENTS

RECENTLY EXHIBITED AT THE

ROYAL MILITARY EXHIBITION, LONDON, 1890

A DESCRIPTIVE CATALOGUE

OF THE

MUSICAL INSTRUMENTS

RECENTLY EXHIBITED AT THE

ROYAL MILITARY EXHIBITION, LONDON, 1890.

C. R. DAY

GYAN

Published by

GYAN

Gyan Publishing House
5, Ansari Road
Daryaganj, New Delhi-110002
Phone: 011-47034999, 9811692060
E-mail: books@gyanbooks.com

Distribution Network
gyanbooks.com
India, USA, Canada, UK, Australia, France

ISBN: 978-93-6280-012-1 (PB)

First Published, 1891

2nd Impression 2023

Printed at: Gyan Press, Delhi.

A DESCRIPTIVE CATALOGUE OF THE MUSICAL INSTRUMENTS RECENTLY EXHIBITED AT THE ROYAL MILITARY EXHIBITION, LONDON, 1890

Author: C. R. DAY

A CATALOGUE

OF

MUSICAL INSTRUMENTS.

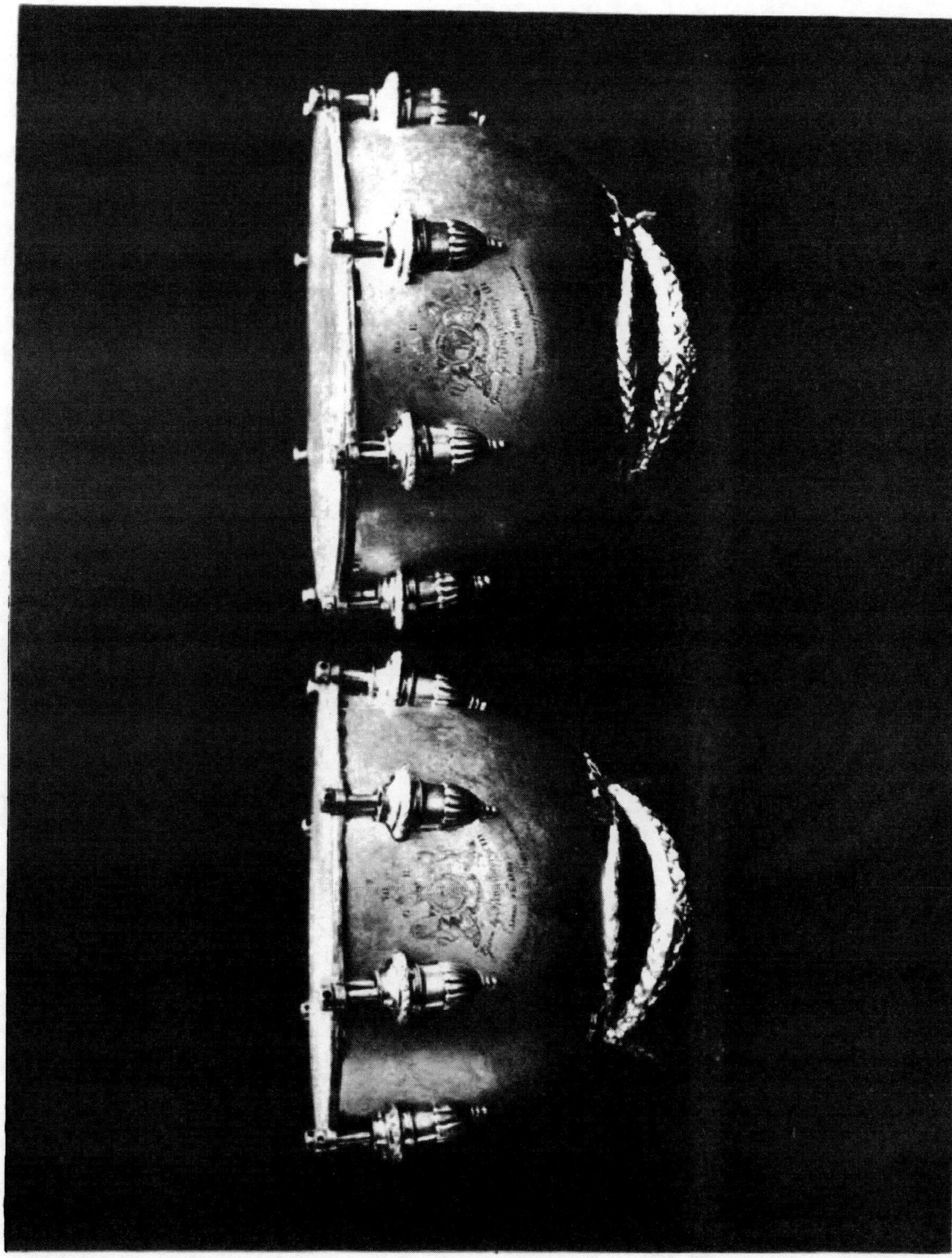

A

DESCRIPTIVE CATALOGUE

OF THE

MUSICAL INSTRUMENTS

RECENTLY EXHIBITED AT THE

ROYAL MILITARY EXHIBITION, LONDON, 1890.

Issued under the orders of COLONEL SHAW-HELLIER, Commandant Royal Military School of Music; and compiled by CAPTAIN C. R. DAY, Oxfordshire Light Infantry.

EYRE & SPOTTISWOODE,
Government and General Publishers,
LONDON—EAST HARDING STREET, FETTER LANE, E.C.

1891.

PREFACE.

WHEN the Royal Military Exhibition of last year was first promoted, I was requested by those in authority to take entire charge of the musical arrangements, and to provide for the performance of varied programmes of popular music, in the grounds of the Exhibition, during the season. As this seemed to me to offer an opportunity, probably unique, for enabling the public to judge of the capabilities of our best military bands, I thought that by introducing music of a higher class into the programmes, and by arranging for a constant succession of different military bands, brought from all parts of the United Kingdom, instead of employing some half dozen bands only, amusement for the frequenters of the Exhibition would be more amply provided for. And, in addition to this, musical critics would have the opportunity of judging of the present state of military music generally, of the requirements of a military bandmaster and of a military musician, and also of the relative merits and demerits of our present system. Accordingly, I suggested this plan, which met with the entire approval of H.R.H. the Commander-in-Chief, who issued the necessary orders to enable me to carry it out. The Exhibition remained open some five months. During these five months no less than 74 different military bands of all branches of the Service were engaged, most of these remaining in London for a week. By these means it has been possible to form a very fair idea as to the general state of military music in this country, and to gain a large amount of material knowledge as to the present system, which could not have been otherwise obtained.

As the development of military music is, like everything else in the army, rapidly progressing, it is becoming more than ever absolutely necessary that military musicians should be in accord and "touch" with the musical profession, and should have some *real* interest as regards what is occurring in the musical world; *and unless this is so, we may look in vain for any real improvement.* That the career of a military musician should offer advantages in a professional point of view must be fully recognised. And that the curriculum at Kneller Hall, *as re-constituted*, offers a sound musical education, and one which may, in its special way, be brought to compare favourably with that offered by the Royal Academy of Music, or Royal College of Music, is a point which time alone can show; and that time *will* show proof of this I venture to believe.

As there is in England, unfortunately, no Conservatoire as comprehensive as that of Paris, and no Museum of Musical Instruments in which students can see the improvements and various experimental stages through which Musical Instruments have passed, the opportunity offered last year by the Exhibition appeared most appropriate for assembling a large collection. And as the military musician has chiefly to deal with Wind Instruments, which in their present state are virtually the growth of the present century, I proposed that the collection should be principally one of Wind Instruments. The matter was fully discussed at a meeting held at the Royal Academy of Music, at which representatives of that excellent society, the Wind Instrument Chamber Music Society, and various leading musicians were present. It was accordingly decided that the aim of the collection should be to set forth the gradual history and development of Wind Instruments from the earliest times *to the most recent improvements of the day*; a point which appears of the greatest importance, and cannot be overrated. Thanks to the cordial co-operation of Dr. Mackenzie, Principal of the Royal Academy of Music, of M. Gevaert and M. Mahillon, of the Brussels *Conservatoire*, and various other gentlemen distinguished in the musical world, the collection became a *fait accompli*, and was thrown open to the public in June last.

As there is no text book in English in which the theory and construction of Wind Instruments is treated of, it seemed that a technical Catalogue designed upon the lines of that now issued would be a book of interest, and would also supply a want felt generally among students, too many of whom are, unfortunately, ignorant of anything further than the mere fingering of their instruments.

Unfortunately, the death of Mr. Charles Cousins, the Director of Music at Kneller Hall, which occurred in May last, caused my time to be occupied almost entirely with the affairs of the School of Music, much extra work falling of necessity upon my shoulders. I was therefore unable to devote as much time as I could have wished to the preparation of this Catalogue, and was compelled to place the matter, subject to my supervision, in the hands of Captain C. R. Day, an officer whose services had, on account of his musical knowledge, been placed, specially, at my disposal by H.R.H. the Commander-in-Chief, and whose skill and intelligence more than realised my most sanguine expectations. Certain considerations, over which I had no control, prevented the publication of this Catalogue before; but as they are now happily removed, the work is issued with the hope that it may prove of interest and permanent value.

To those gentlemen, and to those firms of Musical Instrument makers, who have so generously assisted us in carrying out this work, I desire to convey my fullest thanks, both for their disinterested help, and for the kindness and courtesy with which they have met us upon all occasions. The names of these gentlemen, and the nature of their assistance, are more fully explained in a note of Captain Day's, which I requested him to draw up, and which I therefore judge better to give at length below.

T. B. SHAW-HELLIER, *Colonel*,
Commandant, Royal Military School of Music.

NOTE.—In the compilation of this Catalogue much valuable assistance has been received from various gentlemen, many of whom, at considerable personal inconvenience, unselfishly gave up valuable time and devoted themselves to minute examination of the instruments described in the following pages. I wish especially to thank Mr. RICHARD ROCKSTRO, who very kindly undertook the whole of Section II., relating to Flutes, and who not only furnished the necessary details and "copy," but contributed the admirable prefatory Essay to that Section, revising and seeing all through the press. Especial thanks are also due to the Rev. F. W. GALPIN, F.L.S., for his energy and labour in connection with Sections I. and IX. The details and measurements of almost all the instruments described in these Sections were furnished by him, and his varied and practical knowledge has been of the greatest value.

Of the assistance and co-operation of Mr. D. J. BLAIKLEY, the able manager of Messrs. Boosey and Co's manufactory, it would be impossible to speak too highly. His knowledge of acoustics and his unique practical experience he generously placed at my disposal, and the value of his help, not in one Section alone but throughout the work, cannot be overrated. The learned and exhaustive Essay upon Musical Pitch, a subject of ever-increasing importance, and printed in the Appendix, is from Mr. BLAIKLEY's pen, and has been written by him especially for this work.

Valuable assistance has been rendered by M. VICTOR MAHILLON, the *Conservateur du Musée* of the Brussels *Conservatoire,* and the kindness of this gentleman in coming over, especially, from Brussels was very great. Thanks are also due to Mr. HENRY CARTE for much important information; and to Mr. GEORGE CASE, whose knowledge in connection with instruments of the Trombone family is well known. Thanks are due to Messrs. BESSON and Co. for their courtesy in affording facilities for the examination of various important documents and foreign patent specifications. Acknowledgment is due also to Mr. KÖHLER, to Mr. HENRY POTTER, to Mr. GEORGE POTTER, to Mr. GLEN, and to various others too numerous to mention individually.

In conclusion, I must thank Mr. A. J. HIPKINS, F.S.A., for the sound criticism and judicious advice so freely given by him upon all occasions, and for his kind help and experience, which has been of the most material assistance.

C. R. DAY, *Captain,*
Oxfordshire Light Infantry.

CONTENTS.

LIST OF LENDERS.

Her Majesty the Queen.
Rev. H. F. Armfield, F.S.A.
W. Ringrose Atkins, Esq., F.C.A.
C. A. Barry, Esq.
W. Bateson, Esq.
Messrs. Besson and Co.
Messrs. Boosey and Co.
C. Brock, Esq.
Thomas Bryant, Esq.
G. Butler, Esq.
D. M. Carmichael, Esq.
G. Case, Esq.
Mr. E. Cawley, Bandmaster 2nd Royal Scots.
Mr. Q. Cecconi.
S. A Chappell, Esq.
The Conservatoire Royal de Musique, Brussels.
T. Davidson, Esq.
The Director of Artillery.
G. Donaldson, Esq.
J. W. Eagles, Esq.
The Edinburgh University (Chair of Music).
Rev. F. W. Galpin, M.A., F.L.S.
Messrs. J. and R. Glen.
Colonel Grant (*for the Officers of the* 7th Dragoon Guards).
Rev. W. B. Grenside.
The Grossherzogliches Museum, Darmstadt.
Thomas Harper, Esq.
Alfred Hays, Esq.
Messrs. Higham and Co.
Colonel Hill, C.B.
The Honourable Artillery Company.
E. Hooker, Esq.
D. L. Isaacs, Esq.
Messrs. Köhler and Son.
Henry Lazarus, Esq.
H. Mackeson, Esq.
Messrs. Mahillon and Co.
T. S. Mann, Esq.
G. Miller, Esq., L.R.A.M.
Mr. Alfred Morton.
The Officers of the Royal Horse Guards.
The Officers of the XXth Regiment. (*Now* Lancashire Fusiliers.)
Messrs. George Potter and Co.
Messrs. Henry Potter and Co.
E. Renton, Esq.
Corporal Roberts, 4th Hussars.
Miss G. M. Rockstro.
Messrs. Rudall, Carte and Co.
Colonel Shaw-Hellier.
H. A. Smith, Esq.
M. Césare Snoeck.
T. L. Southgate, Esq.
W. Hugh Spottiswoode, Esq.
Cyril Spottiswoode, Esq.
Sir Arthur Sullivan.
C. Van Raalte, Esq.
H. Veysie, Esq.
Messrs. R. Ward and Sons.
Mrs. Carli Zoeller.

A CATALOGUE

OF

MUSICAL INSTRUMENTS.

I.

CLASS—FLUTES.

FAMILY: *Flûtes-à-bec.*

THE *flûte-à-bec,* or *flûte douce,* so much in use some centuries ago, survives now only in the fast disappearing flageolet. The name flute is, according to Hawkins, derived from the Latin *fluta,* a small eel found in the Sicilian seas, which has seven breathing holes, and thereby resembles the instrument; the word *bec* is an old Gallic word meaning the beak of a bird. Hence the term *flûte-à-bec,* or beak flute, is very appropriate. Philologists, however, dispute this derivation, and possibly with some reason. Instruments of this description were called by the Germans *plockflöten,* and according to Vincentio Galilei (*Dialogo della Musica antica e moderna,* 1581) *flauti diretti,* in contradistinction to the *flauti traversi,* now generally known as "flutes."

The application of the whistle to the pipe goes back to a higher antiquity than has been supposed, and flutes sounded by this means were known in the East at a period almost prehistoric. Among the ancient Aryans an instrument thus constructed was known by the name of Algoa, and is described in many of the Sanskrit treatises upon music that are still extant. It figures frequently upon ancient Hindu sculptures, and, according to recent investigation, would appear also to have been known in China at a period equally remote. Among the ancient Greeks flute playing was looked upon as the fashionable pastime of the *élite,* and consequently the instrument was considerably improved by various players from time to time; and flutes of the most careful and delicate workmanship have been discovered, and prove this to have been the case.

From Greece the instrument appears to have been adopted by the Romans, who, indeed, borrowed all that was beautiful in Greek art; and we learn from Tacitus that even the Emperor Nero himself did not disdain the drudgery of practice. With Roman conquests came also the adoption of Roman manners and Roman arts. Hence the instrument spread throughout the civilized world, and its use became common. Père Mersenne, who wrote in 1636–7, calls it the English flute, possibly because its use in England was common at that time. Ottomarus Luscinius (Nachtgall), a Benedictine monk and a native of Strasburg, published in 1536 a treatise entitled *Musurgia seu praxis Musicæ*, and which was in reality a translation of the earlier work of Virdung, written in 1511. Luscinius has in the work given drawings of a set of these *flûtes-à-bec*, and these instruments do not appear to differ from the earliest specimens exhibited in this collection. These flutes were usually played in complete sets, or families, of soprano, alto, tenor, and bass. Sometimes a larger or contrabass was introduced, and this practice evidently obtained at the time when Prætorius wrote (*Syntagma Musicum, Wolffenbüttel*, 1618). In England, he tells us, the *flûte-à-bcc* was known as the Recorder; how this name came to be given to it is impossible to say. Possibly it is from the old expression "to record," which, in the English of some centuries ago, meant "to sing," and was usually applied to birds singing.

According to Prætorius there were eight different kinds of these instruments; viz., the *small flute*, whose pitch was two octaves above that of the cornetto; the *discant flute*, a fourth lower; the *discant flute*, a fifth lower than the first; the *alt flute*, an octave lower than the first; the *tenor flute* a fifth below the alt flute; the *bassct flute*, which had a key enclosed within a box, and was a fifth below the tenor flute; the *bass flute*, a fifth below the basset flute; and the *great bass flute*, an octave below the basset flute. Such a set of flutes, he tells us, could be purchased in Venice, where the best of them were made, for eighty thalers. The usual compass of all these instruments was two octaves, but, by the aid of cross fingering, good players could extend the compass four or even seven notes higher. Upon the larger instruments the fundamental harmonics from the lower holes were obtained with difficulty, and were of little practical use, as they could only be obtained *pianissimo*.

In the time of Père Mersenne (*Harmonie Universelle*, 1636-7) we find that *flûtes-à-bec* were played in sets of four or even more. They had, nevertheless, undergone considerable improvement as regards their construction, both in the manner of keying, and also in the method of boring. Mersenne tells us how performers sometimes hummed the bass to an air as they played, but with no articulation of the voice, the wind proceeding from the mouth being sufficient to make the instrument sound, so that one player could perform a duet thus. The bore had come to be almost invariably an inverted cone; a cylindrical bore was, however, applied to little instruments, having three finger-holes only, and which will presently be described.

There were usually upon all *flûtes-à-bec* seven finger-holes upon the top, of which the lowest (for the little finger) was made in duplicate, in order that the instrument might be played upon by either right or left handed persons; there was also a thumb-hole at the back. The duplicate hole not used was stopped with wax. The instrument at a later time was made with the lower joint moveable, and this hole could therefore be adjusted to the side at which it was required. A device of this kind was almost always to be met with upon the English *Recorders* of the 17th century. The *flûtes-à-bec* thus constructed were simple enough in appearance, but yet by the aid of cross fingerings were capable of giving a scale of considerable compass. Humphry Salter, in the *Genteel Companion* (London 1683), has given a very complete method for the Recorder, which at that period, and since, was generally constructed in *f*; and from the *Genteel Companion* it seems that the fingering then commonly employed, in some respects, differed from that given by Mersenne.

In the larger varieties of *flûtes-à-bec* the lower finger-holes were closed by means of keys, which, though of rude construction, nevertheless fulfilled their purpose adequately enough. These keys had usually double touch-pieces, to suit right or left-handed players, and they were protected by means of a wooden envelope pierced with holes to allow full egress for the sound. The lowest note upon the *flûte-à-bec* had, at the beginning of the last century, come to be called *f*, whatever might have been its real pitch. The instrument appears to have been used in concerts in conjunction with viols and also violins, though not very generally. The elder Stanesby, the instrument maker, invented, about

1732, a system which obviated the necessity of transposing the flute parts for flutes other than concert flutes, which until that date had been the practice. However, the use of the *flute traversière* or *German flute* had for some years been gradually supplanting that of the *flûte-à-bec*, and Stanesby's endeavours to introduce the new instrument met with scant success.

About the beginning of the 17th century an important alteration was made in the fingering of the *flûte-à-bec*, or rather a fresh instrument of the kind, with a fingering entirely new, appears to have been invented. This was called by Mersenne the *Flageolet;* and the same fingering still survives in the French flageolet of the present day, an instrument seldom to be met with, except, perhaps, in a few dance orchestras upon the continent. The French flageolet differs from the ordinary Recorder, in that it has but four finger-holes in front, and two thumb-holes behind. The upper thumb-hole is placed at the back nearest the mouthpiece, then follow two finger-holes upon the top; these are played by the left hand. The fourth finger-hole is placed upon the top, then a thumb-hole at the back, and lastly the sixth finger-hole near the lower end of the flageolet.

The most celebrated player and maker of flageolets in the time of Mersenne was one Le Vacher. These instruments were made of various sizes, the smaller varieties being used for teaching birds to sing. A more detailed description of the flageolet can be found in the *Pleasant Companion for the Flageolet* (London 1682), and from this work it seems that both the Recorder and flageolet were in use at the same epoch. According to Dr. Burney the invention of the flageolet is ascribed to the Sieur Juvigny, who played it in the famous "Ballet Comique de la Royne" in 1581. That the instrument achieved great popularity is beyond doubt, for it remained in constant use till the beginning of this century, when Bainbridge constructed double and even triple flageolets, of which specimens are noticed in detail later on in this Catalogue.

There is yet another instrument of the same family, whose use was once almost universal. The *Galoubet*, or in German *Schwegel* or *Stamentienpfeiff*—called in England simply *pipe*, and generally employed in conjunction with the tabor—is of great antiquity. It is known to have been in use in the thirteenth century, and a representation of it occurs in a MS. of that date now in the National Library at Madrid

(*Cantigas de Santa Maria*). Instruments of this kind were, in the time of Prætorius, used in sets of two or three, and are mentioned later by Mersenne. Essentially of Provençal origin, the use of the pipe and tabor spread rapidly, and was carried into England by bands of travelling minstrels. Many references to, and some illustrations of, the use of these instruments are given by Strutt in his *Sports and Pastimes*, and it is only within the last fifty years that the pipe and tabor have ceased to be in common use. The peculiarity of the tabor-pipe is that it has but three finger-holes, two in front and one behind, all being placed very near the end furthest from the mouthpiece. The instrument speaks, therefore, in the upper harmonic octave, the fundamental sounds being impossible to produce. This will be better understood by the help of the following scale, which gives the various sounds produced with the same fingering; since the fundamental *d''* was impossible to produce, the instrument took *d'''* as its pitch. Allowing for the more recent rise in pitch, it became nearly our *d'''*♭. The notation, here given, therefore sounded two octaves higher:—

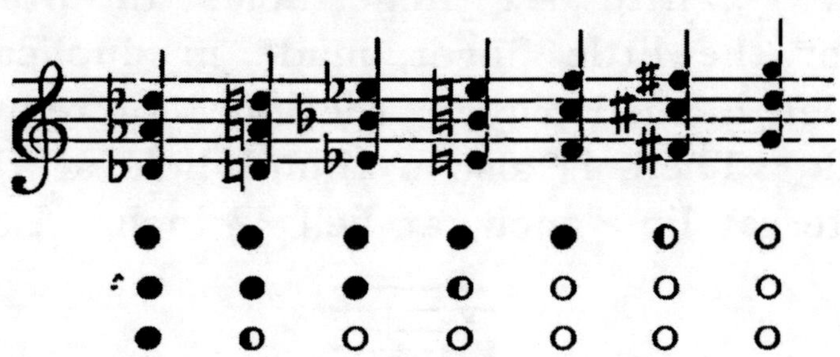

The tabor-pipe is held in the left hand, and the finger-holes are stopped by the thumb and two first fingers; and by the best players an occasional use is made of the little finger, which is employed to half cover the mouth of the pipe. The tabor is beaten by means of a short stick; both stick and tabor being held in the right hand.

The capability of the tabor-pipe was very great, and there were even *virtuosi* who could produce wonderful effects. Such a performer, named John Price, is mentioned by Mersenne, who states that he heard him ascend to the compass of a twenty-second upon this instrument! The pipe and tabor have been occasionally introduced into the orchestra; and in the comic opera, "Aline, reine de Golconde," composed by Berton, and first performed in 1803, a singularly beautiful effect has been thus produced.

1.

SET OF EIGHT FLUTES DOUCES in Case. These instruments are all exact reproductions of a set of 17th century flutes preserved in the *Germanisches Museum* of Nuremburg. They are all of boxwood, most beautifully made, with black horn tips. The set consists of—

One Sopranino, in *f''*, with seven finger-holes in front and one at the back. Length $9\frac{1}{2}$ inches, diameter of tube at lip $\frac{7}{16}$ inch, diameter at bell $\frac{3}{8}$ inch. Lowest note

Two Soprano, in *c''*, constructed in precisely the same way. Length $12\frac{1}{2}$ inches, diameter at lip $\frac{1}{2}$ inch, at bell $\frac{7}{16}$ inch. Lowest note

Two Alto, in *f'*, with six finger-holes in front, and also an additional one for the little finger, made in duplicate so as to suit either a right or left handed player; the hole not required is, of course, stopped with wax. There is also a thumb-hole at the back. Length 18 inches, diameter at lip $\frac{3}{4}$ inch, at bell $\frac{11}{16}$ inch. Lowest note

Two Tenor, in *c'*, made in a similar way to the Alto. Length $23\frac{1}{2}$ inches, diameter at lip $\frac{15}{16}$ inch, at bell $\frac{13}{16}$ inch. Lowest note

One Bass, in *f*, with six finger-holes in front, and a brass key having left and right handed touch-pieces at the lower end; this key works within a box, as is usual with contemporary instruments. There is also a thumb-hole at the back. Length $35\frac{1}{2}$ inches, diameter at lip $1\frac{3}{8}$ inch, at bell 1 inch. Lowest note

Lent by the *Conservatoire Royal de Musique*, Brussels.

2.

Flute Douce, in g'. This beautiful instrument is made of ivory, finely carved with foliated designs. The mouthpiece is also carved, and takes the form of a fish's head. The bell is very elaborately decorated. There are six finger-holes, also one placed slightly to the side, for the little finger, and a thumb-hole behind. Length 17 inches, diameter at lip $\frac{5}{8}$ inch, at bell $\frac{3}{8}$ inch. Lowest note

Probably of German make and 18th century.

Lent by the Rev. F. W. Galpin, M.A., F.L.S.

3.

Flute Douce, in f'. Of ivory, most artistically decorated and carved with foliated designs. There are six finger-holes in front, also an additional hole for the little finger, and a thumb-hole at the back. Stamped "J. O. Denner." Length $19\frac{1}{2}$ inches, diameter at lip $\frac{3}{4}$ inch, at bell $\frac{1}{2}$ inch. Plate II., fig. F. Lowest note

Of German make, and late 17th century. This maker was resident at Leipzig from 1655 to about 1707, when he appears to have been at Nuremberg.

The flute in f' was that in ordinary use, and is the instrument scored for by Bach, who writes the part in the  clef, which he places upon the first line instead of the second. The instrument is used also by Handel, who employs also the bass flute—exactly two octaves lower—on a few rare occasions.

Lent by G. Donaldson, Esq.

4.

Flute Douce, in f'. Of beautifully decorated and carved boxwood. The carving consists chiefly of grotesque figures of fishes; below the mouthpiece there is a carved representation of a face. There are the usual six finger-holes, with the hole for the little finger, and thumb-hole at the back. Length 19½ inches, diameter at lip ¾ inch, at bell $\frac{9}{16}$ inch. The compass and pitch are the same as in the preceding instrument. Stamped "J. W. Oberlender," with the usual initial "O." German 18th century.

Lent by G. Donaldson, Esq.

5.

Flute Douce, in *f'*. Of carved ivory, with six finger-holes in front, and the additional hole for the little finger; also a thumb-hole at the back. The bell is made slightly expanding at the mouth. Length 18¼ inches, diameter at lip ¾ inch, at bell ½ inch, opening to 2¾ inches. The pitch and compass are as described for the instruments above. Stamped with a figure of a crown, and immediately below the maker's name, "J. Hertz." German or Austrian, 18th century.

Lent by Messrs. Rudall, Carte and Co.

6.

Flute Douce, in *f'*. This beautiful instrument is made of wood, and covered with polished tortoiseshell; it is tipped with ivory. The compass and description of this instrument do not differ from the usual flutes douces in *f'*. Length 20½ inches, diameter at lip ¾ inch, at bell $\frac{7}{16}$ inch. German, 18th century.

Lent by the *Grossherzogliches Museum*, Darmstadt.

7.

Flute Douce, in *f'*. Of wood, covered with polished tortoise-shell. This instrument resembles in every way that immediately preceding.

Lent by the *Grossherzogliches Museum*, Darmstadt.

8.

Flute Douce, in *f'*. Of ivory, and richly carved with ornamental beadings and conventional designs. There are six finger-holes in front, but in place of the additional hole for the little finger there is a key, which, in its normal position, is open. This key is of ivory, overlaid with carved mother-of-pearl. There is also a thumb-hole at the back. Length 20½ inches, diameter at lip ¾ inch, at bell ½ inch. Stamped "Villars." Of French make, of the latter half of the 18th century. Plate II., fig. B.

Lent by G. Donaldson, Esq.

9.

Flute à Colonne, in *f'*. This curious instrument is made in the form of a column, with a base and a capital. There are six lateral holes and a key upon one side, and a thumb-hole upon the other. The key, which has both left and right handed touch-pieces, works within a perforated brass box in front of the instrument. In this same box is also the vent or bell. The mouthpiece is placed at the side of the capital of the column; the whistle, placed in front just below the capital, is concealed by a box of pierced brass artistically designed. The instrument gives the following fundamental intonations, the key giving *g'*:—

Height of column 20½ inches, diameter $\frac{11}{16}$ inch. Marked with a trefoil, but with no maker's name. Probably 16th or early 17th century. Plate IV., fig. F.

Flutes of this description do not appear to have been mentioned by any of the early writers, such as Prætorius or Mersenne. There are two specimens of larger size, in *e'*♭ and *b*♭, in the Museum of the Paris *Conservatoire*, and which are described by M. Chouquet in his catalogue. It seems probable that these instruments were made, as a novelty of shape, by some maker to satisfy the caprice of some wealthy amateur of the time. They are, nevertheless, extremely interesting as musical curiosities.

Lent by the *Conservatoire Royal de Musique*, Brussels.

10.

FLUTE DOUCE, in *c'*. Of stained wood, made entirely in one piece, with six finger-holes, and an additional double hole for the little finger to suit right or left handed players, and a thumb-hole at back. Length $24\frac{3}{4}$ inches, diameter at lip 1 inch, at bell $\frac{7}{8}$ inch. Plate III., fig. H. The lowest note is

German, 16th or 17th century.

Lent by the *Conservatoire Royal de Musique*, Brussels.

11.

FLUTE DOUCE, in *c'*. This instrument is made of boxwood, entirely in one piece. There are the usual six finger-holes in front; also the additional double hole for the little finger, to suit right or left handed performers, and a thumb-hole at the back. The compass and pitch of this instrument are precisely as described for the flute immediately preceding. The peculiarity of this instrument consists in the fact that the whistle and mouthpiece are placed at the back of the flute, instead of in front, as is usually the case. Length 25 inches, diameter at lip 1 inch, at bell $\frac{7}{8}$ inch. German, 16th or 17th century.

Lent by Messrs. Rudall, Carte and Co.

12.

FLUTE DOUCE, in *a*. Of stained wood. There are six finger-holes in front, and a brass key, with left and right handed touch-pieces, working within a perforated wooden box; there is also a thumb-hole at the back. The lowest note given by this instrument is

Length 28 inches, diameter at lip $1\frac{1}{16}$ inch, at bell $\frac{15}{16}$ inch. Plate III., fig. G. 16th or 17th century.

Lent by the *Conservatoire Royal de Musique*, Brussels.

13.

Flute Douce, in *a*. Of dark stained wood, with six finger-holes and one open brass key upon one side, and a thumb-hole upon the other. This instrument is of English make, and is stamped "Stanesby, junior." It was probably made about 1730. The compass is

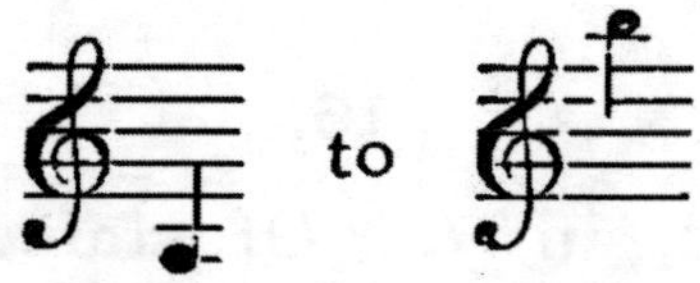

Length $29\frac{1}{2}$ inches, diameter of tube at lip and at top of middle joint, $\frac{3}{4}$ inch, at bell $\frac{1}{2}$ inch.

This instrument appears to correspond exactly, as regards size and appearance, with that shown in the hands of the Recorder player, in the frontispiece given by Humphrey Salter in the *Genteel Companion*, published in 1683. The same plate shows a smaller instrument, of a somewhat similar kind, lying on the table at the player's side.

Lent by the Rev. F. W. Galpin, M.A., F.L.S.

14.

Flute Douce, in *g*. Of stained wood, with six finger-holes upon one side. There is also upon the same side a key having left and right handed touch-pieces, and which works within a perforated box. There is a thumb-hole at the back. Length 37 inches, diameter at lip $1\frac{5}{16}$ inch, at bell $1\frac{1}{4}$ inch. Plate III., fig. F. This instrument is sounded by means of a short brass crook placed at the top of the whistle. The lowest note is

16th or 17th century.

Lent by the *Conservatoire Royal de Musique*, Brussels.

15.

Flute Douce, in *g*. Of stained wood, with six finger-holes in front and a thumb-hole at back. There is also, in front, a key, with left and right handed touch-pieces, working inside a perforated box.

The compass and pitch of this instrument are as described for the flute immediately preceding. The length is 36 inches, diameter at lip 1$\frac{3}{16}$ inch, at bell 1 inch. This flute was sounded by a metal crook as described above. 16th or 17th century.

Lent by the *Grossherzogliches Museum*, Darmstadt.

16.

Tenor Flute Douce, in *f*. Of stained wood, with six finger-holes and a key, right or left handed, in front, and a thumb-hole at back. The key in this specimen is not covered by a box, as was the case with the earlier flutes. This instrument was sounded with a brass crook, which is now missing. The lowest note is

Length 40 inches, diameter at lip 1$\frac{5}{16}$ inch, at bell $\frac{7}{8}$ inch. Stamped "J. Steenbergen"; probably about the commencement of 18th century.

Lent by the *Grossherzogliches Museum*, Darmstadt.

17.

Tenor Flute Douce, in *f*. Of dark stained wood, with six finger-holes and a brass key (single touch-piece) in front, and a thumb-hole at back. There is also an ivory ring round the top of the instrument. The crook is missing. The compass and pitch of the flute are as described for the instrument above. Length 39 inches, diameter at lip 1$\frac{5}{16}$ inch, at bell $\frac{7}{8}$ inch. 18th century.

Lent by the *Grossherzogliches Museum*, Darmstadt.

18.

Bass Flute Douce, in *c*. Of wood, with six finger-holes in front; also a flat brass key, with right or left handed touch-pieces, working within a perforated box. There is also a thumb-hole at the back. Length of instrument, without crook, 48$\frac{1}{2}$ inches, diameter at lip 1$\frac{9}{16}$ inch, at bell 1$\frac{1}{4}$ inch. The length of the crook and mouthpiece is 15 inches, but this of course does not affect the pitch. Plate III., fig. E. The lowest note is

Lent by the *Conservatoire Royal de Musique*, Brussels.

19.

GREAT BASS FLUTE DOUCE, in *C*. This is an exact reproduction of an instrument now in the *Musée du Steen*, at Antwerp. It is of stained wood, with six finger-holes on the upper side, and two open brass keys, both of which have the usual double touch-pieces, and which work inside a perforated box. The keys give *C*♯ and *C*♮. The flap of the *C*♮ key rests upon that of the *C*♯, so closing the latter automatically when depressed. There is a thumb-hole, as usual, at the back. Lowest note

Length, not including crook, 8 feet 7 inches, diameter at lip 2 inches, at bell 1¾ inch. The crook itself is 35 inches in length.

Lent by the *Conservatoire Royal de Musique*, Brussels.

20.

PICCO PIPE. This extremely small instrument is only 3½ inches in length, and has a cylindrical bore opening out at the bell to ⅞ inch in diameter. There are two finger-holes in front and one at the back. The compass extends to two octaves, and the scale is completed by inserting the second finger of the right hand into the bell. The lowest note, which is formed by placing the hand over the bell and closing the pipe, is either

 or 

The pipe upon which the celebrated Picco played himself was somewhat larger than the present specimen. Prætorius mentions that at

the commencement of the 17th century pipes of a similar description were made with three holes in front and one at the back, and the additional hole is still preferred by some players. The bore of these pipes, and that of the tabor-pipe and galoubet, is cylindrical.

Lent by the Rev. F. W. Galpin, M.A., F.L.S.

21.

TABOR-PIPE. Of light stained wood, with two finger-holes in front and one at the back. Stamped "Robert Cotton, London." The lowest note is

Length 12½ inches, diameter of bore $\frac{5}{16}$ inch. English. 17th or early 18th century.

The tabor pipe (called in France Galoubet, and in Germany Schwegel) is held and played by one hand, while the other beats a small drum or tabor. Though no longer used in England, pipes of this description are still employed in the Basque provinces, where they are used in conjunction with the tambourin, a kind of dulcimer.

Lent by Messrs. H. Potter and Co.

22.

TABOR-PIPE. Of stained wood, with the joint of ivory. There are two finger-holes in front and one at the back. The size and compass of this pipe do not differ from that just described. It is stamped "Heny. Potter, 2, Bridge Street, Westminster," but is probably not made by him, but of earlier date. 18th century.

Lent by the Rev. F. W. Galpin, M.A., F.L.S.

23.

TABOR-PIPE. This very beautiful little instrument is made entirely of ivory, and is most artistically carved with bands of foliated scroll-work and figures of musical instruments. There are two finger-holes in front and one at the back. In its proportions and compass it does not differ from the two instruments above. The ornamentation and general design prove it to be French, and it dates probably from the latter end of the 18th century. Plate II., fig. D.

Lent by G. Donaldson, Esq.

24.

Bass Galoubet, in c'. This very rare instrument is of wood, and has been most carefully restored. There are two finger-holes upon one side and a thumb-hole upon the other. The instrument is played with a brass crook. The lowest note is

Length, not including crook, 30 inches, diameter of bore $1\frac{1}{16}$ inch. The bell of the instrument opens out to $\frac{3}{4}$ inch. The length of the crook is $23\frac{1}{2}$ inches.

Lent by the *Conservatoire Royal de Musique,* Brussels.

25.

Flageolet. Of boxwood, tipped with ivory. There are four finger-holes in front and two at the back, also four brass cup-shaped keys on knobs, giving $d''\sharp$ and $a'\sharp$, the two others being shake keys. The lowest note is g'', and there is a compass of two chromatic octaves and three semitones. Stamped "D'Almaine & Co., late Goulding & D'Almaine, Soho, London." Length $14\frac{1}{4}$ inches, diameter at bell $\frac{7}{16}$ inch, at lip $\frac{1}{2}$ inch.

This instrument, now known as the French flageolet, preserved the peculiar fingering of the original instrument, invented in the 16th century, and described in the *Pleasant Companion for the Flageolet* in 1682. The French flageolet is not a transposing instrument, but simply a flageolet in c''' descending to g'', which is written

the music for the flageolet being written an octave below the real sounds. The ordinary flageolet is merely a small flûte-à-bec, or even flûte traversière, played with a whistle.

Lent by Messrs. Rudall, Carte and Co.

26.

Piccolo Flageolet, in c'''. Of dark wood, with ivory tips and mouthpiece. There are six finger-holes in front, and an extra one at the lower end for the little finger. There is a single cup-shaped key, of silver, on knobs at the back. There are also five silver studs or guides in front. The total length of the instrument is only 9 inches, and its lowest note is c'''. Its compass extends to an octave and a sixth.

This little instrument stands an octave above the piccolo, and was formerly used for teaching birds to sing. The finger-holes vary greatly in size, in order to ensure correct intonation. The key at the back gives the sharps to most of the notes without cross fingering. Bainbridge took out a patent in 1807 for a key which produced the same effect.

Lent by the Rev. F. W. Galpin, M.A., F.L.S.

27.

Flageolet, in c''. Of boxwood, with seven finger-holes in front and one silver key, giving $e''\flat$, also a thumb-hole at the back. There are five small ivory guides between the finger-holes in front. There is a large ivory plate or ring at the bell end of the instrument, apparently so that it can stand on end when not in use. The lowest note is

Length $16\frac{1}{2}$ inches.

Lent by Messrs. H. Potter and Co.

28.

Flageolet, in c''. Of black wood, with six finger-holes in front. There are four keys, of white metal and cup-shaped, in front, and one at the back. The keys give $b''\flat$, $g''\sharp$, f'', $e''\flat$, and $c''\sharp$; the top hole is three-quarters closed, and so gives c''' instead of $c'''\sharp$. The lowest note is d''. Length $16\frac{3}{4}$ inches.

Lent by G. Butler, Esq.

29.

Flageolet, in *a′*♭. Of boxwood, with six finger-holes and an additional hole for the little finger in front, and a thumb-hole at the back. There are four flat brass keys on knobs giving *b″*♭, *g″*♯, *f″*, and *c″*♭; also five ivory studs or guides, and an ivory mouthpiece. Length, including mouthpiece, 19¾ inches. Stamped "T. Prouse, Hanway St., London. New Patent." The lowest note is called *c*♯, and actually sounds

The fifth hole is made of rather larger size, thereby giving *f*♯, instead of *f*♮, as in the flute douce. This improvement was patented by Bainbridge in 1803.

Lent by the Rev. F. W. Galpin, M.A., F.L.S.

30.

Flute Flageolet, in *c′*. Of boxwood, and tipped with ivory. There are six finger-holes, arranged as in the flute traversière. There is also one square-flapped silver key giving *e′*♭. The lowest note of this instrument is *d′*. The mouthpiece resembles that of the more early flutes douces, and the instrument is held in a similar manner. It is stamped "S. French, London," and is of the early part of the present century. Length 22 inches.

Lent by the Rev. F. W. Galpin, M.A., F.L.S.

31.

Flute Flageolet, in *c′*. Of boxwood, with six finger-holes in front, also a brass square-flapped key giving *e′*♭. This instrument is blown by means of a small ivory mouthpiece placed at the side, and it is held as a flute traversière. Its lowest note is *d′*. It is stamped "Bainbridge & Wood, 35, Holborn Hill, London. New Patent." This is Bainbridge's patent of 1807.

Lent by Messrs. Rudall, Carte and Co.

32.

DOUBLE FLAGEOLET, in *c''*. This curious old instrument, the prototype of the elaborate double flageolets of the early part of this century, is made from a single piece of wood. There are two channels pierced parallel, and both sounded by whistles. The two tubes are pitched a third apart, the lowest notes being

The larger pipe is placed on the player's right. There are seven holcs to each pipe in front, and they are placed in pairs side by side. There are two holes, one for each pipe, at the back. Length 12 inches. Diameter of right-hand tube, at bell $\frac{7}{16}$ inch, at lip $\frac{9}{16}$ inch; of left-hand tube at bell $\frac{3}{8}$ inch, at lip $\frac{1}{2}$ inch. Plate IV., fig. H.

There is a representation of a double flageolet of this kind in the *Encyclopèdie Méthodique* of 1785.

Lent by the *Grossherzogliches Muscum*, Darmstadt.

33.

DOUBLE FLAGEOLET, in *c''*. Of boxwood, with two parallel tubes, of unequal length, fixed in the same stock. The left tube is pierced with seven finger-holes, and has two silver keys, which give *d''* and *e''*♭. The tube on the right hand has four finger-holes, with an additional hole for the little finger, and three silver keys giving *c'''*, *b''*, and the *c''*♭ below. The lowest note upon the instrument is

It was probably made by Bainbridge about 1810, but it is stamped "Metzler, London, 105, Wardour Street. Patent." In this instrument, and also in all of the double flageolets described hereafter, either tube can be silenced at will by a cut-off shutter, which acts upon the whistle. Length 15¾ inches.

Lent by T. L. Southgate, Esq.

34.

DOUBLE FLAGEOLET, in *a'*♭. Of boxwood, and tipped with ivory. Both the tubes are of equal length, and are fixed parallel in one stock, which contains both the whistles. The left tube is pierced with six finger-holes, and one for the little finger in addition. There are also two silver keys, which give *d''* and *e''*♭. The tube on the player's right has only four finger-holes, with one for the little finger; there are three silver keys, which give *c'''*, *b''*, and the *e''*♭ below. The lowest note is called *c*♯, and sounds

Length 18¾ inches. Stamped "Bainbridge & Wood, 35, Holborn Hill, London."

Lent by the Rev. F. W. Galpin, M.A., F.L.S.

35.

DOUBLE FLAGEOLET, in *a'*♭. Of boxwood, with two tubes of equal length fixed parallel in one stock. The left-hand tube is pierced with six finger-holes, and with one in addition for the little finger. There are also three silver keys, giving *d''*, *f''*, and *e''*♭. The right-hand tube has four holes, and an additional hole for the little finger. There are four keys, which give *c'''*, *b''*, *f''*, and *e''*♭. Length 19⅛ inches. The lowest note sounds *a'*♮, as in the preceding instrument. Stamped "Simpson, from Bainbridge's, 26, Oxford Street. Patent."

Lent by Messrs. Besson and Co.

36.

DOUBLE FLAGEOLET, in *c''*. Of boxwood, with two tubes of equal length. The tube for the left hand is pierced with six finger-holes, with an additional hole for the little finger. There are also four silver keys, which give *d'''*, *c'''*, *f''*, and *d''*♯. The right-hand tube has five holes and four keys, which give *c'''*, *b''*, *f''*, and *c''*♭. Stamped "Bainbridge, Inventor, Holborn Hill." The lowest note is

Length 16 inches. This instrument is fitted with the "New *C*♮ key" on the left pipe, between the whistle and the first finger-hole. This was an improvement patented by Bainbridge in 1819.

Lent by G. Butler, Esq.

37.

Double Flageolet, in *a'*♭. Of boxwood, stained black and tipped with ivory. There are two tubes, but of unequal lengths. The shorter pipe is pierced with six finger-holes, and has four silver keys, which give *d'''*, *f''*, *c''*♭, and the *c''*♯ below, the latter being an open key. The larger of the two pipes has but four finger-holes, and there are five silver keys, which give *c'''*, *b''*, *f''*, and the *c''*♮ and *b'*♮ below. The lowest notes are, on the two tubes,

Length 21½ inches. Stamped "Simpson, 266, Regent Street, Oxford Street, London. Patent." This was probably made about 1830. It includes Bainbridge's patent extension to the "low *B*♮" on the right tube, an improvement patented in 1819.

Lent by the Rev. F. W. Galpin, M.A., F.L.S.

38.

Double Flageolet, in *a'*♭. Of boxwood, with two tubes of unequal length. The shorter tube has six finger-holes, and five closed keys, *e'''*♭. *d'''*. *c'''*, *f''*, *d''*♯; also an open key giving *c''*♯. The longer tube has four finger-holes and four keys, which give *d'''*, *c'''*, *f''*, and *c''*. Stamped "Simpson, Regent Street, Oxford Street." The lowest notes are

Length 21¾ inches. In place of the usual cut-off shutter for silencing either pipe at will, there is a contrivance like a key, which covers the whole aperture of the whistle, and is worked by a lever. This instrument has also the "patent *C*♮" key of 1819.

Lent by Messrs. H. Potter and Co.

39.

Double Flageolet, in *a'*♭. Of boxwood, and tipped with ivory. There are two tubes of unequal length, the shorter of which is pierced with six finger-holes, and has also five keys, which give *c'''*♭, *d'''*, *c'''*, *f''*, *d''*♯, and *c''*♯; the latter is an open key. The longer tube has four finger-holes only, and has also five keys, giving *c'''*, *b''*, *f''*, and the low *c''* and *b'*; the *b'*♮ key is open. Stamped "Hastrick, late Bainbridge, Inventor, 35, Holborn Hill, London. Patent." The lowest notes are

Length 21 inches. The "patent *C*♮" key is also upon this instrument.

Lent by Messrs. Rudall, Carte and Co.

40.

Double Flageolet, in *a'*♭. Of boxwood, with ivory tips. The general construction of this instrument does not differ from that mentioned immediately before. Stamped "Hastrick, 35, Holborn Hill, New Patent."

Lent by Messrs. Köhler and Son.

41.

Triple Flageolet, in *c'*. This instrument is made of boxwood, and is tipped with ivory. It is constructed of three separate tubes, all being blown from the same mouthpiece. The general look of the instrument is that of an ordinary double flageolet, but with an additional tube of greater length hanging parallel, and communicating with the upper part of the top joint by a lateral tube. The shortest of the tubes has seven finger-holes, and the usual five flat brass keys (closed). There are also three long levers, which close the f'', e'', and d'' holes. The second tube has four holes and three brass keys (closed), which give b'', f''♮, and the low e''; a key placed at the back gives b'. The third tube has only one open hole, and four closed brass keys, which are worked by the thumb of the left hand. The keys give d'', c'', a', and g'. Any of the tubes can be stopped off at pleasure. The instrument is supported upon a rest. Length, including rest, 22½ inches. Stamped "Bainbridge, Inventor, 35, Holborn Hill, London." The lowest notes given by all three tubes are

Lent by Messrs. Rudall, Carte and Co.

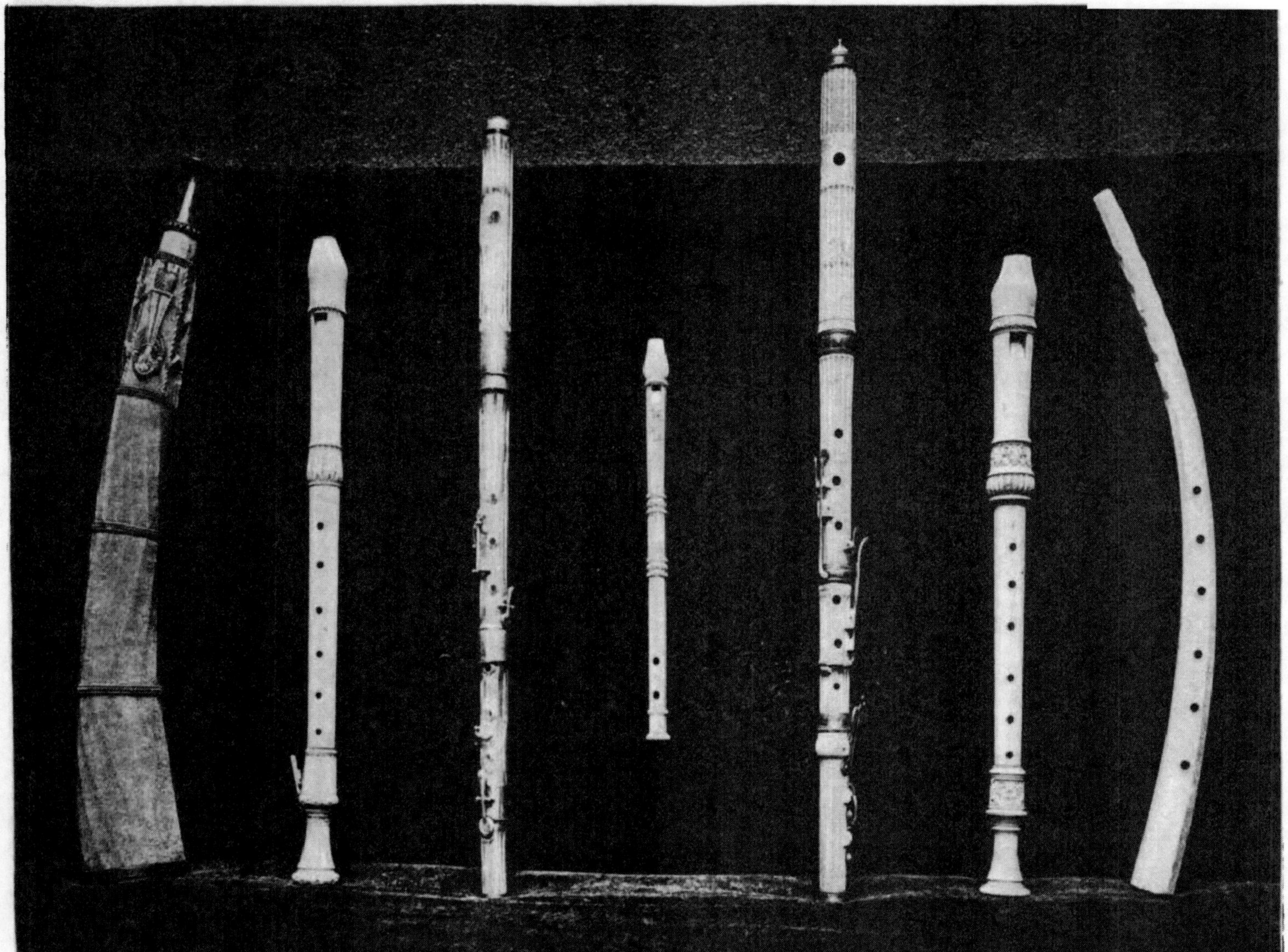

A B C D E F G

Eyre & Spottiswoode Publishers London E.C.

II.

CLASS—FLUTES.

FAMILY: *Transverse flutes;* flûtes traversières, *or German flutes, now generally known as "flutes."*

THE flute of the present day has little in common with the *flöte*, the *schwegel*, the *flûte droite*, or the *flûte-à-bec* of early times, these being simply whistles, whereas the distinguishing characteristics of the modern flute, like those of its prototype the *zwerchpfeiff* or *schweitzer-pfeiff*, are the complete closing of the extreme upper end of the instrument, and the lateral mouth-hole, or *embouchure*. The flute of our time may be described as a tube closed at one end by a "stopper" of cork or other material (which for the last century and a half has generally been made moveable), and provided with seven or more lateral apertures. These, with the exception of that nearest to the closed end of the flute (the mouth-hole), are governed by the fingers, either directly or with the aid of "keys." The form of the mouth-hole has varied greatly at different periods and places. Oval is now the favourite shape in this country, but on the Continent an oblong, slightly rounded, is often used. In order to sound the instrument it is necessary to blow across this opening, which, being always partly open when the flute is in use, renders the tube, in an acoustical sense, open at both ends, consequently the harmonic sounds of the flute are the same as those of a stretched string, whatever, within very wide limits, the form of the bore may be. The passing of the breath directly from the lips to the edge of the mouth-hole, without the intervention of the rigid mouth-piece common to all instruments of the whistle type, gives to the skilful flute-player absolute command over the tone of his instrument.

The bore of the early flute was invariably cylindrical throughout, or as nearly cylindrical as it could be made. At a period approaching the close of the seventeenth century the lower portion of the tube was gradually contracted in diameter so that it became conoidal, while for the upper part, or "head-joint," the original cylindrical form was retained. The advantages of the conoidal bore were so great that it was soon generally adopted, excepting for military fifes; these, until recently, were made entirely cylindrical; hence, for the sake of distinction, the term "flute" came to be applied to transverse flutes of all sizes, with bore wholly or partly conoidal, while the smaller cylindrical instruments of the same genus were, and are, designated "fifes." The true fife is, however, almost obsolete, the instruments used in the so-called "drum and fife bands" being flutes of various sizes, with the bore usually described as "conical."

In the year 1847 an important change was made in the bore of the flute by the late Theobald Boehm of Munich. This change almost amounted to a complete reversal of the proportions which had been adopted for the previous century and a half, the head-joint being reduced in diameter at the upper part, while for the lower part, or "body," of the flute the original cylindrical shape was restored. The "cylinder flute with parabola head," the name by which such instruments are generally known, possesses, under certain circumstances, a most decided and indisputable preponderance of advantages over the "conical flute," and it has become deservedly popular in England, France and America; it is, however, but little esteemed in Germany.

One of the most interesting facts relating to the history of musical instruments is the almost complete immunity from change which has been maintained in the diameter of the cylindrical part of the bore of the "concert-flute," that is, the flute which gives the notes as they are written and fingered. The earliest, and the smallest, recorded measurement of the bore of this instrument, that given by Mersenne (*Harmonie Universelle,* Paris, 1636-7), is ·71 inch, and there is no reason to believe that the diameter of the cylinder has ever exceeded ·75 inch. The largest part of the bore of a concert-flute of the latest pattern has a diameter of 19 millimetres, ·748 inch.

The primitive flutes were provided with six "finger-holes" only: these, being covered or uncovered successively, gave a descending or ascending diatonic scale of an octave, less one note, the open end of the flute giving the key-note. The second series of notes was formed, as at present, by the harmonic-octaves of the first series; the third, or as much of it as was possible, by the higher harmonics, assisted in their production by the opening of certain finger-holes as "vent-holes." The holes of the flutes of the sixteenth century were exceedingly small.

No. 44 is a most interesting specimen of these very early instruments. In the following century the finger-holes were much increased in size, those of the flute described by Mersenne varying from ·266 to ·444 inch in diameter. Probably with a view to improving what are termed "fork-fingerings" the holes were afterwards reduced in size. Those of the Monzani flute, No. 65, vary from ·18 to ·36 inch. The size was again increased by the celebrated Nicholsons, father and son, the largest hole (that for *f'*♯) of the Nicholson flutes being often ·45 inch in its exterior diameter. The best modern concert-flutes, in the writer's opinion, have equal-sized holes (with the exception of the highest three) of ·64 inch. The main advantage of this increase and uniformity is the preservation of perfect intonation in the several octaves.

In the times when Mersenne, Hotteterre and Quantz wrote, 1636 to 1752, the compass of the flute was considered to extend for about two octaves and a half; we have now three octaves of good notes, with a few higher sounds of inferior quality of tone.

About the year 1660 the first step was taken in the direction of rendering the flute a chromatic instrument. This was the addition of a seventh finger-hole, giving *d'*♯, governed by a closed key which was opened by the little finger of the right hand. The name of the inventor of this key is unknown, but no great ingenuity had been exercised in its application to the flute, as similar keys had long previously been applied to other wind-instruments. We are told by Quantz that about the year 1722 the flute was lengthened in order that *c'*♯ and *c'*♮ might be obtained. The holes for these notes were governed, as at present, by open keys. No. 50 is an early example of a flute with the *c'*♯ key. The well-known keys for *f*♮, *g*♯, and *b*♭ were coming into use at a period not far removed from 1774. The precise dates of their invention cannot be determined, but there is certain evidence that they were made in London by Richard Potter, the grandfather of the renowned Cipriani Potter, before the above-mentioned year. It is also proved by Dr. J. J. H. Ribock, a German doctor of medicine, that these keys were made, at a period before the year 1782, by Tromlitz of Leipsic and by Kusder of London, the maker of the two hautboys numbered 178 and 179. The long key for *f*♮ was invented by Tromlitz before the year 1786. The history of the *c''* key (which was at first an open one, similar to that on most of the modern flutes) is extremely interesting, but too long to be inserted here. The ordinary *c''* key of the "eight-keyed flute" was invented prior to 1806.

The first systematic attempt to battle with the imperfections and difficulties caused by the union of open holes with closed keys, and the adaptation of the positions of the former to suit the convenience of the fingers instead of in accordance with the requirements of the musical scale, was made by Tromlitz, and described by him in 1800. A more important and ingenious effort was made by a German doctor of medicine, named H. W. Pottgiesser, in 1803, but little notice seems to have been taken of either of these attempts to improve the flute, and even a letter from the illustrious C. M. von Weber, in the *Leipsic Musical Gazette,* concerning a new flute by Capeller of Munich, received scant attention, although on this flute was placed, for the first time, the now almost universally adopted key for *d''*. A further experiment by Pottgiesser, in 1824, met with no better reception, and, notwithstanding numerous minor improvements, the flute remained in its old anomalous condition until 1826, when the unfortunate Captain Gordon of Charles the Tenth's Swiss Guards, an amateur passionately devoted to the flute, began to apply himself to the task of devising a rational system of open holes and open keys, founded on the schemes of Tromlitz and Pottgiesser. How Theobald Boehm modified the machinery, while retaining the principal features of the system of Gordon; how he asserted that the invention was, *ab initio,* his own, and that Gordon was utterly ignorant of the principles of flute-construction, are matters which have been amply discussed, and which need no more than a passing allusion here. The "ring-key" (see No. 97) for closing an open key and an uncovered hole by the same finger, an invention often attributed to Boehm, was first applied to a flute by the Reverend Frederick Nolan in 1808. Pottgiesser, in 1824, and Gordon after him, employed a crescent, partly surrounding the hole, for the same purpose. Many of the subsequent improvements and modifications are illustrated by the specimens hereafter described.

It has been the immemorial and almost universal custom to consider the fundamental note of the simple transverse flute as *d'*, whatever its actual sound may have been. The flutes on which the note *d'* (and of course every other note of the scale) sounded as it was written and fingered, were called *d'*, or concert, flutes. Those of other sizes were named after the note actually given when *d'* was fingered. For example: a flute giving *f'*, with the fingering of *d'*, was called an *f* flute, or a flute in *f*, and the music for such an instrument was written a minor third lower than the actual sounds of the notes. This custom still prevails, and has been followed in the descriptions of the flutes in this Catalogue. It should be understood that although a "*c'* clarionet" gives the actual notes, as written and fingered, a "*c'* flute" gives sounds a full tone lower. The names of piccolos and fifes follow the same rule as those of flutes, excepting that those instruments sound an octave higher; the *d''* piccolo, or octave-flute, sounding an octave higher than the *d'*, or concert, flute.

The pitches of the flutes described in the following pages are reckoned from a standard *a'* with 452 double vibrations to the second, corresponding to *c''* with 537·5 vibrations.

FIFTEENTH OR SIXTEENTH CENTURY.

42.

FIFE of dark brown wood, in *b'*♮, without keys. Length from cork 12·7 inches. Diameter of bore ·37 inch. The surface of the wood is flattened from end to end, and on the flattened side the holes are placed. Instruments similar to this are figured by Virdung (*Musica getutscht etc.*, 1511) and by Agricola (*Musica Instrumentalis Deudsch*, 1528, 1532 and 1545). Thoinot Arbeau (Jehan Taburot) gives a quaint description of this kind of fife, and of the manner in which it was played: "Those who perform on this instrument," he writes, "play according to their own pleasure, and it is enough for them to keep time with the sound of the drum." (*Orchesographie*, Langres, 1588.) See plate I., fig. F.

Lent by the *Conservatoire Royal de Musique*, Brussels.

43.

Cylindrical flute of dark brown wood, in one piece, without keys, in *f′*. Length from cork 17·4 inches. Diameter of bore ·57 inch. Precisely similar, excepting in size, to No. 42. See plate I., fig. E.

Lent by the *Conservatoire Royal de Musique*, Brussels.

44.

Cylindrical flute of box-wood, in *b*♭, without keys, mountings, or cap; in one piece. Length from cork 25·4 inches. Diameter of bore ·73 inch. Branded with the name "C. Rafi," surmounting a shield bearing a griffin. A similar device is placed between the *g* and *a* holes. Between the initials C. and R. there is a trefoil. See plate I., fig. D.

This rare and most interesting specimen is evidently of a much earlier date than the cylindrical flute described by Mersenne (*op. cit.*) It is probably one of the oldest transverse flutes in existence.

Lent by the *Conservatoire Royal de Musique*, Brussels.

SEVENTEENTH CENTURY.

45.

Model of a cylindrical flute, in one piece, without keys, giving *f*♯ as its lowest note. Length from cork 32·4 inches. Diameter of bore ·95 inch. See plate I., fig. C.

Lent by the *Conservatoire Royal de Musique*, Brussels.

46.

Model of a cylindrical flute, in two pieces, without keys, giving *f*♮ as its lowest note. Length from cork 34·5 inches. Diameter of bore 1·02 inch. See plate I., fig. B.

Lent by the *Conservatoire Royal de Musique*, Brussels.

47.

MODEL of a cylindrical flute, in two pieces, without keys, giving *e♭* as its lowest note. Length from cork 38·4 inches. Diameter of bore 1·02 inch. The holes for the third fingers are double. See plate I., fig. A.

No person of ordinary stature could play on this flute without assistance in stopping the holes, the distance from the lowest hole to the mouth-hole being 30·5 inches.

Lent by the *Conservatoire Royal de Musique*, Brussels.

The models numbered 45, 46, and 47 are exact copies of original instruments preserved in the *Musée Communal* at Verona. Similar flutes are described by Mersenne.

48.

COPIES of a pair of fifes in *g′*. The originals are in the *Carolino Augusteum* at Salzburg.

Lent by the *Conservatoire Royal de Musique*, Brussels.

EIGHTEENTH CENTURY.

49.

CONCERT-FLUTE of box-wood, with tips and cap of black horn, and one brass square-flapped key. This is undoubtedly the oldest conoidal flute in the collection. It is in four "joints," the second of which is marked "2," and was probably the flattest but one of an uncertain number of interchangeable joints of different lengths. Such "*corps de réchange*" were in general use before the invention of the tuning slide. As the flute stands at present, its *a′*, blown at the mean between possible sharpness and flatness, has 440 vibrations. There is no screw-stopper. This instrument was once the property of the celebrated Johann Joachim Quantz, Chamber-musician to Frederick the Second, King of Prussia, from 1741 until his death in 1773. Above the name of the maker, F. BOIE, the word "Quantz" is written in ink. See plate I., fig. G. In the year 1726, while staying in Paris, Quantz invented a second *d'*♯ key, not only in order to make the enharmonic difference between *d*♯ and *e*♭, but also to improve many other notes of the scale. After the date of this invention, of which he was exceedingly proud, Quantz always played on a two-keyed flute; it is, therefore, almost certain that the instrument under discussion was made prior to 1726, and it is at least probable that it was in his possession before he left Dresden for Rome in 1724. It was presented to the late Mr. Carli Zoeller, by Herr Albert Quantz, of Göttingen, grand-nephew of J. J. Quantz.

Lent by Mrs. Carli Zoeller.

50.

CONCERT-FLUTE of box-wood, with tips and cap of ivory, and two square-flapped silver keys on knobs, one being the ordinary closed *d'*♯ key, the other an open key, with a double lever, to close the *d'* hole and thus to cause the open end of the flute to give *c'*♯. The second joint is marked "4," and was evidently one of several interchangeable joints. By Biglioni of Rome, 1725 *ante*.

This instrument was also obtained from Herr Albert Quantz by Mr. Carli Zoeller. It is believed to have been brought from Rome by J. J. Quantz when he left that city in 1725. It has been but little used, which is probably owing to the poverty of its tone, and to the fact that Quantz objected strongly to the flute being carried below *d'*.

Lent by Mrs. Zoeller.

51.

FLUTE of decorated ivory, with one key. Each of the four "joints" is made up of several pieces. There is neither tuning slide nor screw-cork. This flute is exactly a semitone higher than the Boie flute (No. 49); it was probably made at about the same time and place, and was no doubt intended for an *e'*♭ flute.

Lent by the Rev. F. W. Galpin, M.A., F.L.S.

52.

CONCERT-FLUTE of box-wood, with tips of black horn, and one square-flapped brass key. Probably made in Germany.

Lent by the Rev. F. W. Galpin, M.A., F.L.S.

53.

CONCERT-FLUTE of box-wood, with ivory tips and cap, in four pieces. One square-flapped silver key. The proportions of the bore are very peculiar, the diameter at the cork being ·74 inch; at the lower end of the head-joint, ·72 inch; and at the upper end of the second joint, ·79 inch. The *a'* of this flute has but 400 vibrations, 3 vibrations below our present *g'*, but as this pitch is almost identical with that of the flute described by Henri Lambert in his celebrated paper (*Observations sur des flûtes*, Paris, 1775), it may be assumed that the instrument under description was a concert-flute of the period. It bears the name "T. LOT," above a lion rampant. Thomas Lot was one of five "*maîtres constructeurs*" of wind-instruments established in Paris in 1752. He was a member of the "*corporation des luthiers*" of that city in 1770, and he was still carrying on his business in 1785. The late Mr. Carli Zoeller, of whose collection this instrument formed part, estimated the date of its manufacture to be about 1756.

Lent by the Rev. F. W. Galpin, M.A., F.L.S.

54.

FLÛTE D'AMOUR of box-wood, in four pieces, with conoidal bore, and one brass key. There are no tips or mountings of any kind, nor is there any screw to the cork. Length from cork, 27·3 inches. Interior diameter of head-joint, ·78 inch. The *a* and *c* holes are bored obliquely, thus practically increasing their distance from the mouth-hole. The *a'* (*f'*♯ in sound) has 360 vibrations. By Oberlender. This flute is supposed to have been the property of the celebrated violoncellist Krafft, or Kraft, a member of Haydn's band. The name "Krafft" is written inside the cap.

Lent by the Rev. F. W. Galpin, M.A., F.L.S.

55.

CONCERT-FLUTE of ivory, with four square-flapped silver keys, mounted on "knobs," furnished with leathers. This instrument has a screw-stopper but no tuning slide. Its pitch is about a semitone below the present English pitch. By Cahusac of London, 1780 *circa*.

Lent by Messrs. Rudall, Carte and Co.

56.

WALKING-STICK-FLUTE of ivory, without keys. This appears to have been intended to form a flute at the upper end, and a piccolo at the lower, but it has evidently been subjected to injudicious experiment.

Lent by the *Grossherzogliches Museum*, Darmstadt.

57.

WALKING-STICK-FLUTE of light-coloured wood, with four keys fashioned in imitation of stumps of twigs. The *f*♮ key is for the right-hand thumb. The peculiar position of this key was first adopted by Dr. J. J. H. Ribock in 1784, but it never came into general favour.

Lent by Messrs. Henry Potter and Co.

58.

CONCERT-FLUTE of ebony mounted with ivory, in four pieces, with screw-stopper, and one square-flapped key. By Hoffmann.

Lent by the Rev. F. W. Galpin, M.A., F.L.S.

59.

CONCERT-FLUTE of ivory, with eight circular-flapped silver keys including the "long *c''* key"), furnished with leathers, and mounted on "knobs." This flute has a screw-stopper, and a tuning slide in the head-joint, consisting of a single tube of silver which slides in the unlined ivory. By (Richard) Potter of London. See plate I., fig. H.

Lent by the Rev. F. W. Galpin, M.A., F.L.S.

60.

FIFE in $a'\flat$, of German manufacture.

Lent by M. Césare Snoeck.

61.

CONCERT-FLUTE of box-wood, with ivory tips, graduated tuning slide (the outer tube of which is covered with wood), graduated screw-cork, and six silver keys (including those for c' and $c'\sharp$), on knobs, furnished with plugs of soft metal. By (Richard) Potter, Johnson's Court, London.

The graduated slide, the graduated cork, and the metal plugs were patented by Richard Potter in 1785, but tuning slides of various kinds had been in use for half-a-century before the date of the patent, and J. F. Boie, a celebrated flute maker of Göttingen, was the inventor of the metal plugs.

Lent by Messrs. Rudall, Carte and Co.

62.

CONCERT-FLUTE of box-wood, with ivory tips, tuning slide, screw-cork, and four silver keys with plugs of soft metal. By (Richard) Potter, London.

Lent by Messrs. Boosey and Co.

63.

FLUTE in *a*, of ebony, with ivory tips, screw-cork, and four silver keys with plugs. Probably a $b\flat$ flute of its time. By (Richard) Potter of London.

Lent by the Rev. F. W. Galpin, M.A., F.L.S.

NINETEENTH CENTURY.

64.

CONCERT-FLUTE of richly-cut glass, with broad bands of silver, and five silver keys mounted on "pillars," including the long c'' key. The keys have flat, circular flaps with leathers. This instrument has neither tuning slide nor screw-stopper. It consists of four pieces. See plate II., fig. C. By Laurent of Paris. Patented in Paris in 1806.

Lent by G. Donaldson, Esq.

65.

CONCERT-FLUTE of cocus-wood, in three pieces only. The tuning slide is formed at the junction of the head with the second joint. In addition to the ordinary eight keys there are a small key near the *a* hole, the purpose of which is doubtful; a *g*♯ shake key, and a lever for making the shake with the *b*♭ key by the first finger of the right hand. The finger-holes are unusually small for an English flute, the largest open holes being only ·26 inch in diameter. By Monzani of London. On the foot joint is the number 1811, but the date of manufacture is probably 1807 *circa*.

Lent by Messrs. Rudall, Carte and Co.

66.

CONCERT-FLUTE of box-wood, with ivory tips, and eight silver keys with plugs. This flute has the long *f* and *c''* keys, but is in other respects similar to that numbered 61. By William Henry Potter, London.

Lent by Messrs. Henry Potter and Co.

67.

CONCERT-FLUTE similar to No. 61, but the keys are wanting. By William Henry Potter, London.

Lent by Messrs. Henry Potter and Co.

68.

"FLAUTO DI VOCE," an alto flute of box-wood, with ivory tips and cap, and six keys on knobs, in *a*♭. MacGregor's patent of 1810. The head-joint is turned back so as to bring the mouth-hole more easily within reach, the double bore being cut in a single block of wood of oval exterior. There is the usual screw-stopper, but no tuning slide. In addition to the four ordinary closed keys, for *d*♯, *f*♮, *g*♯, and *b*♭, there are open keys for the *e* and *c''*♯ holes, for the purpose of reducing the stretch of the fingers. The keys have the original pads, which are covered with leather, and are probably stuffed with sponge according to the terms of the specification.

"A thin skin, stretched over a large opening at the side, almost opposite to the *c''*♯ hole, imparts a reedy tone. No mention is made of this in the specification of patent, but it is known that some old flutes were thus made, in order to give a sympathetic tone somewhat like that of the hautboy, hence the name, voice flute."—F. W. G.

By Wigley and McGregor, 151, Strand. Date on cap, 1811.

Lent by the Rev. F. W. Galpin, M.A., F.L.S.

69.

"BASS FLUTE" of box-wood, with ivory tips and cap, and eight brass keys on knobs. In *d*, therefore an octave lower than the concert-flute. MacGregor's patent of 1810. The head-joint is turned back on itself, by means of a curved tube of brass, in order to bring the mouth-hole within reach of the player. Besides the four ordinary closed keys, for *d*♯, *f*♮, *g*♯, and *b*♭, there are open keys for the *e*, *g*, *a*, and *c''*♯ holes, which would otherwise have been out of the reach of the fingers. See plate I., fig. K. The tone of the lowest octave is rather full, but that of the second and third octaves has an unpleasantly nasal character. The dimensions of a similar flute are given in the description of No. 70. By Wigley and McGregor, 151, Strand. 1811–16.

Flutes of this pattern were made in France before 1751, and in a volume of plates of that date, forming part of the great Encyclopædia of Diderot and D'Alembert, there is a good engraving of a flute in *g* which closely resembles that described above, excepting that, of course, there are no keys for *f*, *g*♯, or *b*♭. A similar flute, with an entire length of fifty inches, made by the celebrated Delusse about the year 1760, is now in the Museum of the Paris *Conservatoire*.

Lent by the *Conservatoire Royal de Musique*, Brussels.

70.

"BASS FLUTE" of box-wood, similar to that numbered 69, excepting that there is no cap, and that in place of the usual screw-stopper there is a solid ingot of gun-metal, with a deeply concave surface. The entire interior length, supposing the presence of an ordinary stopper correctly placed, is 43·5 inches. The bore is conoidal, its greatest diameter being 1·07 inch, and its least ·67 inch. By Wigley and McGregor, 151, Strand. 1811–16.

Lent by Messrs. Rudall, Carte and Co.

71.

CONCERT-FLUTE of glass. This instrument has the "long *f* key"; in other respects it closely resembles the flute numbered 64. By Laurent of Paris, 1812.

Lent by Messrs. Rudall, Carte and Co.

72.

CONCERT-FLUTE of ivory, elaborately ornamented, with eight silver keys mounted on "knobs," six of which have flat, circular flaps with leathers. The keys for *c'* and *c'*♯ have metal plugs. The head-joint, which is furnished with a screw-cork, is in one piece, the tuning slide being at the junction of the head with the second joint. This slide is a "double cylindrical tube" of silver, which was patented in 1814. The specification sets forth certain apocryphal advantages alleged to accrue from the application of such tubes to all the joints of a flute, but this specimen has only the one above mentioned, the other joints being united by the ordinary "pin and socket" with thread "lapping." See plate II., fig. E. The pitch of this flute is about a semitone below the present English pitch. By Wood of London.

Lent by G. Donaldson, Esq.

73.

FIFE of box-wood, in *b'*, no doubt a *c''* fife of the period.

Lent by M. César Snoeck.

74.

FIFE of brass, in *e''*♮, no doubt the *f''* of its time.

Lent by M. Césare Snoeck.

75.

FIFE in *g'*, by Carl Sattler.

Lent by M. Césare Snoeck.

76.

CONCERT-FLUTE of ebony, with broad fluted silver bands, tuning slide, screw-cork, and eight silver keys, on knobs, with flat circular flaps and leathers. The head-joint is fluted in imitation of an Ionic column, and is furnished with a silver lip-plate. The *b*♭ key has an extra lever for the first finger of the right hand. By Monzani. 1815.

Lent by Messrs. Rudall, Carte and Co.

77.

CONCERT-FLUTE of box-wood, with ivory tips and one brass key. By Willis of London. 1815.

Willis was the maker of the first flutes that were branded with the name RUDALL.

Lent by Messrs. Rudall, Carte and Co.

78.

CONCERT-FLUTE of box-wood, with ivory tips, screw-cork, and four square-flapped keys of silver. By Wafford.

Lent by Messrs. Rudall, Carte and Co.

79.

FLÛTE D'AMOUR of box-wood, tipped and capped with ivory. The tips are covered with silver. This instrument resembles the *flûte d'amour* by Oberlender (No. 54) excepting in the following particulars: it consists of three pieces only; the pin of the upper joint forms part of the head, which has a screw-cork, the socket being in the middle piece; it has four square-flapped silver keys mounted on knobs. The pitch is almost identical with that of No. 54. Length from cork 27·15 inches. Interior diameter of the head ·77 inch. By Clementi and Co. of London. 1819.

Lent by the Rev. F. W. Galpin, M.A., F.L.S.

80.

CONCERT-FLUTE of cocus-wood, with embossed silver tips, and eight cupped silver keys on knobs. The bore, at the upper end of the second joint, measures only ·7 inch. Made by Cornelius Ward under the direction of the celebrated Louis Drouet, who was established as a flute-maker at 23, Conduit Street, for about a year, 1818.

Lent by Messrs. Rudall, Carte and Co.

81.

FIFE of box-wood, in *g'*, in two pieces. By Christian of Amsterdam.

Lent by M. Césare Snoeck.

82.

FIFE of box-wood, in *a'*♭. By Key of London.

Lent by Messrs. Rudall, Carte and Co.

83.

FIFE of massive iron, with seven finger-holes, including one for the left-hand thumb. A hole, which once existed in the middle of the instrument, has been neatly plugged with iron. The holes, successively opened, give the following series of notes, *g'* (from the open end), *b'*, *c''*♯, *c''*♭, *g''*, *b''*♭, *c'''*♯ (from the thumb-hole), *d'''*♯. Evidently the work of a person totally unskilled in the construction of musical instruments.

Lent by M. Césare Snoeck.

84.

Concert-flute of cocus-wood, with eight cupped keys of silver, and an extra *b*♭ lever for the first finger of the right hand, all on knobs. This instrument is branded: "C. Nicholson's Improved," but it has not the large holes of most of the Nicholson flutes. The head-joint is turned in rings, like the rails of an "early English" chair, and the narrow silver bands are embossed. By Clementi, London.

Lent by Messrs. Boosey and Co.

85.

Concert-flute of box-wood, with ivory tips, screw-stopper, tuning slide, and six keys with metal plugs, including the "*c'* and *c'*♯ keys." By Astor and Horwood of London. The elder Nicholson preferred the flutes of Astor to those of any other maker, and his son, the celebrated Charles Nicholson, considered them superior to those of Potter.

Lent by the Rev. F. W. Galpin, M.A., F.L.S.

86.

Concert-flute of cocus-wood, with tuning slide, screw-cork, and six square-flapped keys of silver, on knobs, including the "*c'* and *c'*♯ keys." Four of the keys have leathers; the lowest two have plugs. By Key and Co. 1820.

Lent by Messrs. Rudall, Carte and Co.

87.

Concert-flute of box-wood mounted with ivory, in four pieces, with one key. By Millhouse of London.

Lent by Mr. E. Cawley, Bandmaster 2nd Royal Scots.

88.

CONCERT-FLUTE of ebony, with thirteen silver keys, descending to the *g* of the violin. The extra five keys of the foot-joint are given: one to the little finger of the right hand; two to the little finger of the left hand, and two to the left hand thumb. All the keys are furnished with metal plugs. The lower end of the flute is turned back, the reversed portion extending from below the *b*♮ hole almost as far as the *d'*♯ hole. By Koch of Vienna. 1827 *ante*. Once the property of the well-known Sedlatzek.

Lent by Messrs. Rudall, Carte and Co.

89.

CONCERT-FLUTE of box-wood, with ivory tips and cap, tuning slide, screw-cork, and six silver keys, on knobs, including the "*c'* and *c'*♯ keys." The last mentioned keys have plugs; the others have flat, circular flaps, which, nevertheless, are furnished with stuffed pads. By Rudall and Rose, 15, Piazza, Covent Garden. 1830 *circa*.

Lent by Messrs. Rudall, Carte and Co.

90.

CONCERT-FLUTE of cocus-wood, with screw-cork, tuning slide, and eight silver keys mounted on pillars. Six of the keys have cups of shell-pattern. The "*c'* and *c'*♯ keys" have metal plugs closing on square plates. The holes are very small. By Sax *père* of Brussels. Marked "J. S."

Lent by E. Hooker, Esq.

91.

CONCERT-FLUTE of box-wood, with silver tips and cap, and eight silver keys, on knobs, five of which have cups with pads, while the three foot-keys have plugs and square plates. This flute is of Charles Nicholson's model, that is, a "large-holed flute" of its time, about 1840. There is an excavation for the reception of the left hand first finger, as always used by Nicholson. Although the flute has the ordinary tuning slide and screw-stopper the cap is embossed in the same manner as that of the "patent head," which, by means of double screws, enabled the slide and the stopper to be adjusted simultaneously by merely turning the cap. This patent is dated 1832. By Rudall and Rose.

Lent by Messrs. Rudall, Carte and Co.

92.

FLUTE of box-wood, in *a'♭*, in three pieces, with conoidal bore. By Collard and Collard, London.

Lent by M. Césare Snoeck.

93.

FLUTE of box-wood, in *f'*, with tips of horn, and one brass key.

Lent by the Rev. F. W. Galpin, M.A., F.L.S.

94.

FLUTE, in *a'♭*, in three pieces, with conoidal bore. By C. E. Purday, London.

Lent by M. Césare Snoeck.

95.

FIFE of brass, in *c''*. By Potter, London.

Lent by Messrs. Henry Potter and Co.

96.

FLUTE of box-wood, in one piece, with six finger-holes only. In *c''*. In outward form a fife, but with conoidal bore. By Potter, 30, Charing Cross.

Lent by Messrs. Henry Potter and Co.

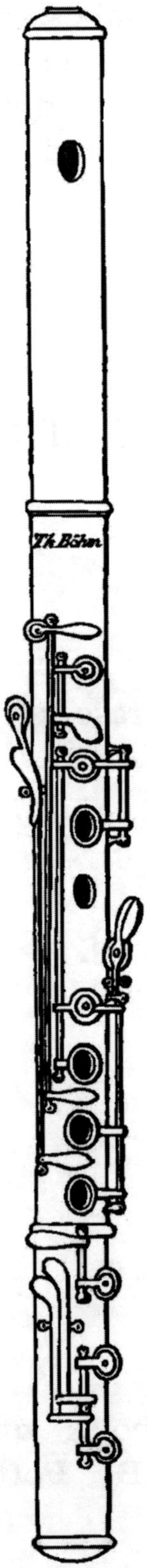

No. 97.

97.

CONCERT-FLUTE of cocus-wood, with conoidal bore, silver keys, &c. This is almost an exact copy of the so-called "Boehm flute," as made by Th. Boehm between the years 1835 and 1846. It bears little resemblance, either in the positions of the holes or in the fingering, to "Boehm's newly invented patent flute" of 1831–2, but it differs from Gordon's flute very slightly in either respect, the arrangement of the holes being on a similar principle, while the fingering is only changed in the following particulars:—Gordon retained the old fingering for *g*♯, at the same time preserving intact his system of open keys; Boehm adopted the "open *g*♯" of Tromlitz and Pottgiesser. Gordon employed an open *d'*♯ key, and governed the "*c'* and *c'*♯ keys" by the little finger of the left hand; Boehm retained the old fingering for *c'*, *c'*♯, and *d'*♯. The *d''* key, so useful for shakes, was invented by Capeller of Munich, Boehm's instructor, in or before 1811. The valuable *d''*♯ key, which is not shown in the annexed wood-cut, was invented by Victor Côche of Paris, in or before 1838. (See No. 108.) The machinery of this flute, notwithstanding the old-fashioned screw-cups of the keys and the flat brass springs, is an indubitable improvement on that of Gordon's, but those parts of it which were designed by Boehm have long since fallen into disuse. Four of the open finger-holes are furnished with rings instead of the crescents used by Gordon.

The wood-cut is an exact reproduction, on a reduced scale, of Boehm's engraving of 1847.

By Rudall and Rose, 1, Tavistock Street, Covent Garden. 1844 *circa*.

Lent by H. Veysie, Esq.

98.

CONCERT-FLUTE of cocus-wood, with conoidal bore and silver fittings. Ward's patent of 1842. The inventor's object was to construct a flute, on the "open-keyed" system, with greater mechanical facilities than had previously been obtained, but although there are many points of excellence in this instrument, it is not equal, as a whole, to the inventions it was intended to supersede. In some respects it bears strong resemblance to the flutes of Pottgiesser, particularly in regard to the four open holes for the fingers of the right hand, and the *d'*♯ and *g*♯ levers for the left-hand thumb. Its best point is the appropriation of the touches of the *c'* and *c'*♯ keys to the left-hand thumb. These keys are closed by traction-levers similar to those known to have been employed by Captain Gordon. Ward, "in 1839, began to make what is called the Boehm-flute in London," and he was the first in this country to make the valuable and now well-known "needle-springs." The flute here described has an extra *b*♮ lever for the first finger of the left hand, and extra *g*♯ levers for the third and fourth fingers of the right hand. These additions were suggested by the writer in 1844. A lever precisely similar in its object to the extra *b*♮ lever of this flute is now in use on the instrument numbered 108. The "stopper" of Ward's flute is moved by means of an excentric disc, within the head, which is connected with an index-lever outside. This moves on a dial furnished with numbers which correspond to others on a graduated tuning slide. The annexed wood-cut is copied from Ward's pamphlet, *The Flute Explained*, London, 1844. By Cornelius Ward of London. 1845 *circa*.

Lent by Messrs. Rudall, Carte and Co.

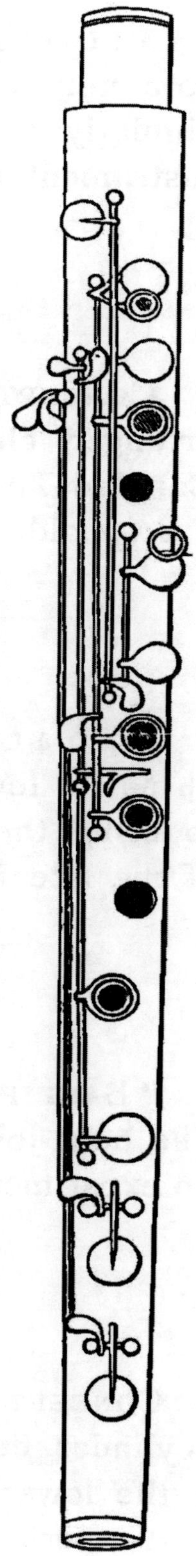

No. 98.

99.

FLUTE of cocus-wood, in *c'*, descending by means of two extra keys to a nominal *b♭*, *a♭* in sound. The foot-joint is turned back on itself similarly to that of the flute numbered 88. In other respects the instrument resembles No. 98. By Cornelius Ward, London.

Lent by Messrs. Rudall, Carte and Co.

100.

CONCERT-FLUTE of light-brown wood, with uncovered finger-holes arranged chromatically. An experiment of the late Dr. Burghley, of Camden Town, the first to suggest (in 1845) the idea of the well-known "Briccialdi *b♭* key."

Lent by the Rev. F. W. Galpin, M.A., F.L.S.

101.

ALTO FLUTE of light brown wood, with six keys of ebony, giving *a♭* as its lowest note. The head-joint is bent back on itself in order to bring the mouth-hole within reach of the player. An experiment of the late Dr. Burghley.

Lent by Messrs. Rudall, Carte and Co.

102.

"BASS FLUTE" of light-brown wood, with eleven keys of ebony. The head-joint is bent backwards like that of the flute numbered 101. An experiment of the late Dr. Burghley.

Lent by Messrs. Rudall, Carte and Co.

103.

CONCERT-FLUTE of metal, with silver mouth-plate, the so-called "cylinder flute." For the restoration of the original cylindrical form to the lower portion of the bore, and the union therewith of a head-joint tapering towards the stopper, Boehm obtained an English patent in the name of John Mitchell Rose (one of the founders of the firm of Rudall, Carte and Co.), in the year 1847.

The cylindrical part of the bore has a diameter of ·748 inch. The diameter of the head-joint at the mouth-hole varies considerably in different specimens, but Boehm laid down a rule that it should measure ·669 at the centre of the mouth-hole, and he considered that the lines of the interior of the head should form a portion of a parabola. The specimen here shown is of the original pattern, and was made by Boehm, probably about the year 1848. The fingering is the same as that of the flute numbered 97, but this bore is only adapted for holes of a larger size than the unaided fingers could conveniently cover, therefore it was necessary that every hole should be covered by a key. Boehm's machinery for effecting this object is of the rudest construction, and extremely uncertain in its action, but, by the successive improvements of various constructors of Paris and London, the "stopping" of the keys has been rendered perfect. The holes vary irregularly in size from ·46 inch, for the *c''* hole, to ·54 inch, for the *d'* hole. The *c'*♯ hole measures ·535 inch. The distances between the holes are also extremely irregular, and appear to have been arranged on no system whatever. Until the year 1864 the best flutes of this pattern were made with holes, from that for *c''*♮ downwards, of the uniform diameter of ·52 inch.

The "crutch" for the left-hand thumb is a contrivance invented by Boehm for the purpose of rendering the instrument steady during performance. It is absolutely unnecessary, and has long been discarded in England, even by the few who ever used it.

A flute similar to this gained, in spite of its imperfections, the Council-medal of the Great Exhibition of 1851. See plate I., fig. I.

Lent by Alfred Hays, Esq.

104.

CONCERT-FLUTE of metal. Crutch wanting. Excepting that it has a rude imitation of the "Briccialdi *b*♭ key," and a hollowed mouth-piece of ivory entirely surrounding the head-joint, this instrument exactly resembles that numbered 103. By Theobald Boehm, Munich. 1850 *circa*.

Lent by Alfred Hays, Esq.

105.

CONCERT-FLUTE of cocus-wood, with improved "cylinder bore" and silver fittings. All the finger-holes are covered by keys. Carte's "1851 flute." The object of the inventor of this flute was to "design a mechanism which should retain the open keys . . . of Boehm's flute, and yet secure a greater facility of fingering," and he claims in his specification that "the fingering is easier than that of the Boehm or of the old system. It is, at the same time, a smaller departure from the latter." Mr. Carte gained a prize-medal for this instrument at the Exhibition of 1851. The construction of the flute will be best understood by an examination of the wood-cut (see page 47). The now well-known "open *d''*" first appeared on a flute, patented in 1850, which was the immediate precursor of, and which did not differ greatly from, the flute of 1851. In this same year a well-known amateur suggested a nearer approach to the fingering of the old flute, and to this end he had an instrument made with a "closed *g*♯ key" and without the open *d''* key, in place of which he substituted the ordinary closed shake-key, but in other respects the same as the 1851 flute. In this form the instrument is still made, but it may be considered to have been superseded by the flute of 1867 (No. 106), which is vastly superior to it. By Rudall, Rose, Carte and Co.

Lent by Messrs. Rudall, Carte and Co.

106.

CONCERT-FLUTE of silver, with improved "cylinder bore." All the finger-holes are covered by keys. This instrument, which is generally known as the "1867 patent" (see page 47), combines, in its fingering, the principal features of Mr. Carte's flute of 1851 (see No. 105) with many of the best points of the so-called "Boehm system." Its greatest advantages over the flute of 1851 are gained by the abandonment of the long *f*♮ key of that instrument (see the engraving), and the substitution of the *f*♮ of the "Boehm-flute." In tuning and tone it does not differ from other well-constructed flutes of the period. By Rudall, Carte and Co.

Lent by Messrs. Rudall, Carte and Co.

No. 105.
Mr. Carte's Patent of 1851.

No. 123.
"Radcliff Model."

No. 106.
Mr. Carte's Patent of 1867.

No. 107.

107.

"Bass flute," or, more correctly, alto flute, of silver, in *a*, descending by means of the "*c′*♯ and *c′*♮ keys" to the *g* of the violin. The bore of this flute was designed by Boehm. The position and the size of the holes, as well as the entire mechanism, have been arranged and most ingeniously designed by Mr. Henry W. Carte. The fingering is that of the flute of 1867. Length, from the face of the stopper to the open end, 31·63 inches. Diameter of the cylindrical part of the bore 1·035 inch. Diameter of the narrowest part (at the stopper) ·906 inch. The finger-holes, with the exception of those for *c″*♯ and *d″*, have a uniform diameter of ·744 inch. By Rudall, Carte and Co.

Lent by Messrs. Rudall, Carte and Co.

108.

Concert-flute of ebonite, with improved "cylinder bore" and silver fittings. "Rockstro's model." All the finger-holes are covered by keys, but five of these are perforated in the centre, an old French custom, so that partial opening may be effected when desired. The writer's chief object in designing this flute was to perfect a system of tuning which he initiated in 1852 and improved in 1858. The system could only be carried out by giving all the holes, but the three highest, a uniform diameter of approximately ·64 inch, and this was done in 1864. This method of tuning is now constantly employed, though not in its full perfection, on flutes with smaller holes. The general fingering of this model is precisely the same as that of the flutes numbered 97 and 103, but there are changes in, and additions to, the mechanism which afford certainty in action and facility in execution. Chief among the additions are the following: an extra *f*♯ lever for the third finger of the right hand; an extra *b*♮ lever for making that note without the use of the thumb; a large hole, with a closed key connected with the ordinary *d''* key, which is useful in alternations of *d''* and *d'''* with certain notes below them; a lever partly closing the *c''*♮ hole by the action of the second finger of the left hand, and thus giving an easy *f'''*♯ in alternation with *e'''*, besides other important advantages. The instrument exhibited has the latest addition to the flute, namely, "the tubular extension of the *c''*♯ hole," which was contrived by the writer in 1889. The advantages of this may be thus summed up shortly: the enlargement of the hole greatly improves the *c''*♯ as well as the *c'''*♯, and the added tube renders the hole more generally useful than before, while there are no resultant disadvantages. The annexed wood-cut was made prior to the date of this improvement. Made by Rudall, Carte and Co. in 1877. Completed in 1889.

Lent by Miss G. M. Rockstro.

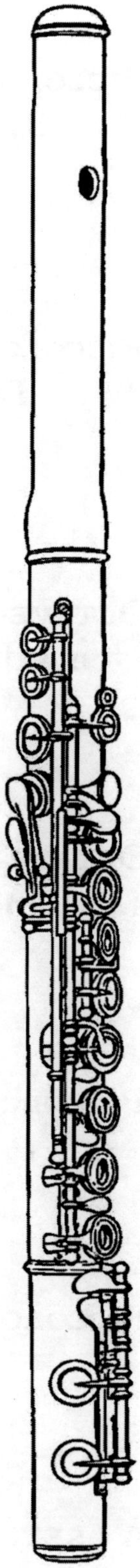

No. 108.

109.

FLUTE of cocus-wood, with four brass keys. In *f'*. By Rudall, Carte and Co.

Lent by Messrs. Rudall, Carte and Co.

110.

PICCOLO of cocus-wood, with four brass keys on knobs. In *f''*.

Lent by Messrs. Rudall, Carte and Co.

111.

PICCOLO of cocus-wood, with six German silver keys on pillars. In *e''*♭. By Rudall, Carte and Co., 23, Berners Street.

Lent by Messrs. Rudall, Carte and Co.

112.

PICCOLO of cocus-wood, with six German silver keys on pillars. In *f''*. By Rudall, Carte and Co., 23, Berners Street.

Lent by Messrs. Rudall, Carte and Co.

113.

PICCOLO of cocus-wood, with six German silver keys on knobs. In *c''*♭. By Rudall, Carte and Co., 23, Berners Street.

Lent by Messrs. Rudall, Carte and Co.

114.

OCTAVE-FLUTE (piccolo in *d''*) of cocus-wood, with six German silver keys on pillars.

Lent by Messrs. Rudall, Carte and Co.

115.

OCTAVE-FLUTE (piccolo in *d''*) of cocus-wood, with six German silver keys on knobs.

Lent by Messrs. Rudall, Carte and Co.

116.

PICCOLO of cocus-wood, with four brass keys on knobs. In *c''*♭.

Lent by Messrs. Rudall, Carte and Co.

117.

PICCOLO of ebonite, with six German silver keys on pillars. In *c''*♭.

Lent by Messrs. Rudall, Carte and Co.

118.

A SET OF TWO FLUTES AND A PICCOLO, of cocus-wood, with conoidal bore. "Boehm-fingering," with the open *g*♯ key. The flutes are in *c'*♭ and *f'*; the holes of these are all covered by keys. The piccolo is in *e''*♭, and has ring-keys, somewhat similar in their appearance to those of No. 97 but very much improved in their construction and action. By Rudall, Carte and Co., 23, Berners Street.

Lent by Colonel Shaw-Hellier.

119.

FLUTE of cocus-wood, with four brass keys. In *b'*♭.

Lent by Messrs. Rudall, Carte and Co.

120.

FLUTE of ebonite, in *e'*♭, with eight keys on pillars. Conoidal bore.

Lent by Messrs. Rudall, Carte and Co.

121.

FLUTE of ebonite, similar to that numbered 120.

Lent by Messrs. Rudall, Carte and Co.

122.

CONCERT-FLUTE of cocus-wood, with "cylinder" bore, and eight keys on pillars. By Rudall, Carte and Co.

Lent by Messrs. Rudall, Carte and Co.

123.

CONCERT-FLUTE of cocus-wood, with conoidal bore. By Rudall, Carte and Co. "Radcliff Model." This flute is thus described by Mr. John Radcliff:—"The fingering is a near approach to the old system (eight keyed) but it carries out the modern method of venting; through the *B* and *C* shake being made by a separate lever, the *C* hole can be opened when the first finger of the right hand is down. It is contrived that the duplicate *G*♯ hole shall be closed in making the top *E*♮, so as to prevent the breaking of that note. This flute was first made in 1870." The woodcut upon page 47 shows a silver flute of this model.

Lent by Messrs. Rudall, Carte and Co.

124.

CONCERT-FLUTE, "Boehm Model," of ebonite, with German silver keys, closed *g*♯. 1890. By Boosey and Co., who have kindly supplied the following description:—

"The novelty in this instrument consists in the style of pad. Hitherto the centres of the pads have been prevented from bulging by being screwed down against a boss in the cup with a screw carrying a large flat washer. The pads in this flute are kept in shape by rivets and washers of aluminium, and the boss in the cup is dispensed with. By this means the pads are kept both very light and very air-tight."

Lent by Messrs. Boosey and Co.

III.

CLASS—BAGPIPES.

INSTRUMENTS with enclosed reeds, blown from a reservoir of air, and known at the present day by the generic term of "Bagpipe," are of very remote antiquity. They were certainly known and used by the ancient Babylonians, and in the many Sanskrit treatises upon music that are still remaining the bagpipe is described. It would appear to have been carried into India by the Aryans, and it is now known under the name of "Moshuq"; and in Southern India as the "S'ruti upanga."

It is even possible that Bagpipes were used by the Hebrews in the Temple service, and upon an ancient terra-cotta, discovered some years since at Tarsus, in Asia Minor, is a representation of what is probably the bagpipe commonly in use at that period, about 200 B.C. By the Greeks the bagpipe was usually called ἄσκαυλος or συμφώνια; while among the Romans it took the characteristic name of "Tibia utricularis," and it is said to have been a favourite instrument of the Emperor Nero, whose love for music has been noticed freely by Tacitus and other historians. Whether we should regard the bagpipe as a Roman importation to this country or not seems an exceedingly doubtful point. But it is certain that it was very well known here shortly after the Roman conquest, and it is a singular fact it is mentioned by Procopius as the instrument of war of the Roman infantry.

During the Middle Ages the bagpipe was used both in England and on the Continent largely, and appears to have been found in monasteries and religious houses, where it served as an accompaniment to the chanting. An illustration of an instrument of this kind of the 9th century is given by Gerbert, Abbot of St. Blaise (*De Cantu et Musica Sacra*), and called by him "*Chorus*." The bagpipe appears to have retained its popularity for some centuries later, and to have been in general use, for on the Minstrels' gallery in Exeter Cathedral another representation of it is seen. This gallery dates from the 14th century, and was constructed during the reign of King Edward III. The bagpipe is held by the player much as at the present day. The single drone rests upon his left shoulder, the bag being beneath his left elbow. The instrument is inflated from the mouth, and he is holding the chanter and playing upon it; the position of the hands is noticeable, the right hand being uppermost; and the right thumb is evidently stopping a hole on the underside of the chanter.

Of the advent of the bagpipe into Scotland or Ireland it is difficult to say much with certainty. It appears to have been, from very early times, a special instrument with the Celtic races, and a very interesting old Celtic pipe of the 15th century is presently described. This pipe appears to be almost the only instrument of that age in existence, and it is in a singularly good state of preservation. Its authenticity is beyond doubt. The bagpipe appears to have been in use in Ireland about the same time, for in an ancient Irish MS. of the year 1300, known to the late Mr. Carl Engel, is a representation of a pig gravely employed in playing the bagpipe. In the following century the pipes were in common use as a military instrument; and Derrick, who wrote in 1581, gives, in his "Image of Ireland," a picture of a band of Irish warriors marching out preceded by a piper. The pipe in this case has two drones held over the left shoulder, and is inflated from the mouth.

That the bagpipe appears to have come into Ireland from Scotland, is an opinion advanced by Mr. Walker in his *Historical Memoirs of the Irish Bards* (Dublin 1786), where the subject has been very fully treated of. According to Aristides Quintilianus, the instrument prevailed from very early times in the Highlands of Scotland. Mr. O'Connor, the eminent antiquarian, informs us (*Dissertation on the History of Ireland*) that one of the instruments in use amongst the Scots, or ancient Irish, was the *Adharcaidh Cuil*, that is, a collection of pipes with a bag, or rather a musical bag. We also learn that another instrument, of more simple make, called *Cuisley Ciuil*, was employed as a means of marking the measure for the Rinkey, or field dance, of the ancient Irish. The Irish pipes used prior to the 16th century were blown by means of a pipe held in the mouth of the player. The chanter had six finger-holes only; and there were two drones. The instrument thus made was known by the name of *Piobmala*. Bellows for inflation of the bag appear to have come into use in Europe generally about the 16th century; Irish pipes blown thus were called *Cuislean*, or elbow pipes. Accurate information concerning the development of the Irish bagpipe is, however, exceedingly difficult to procure, but it seems that the instrument underwent gradual improvements until it eventually took the form of the Union pipes, or Irish bagpipe of the present day. The name of Union pipes probably originated from the instrument having appeared about the time of union of the Irish and English Parliaments.

In Germany the bagpipe was known as *Sackpfeiff*, and Prætorius, who wrote in 1618 (*Syntagma Musicum*), describes minutely four or five different varieties, together with the respective compass and tuning of each. The largest bagpipe, he tells us, was called *Bock*, and was inflated by the mouth. The chanter had a compass of one octave from *c* to *c′*; the drone was tuned to *C*; in the *Grosser Bock* the drone was, however, a fourth lower, and sounded *G,*. Another variety of bagpipe, called *Schäffer-pfeiff*, was smaller, but had two drones tuned to *b*♭ and *f′*, and the chanter had a compass from *f′* to *f″*. Prætorius tells us that the notes given by the upper finger-holes upon the chanter of this instrument were of faulty intonation; the reason assigned being that there being no thumb-hole at the back, as in all the other bagpipes, faults of intonation could not be corrected. A smaller bagpipe, called *Hümmelchen*, possessed a compass extending from *c″* to *c‴*, and had two drones tuned to *f′* and *c″*. The smallest instrument of this kind was known as *Dudey*; its three drones were tuned to *e′*♭, *b′*♭, and *c″*♭, and the compass of its chanter was from *f″* to *c‴*.

In Magdeburg and the immediate neighbourhood there was found another species of bagpipe, somewhat similar to the later Calabrian pipes, of which a fine specimen was exhibited in this collection. The Magdeburg pipes somewhat resembled the *Schäffer-pfeiff*, but sounded a third lower in tone. There were two chanters mounted in the same stock, that for the left hand giving the notes *g*, *a*, *b*♭, *c′*, *d′*, and that for the right *d′*, *e′*, *f′*, *g′*, *a′*. This arrangement allowed of simple airs being performed in two parts.

The application of the bellows to the bagpipe appears to have originated in Ireland, whence it was carried to France, where the instrument eventually took the form of the musette, and was further improved and perfected by Hotteterre the elder. The improvements designed by him consisted in the extension of the scale by means of keys, and the addition of a second chanter. The musette thus perfected rapidly made its way, and becoming popular and fashionable in the reign of Louis XIV., was introduced into the orchestra by Lully. A quartet of these instruments was, even in the time of Prætorius, not uncommonly met with; but we are told that the "harmony" thus produced was seldom pleasing to the ear. At the end of the 17th century the musette became to wind instruments what the Vielle was to stringed; and the many beautiful specimens that remain show us what wealth of ornamentation and skilled workmanship was lavished upon them.

An elaborate tutor for the musette was written by Borjon, a distinguished lawyer of the time, and published at Lyons in 1672; and that the instrument retained its popularity is proved by the publication of a similar work by the younger Hotteterre, known also as Hotteterre le Romain. This latter, *Méthode pour la Musctte,* was published at Paris in 1738 in quarto. The best makers of musettes were, according to M. Lavoix (*Histoire de l'Instrumentation,* Paris, 1878), the elder Hotteterre, Perrin, and Lissieux of Lyons. Towards the latter part of the last century the musette gradually became disused, and with the dawn of the 19th century disappeared entirely; and specimens of the instrument are now of value as musical and artistic curiosities only, and as such are eagerly sought after by collectors.

The Scotch Highland pipes are, perhaps, the best known of all the various forms of the bagpipe. The modern form is constructed with three drones, two of which are tuned an octave below the lower *a'* of the chanter; and the longer drone a second octave below. Some works give the tuning as *G*, *d*, *g*, and also *D*, *A*, *d*. The long drone does not appear prior to the 16th century, but of its introduction it is difficult to speak with certainty. The chanter of the Highland pipe is conical in bore, and is pierced with seven finger-holes, and a thumb-hole at the back. The compass consists of but nine notes, from *g'* to *a''* inclusive; and the temperament of the scale thus produced is very peculiar, there appearing to be no definite rule by which the result is obtained. The chanter has a double reed, rather like that of the bassoon; the drone reed is single, and more nearly resembles that of the Egyptain Arghool, or the primitive "squeaker" which children make from pieces of straw.

The prominent feature in all bagpipe music consists in the employment of ornamental or grace notes, termed by Scotch pipers "warblers." Such *fiorituri* are very commonly made use of, and a skilful piper will manage to introduce a "warbler" of eleven notes between the last up beat and the first down beat of a bar. The usual "warbler," however, consists but of five or six notes. The highest form of bagpipe music is the *Piobaireachd*, or, as it is more usually called, *Pibroch*. This is usually difficult of execution, and consists of an air or theme called *urlar*, which is made the subject of variations, three or four in number, and increasing in difficulty and pace. The air is occasionally repeated, and ultimately ends the piece. And the *pibroch* has been recently adapted as a form for orchestral composition by Dr. A. C. Mackenzie, whose well-known and beautiful *pibroch* has been frequently performed within the last few years. The martial character and inspiriting nature of the pipes as an instrument of military music is so well known and so fully recognised that further comment is unnecessary.

125.

Highland Bagpipe. 15th century. This curious and interesting bagpipe consists of two drones and chanter finely ornamented with Celtic patterns carved in circular bands. The drones are inserted in a single stock, formed apparently from a forked branch, the fork giving the proper spread for the shoulder. Carved on the stock are the letters R. McD.; under them is a representation of a galley, and in Roman numerals the date M: CCCC: IX. The letters, both of the initials and date, are of the Gothic type in use during the 15th century. On the reverse side of the stock is a triplet of foliated scroll work. There are round the ends of the forks bands of interlaced work. The lower part of one of the drones has a somewhat similar band in the centre; the corresponding piece of the other drone is not original. The head-pieces of the drones have each two bands of interlaced work, and they terminate in cup-shaped heads ornamented in the same manner. The chanter, which has seven finger-holes in front, and a thumb-hole behind, very much worn, is also ornamented with interlaced bands at both extremities. The nail heads round the bell are decorated with engraved designs. The metal ferrules, with which the instrument is mounted, are original, and nicely engraved with Celtic designs. The drones and chanter are apparently made of thorn. The drones were tuned to *A*, in unison with the note given by the lowest finger-hole of the chanter when uncovered. See plate IX., fig. A.

Lent by Messrs. J. and R. Glen.

126.

MUSETTE, French. This beautiful instrument, formerly in the Tolbecque collection, dates from the latter part of the 17th century. It is blown by means of a bellows held under the right elbow; the bag, covered with red silk brocade, is held under the left elbow of the player. There are two chanters of ivory (called *Chalumeau*) mounted in one stock; the smaller chanter is fixed on to the larger. The larger chanter is pierced with eight holes, which give the following series:

the bell note being of course *f'*. There are seven silver keys, mounted upon knobs, which furnish the following additional sounds:

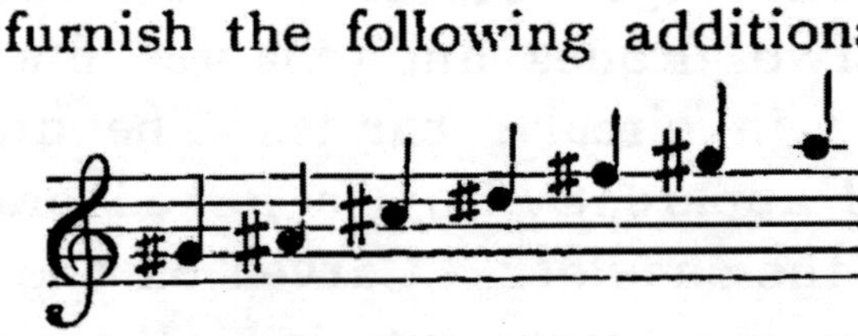

The first hole is made double, so that, by half closing, the *f'*♯ can be obtained. The smaller chanter, fixed parallel to the larger, is flat, and has three keys upon each side, giving the following sounds:

The keys 1, 2, 3 are worked with the thumb of the right hand, the others (shown uppermost in the plate) by the little finger of the left hand.

The drone, called Bourdon, consists of an ivory cylinder pierced with a series of channels of very small diameter, parallel to its axis. These channels are arranged by threes and twos, so as to form four or five separate single tubes of the proper length for the sound to be produced. The channels open by means of longitudinal slits upon the circumference of the cylinder; they are tuned to the required length by means of sliders, termed technically "layettes." The drones are usually tuned as follows:

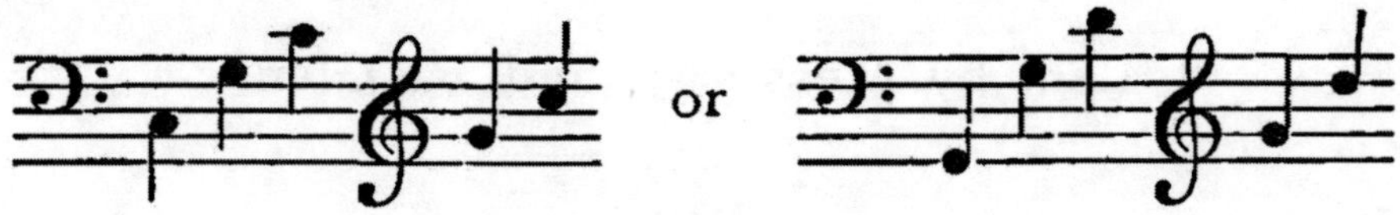

It is interesting to note that the reeds, both chanter and drone, are *double*. This association of a cylindrical bore and double reed would be hardly possible were it not that the bore is singularly small, being only about ⅛th of an inch. As cylindrical tubes, thus employed, speak as *closed* pipes, the depth of the pitch can be thus accounted for. Plate IX., fig. F.

Lent by the *Conservatoire Royal de Musique*, Brussels.

127.

PASTORAL BAGPIPE, French. 17th century. There is one drone only, tuned to the lowest hole of the chanter uncovered. The bag is inflated by the mouth, and when in use is held on the left breast.

Lent by Messrs. J. and R. Glen.

128.

MUSETTE, French. 17th century. This instrument is very similar to that previously described, and appears to be of much the same date. The barrel and chanters are of ebony, with ivory tips most artistically worked. The bag is covered with yellow silk brocade and fringed with gold lace. The "Grand Chalumeau" is fitted with five keys only, the "Petit Chalumeau" with six. The barrel has no less than thirteen sliders, and is apparently made to hold six instead of five reeds.

Lent by C. Van Raalte, Esq.

129.

Musette, French. 17th century. This beautiful instrument is in tuning and make identical with No. 126. The chanters, however, are of ebony, with ivory tips. The barrel differs slightly from that of No. 126, in that it has spaces for four reeds only. The bag is covered with silk brocade and edged with black silk fringe. It is inflated by bellows, the sides of which are beautifully inlaid with devices of fruit, flowers, and butterflies.

Lent by Messrs. J. and R. Glen.

130.

Cornemuse, French. 17th century. The cornemuse differs from the musette, in that it is of simpler construction, and is inflated from the mouth. The drone and chanter are of ivory, and are fixed parallel in one stock. The chanter is pierced with nine finger-holes in front and a thumb-hole at back. The drone was tuned by means of a stopper. The bag is covered with red silk brocade, worked with flowers and fringed with gold lace.

The usual compass of the cornemuse was

or to the e'' above, the drone being tuned in unison with c'. The cornemuse frequently had another drone, giving the octave lower, mounted in a separate stock. Instruments of this description were in use in the 16th and 17th centuries, and were usually played in consort with other wind instruments called in France "Hautbois de Poîtou," the reeds of which were enclosed within a cap, as in the cromorne. Père Mersenne, in his *Harmonie Universelle*, gives a *Cantilena* in four parts, the upper of which is taken by the cornemuse, the others by the instruments just mentioned. Plate IX., fig. E.

Lent by C. Van Raalte, Esq.

131.

Lowland Bagpipe, Scotch. 18th century. The bag is covered with red velvet, and is inflated by the mouth. The chanter, made of light red wood and tipped with horn, contains seven finger-holes and a thumb-hole at the back. The three drones, of the same wood, are tipped with ivory, beautifully engraved, and are mounted in one stock. The Lowland bagpipe is tuned like the modern Highland pipe, the drones, two tenor and one bass, being tuned to *a* and *A*, in accord with the lowest finger-hole on the chanter when uncovered.

Lent by Messrs. J. and R. Glen.

132.

CALABRIAN BAGPIPE. The bag is of goatskin, with very long hair, and is inflated by the mouth. The chanters and the drones are all fixed in one stock. The chanter for the left hand contains three finger-holes and a thumb-hole; that for the right hand is somewhat larger, and has three finger-holes, and a key for the low note, enclosed within a box as in the old bass Pommer. The two drones are somewhat shorter, and are evidently tuned in octaves. The workmanship is curious, and is apparently of the early part of the 18th century.

Lent by Messrs. J. and R. Glen.

133.

UNION PIPES, or Irish Bagpipe. The chanter is of ebony, containing seven finger-holes and a thumb-hole; there are eight brass keys. The drones are mounted all in one stock. The bag is covered with green velvet, and is inflated by means of bellows. The instrument is stamped "Kernia, Dublin." The chanter has a chromatic scale of two octaves as follows:

The drones are tuned to *A* of different octaves; and the regulators, *i.e.* the parts other than the chanter having keys, give the following:

and this arrangement, which allows of a rude harmony of tonic and dominant chords, is manipulated by the elbow of the player.

Lent by Messrs. J. and R. Glen.

134.

UNION PIPES, or Irish Bagpipes. Stamped "Kernia, Dublin." 18th century. This instrument is, in general construction, very similar to that previously described. There are, however, only two regulators instead of three, as in the last specimen. See plate IX., fig. D.

Lent by G. Butler, Esq.

135.

BIGNOU, or Breton Bagpipe. The word "Bignou" is derived from a Breton word, *bigno* (= se renfler beaucoup). The bag is of rough leather, inflated by the mouth. The drone is ornamented with tin, rather curiously worked; the chanter contains seven finger-holes, and is apparently constructed for either a left or right handed player. The drone is tuned to the lowest hole of the chanter uncovered.

Lent by Messrs. Rudall, Carte and Co.

136.

NORTHUMBRIAN OR BORDER BAGPIPE. This beautiful instrument is mounted with silver and ivory. The chanter, which is of black wood, is pierced with seven holes in front and a thumb-hole behind. The chanter is stopped at the lower end, so that when all the holes are closed the pipe is silent. There are seven flat silver keys, working upon knobs, and giving g'', $f''\sharp$, $c''\sharp$, b', d', c'. The compass is from

 to 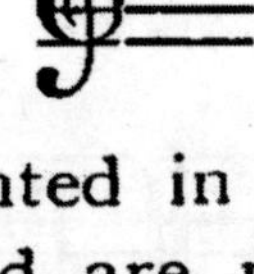

There are four drones, of ivory, mounted in one stock. These drones are tuned by means of stoppers, and are provided with an arrangement so that any one can be shut off at will. They are tuned usually to the tonic and dominant of the natural scale. The drones are

ornamented by long streamers of blue silk; the bag is covered with purple velvet, and is inflated by bellows. 18th century. See plate IX., fig. C.

Lent by the Rev. F. W. Galpin, M.A., F.L.S.

137.

NORTHUMBRIAN OR BORDER BAGPIPE. This instrument has a chanter of ebony, pierced with seven finger-holes and a thumb-hole; there are seven brass keys. The drones are four in number, tuned by means of stoppers, made of ivory, tipped with silver. The compass and construction of this pipe is similar to No. 136. 18th century.

Lent by Messrs. Köhler and Son.

138.

NORTHUMBRIAN OR BORDER BAGPIPE. This instrument has a chanter of ivory, with seven finger-holes and a thumb-hole at the back. There are three drones, mounted in one stock, and tuned by means of stoppers. The instrument is inflated by bellows, and is probably of the early part of the 18th century.

Lent by Messrs. J. and R. Glen.

IV.

CLASS—REED INSTRUMENTS.

Family: *Double reeds,* (α) *with conical bore.*

INSTRUMENTS in which the sound is produced by means of a double reed vibrating between the lips, and set in motion by a current of air, are of great antiquity. The origin of the double reed is decidedly prehistoric, and in Eastern countries it is known to have existed from very remote ages. The double reed is found in China and Japan, as well as in India, Arabia, and other Mohamedan countries. It is mentioned in the Sanskrit musical treatises, and traces of its use may be found among the sculptures and paintings of the ancient Assyrians. Its employment among the ancient Greeks is no less certain; it was at a very early period adopted into Italy, probably by the Tarentines; and from Italy it very possibly became generally used throughout Europe.

At first applied to pipes of short length, and almost invariably of conical bore, the double reed became gradually applied to instruments of better make and more accurate intonation, and the reed instruments used during the latter days of the Greek supremacy were of very fine workmanship. There are, fortunately, several fine examples of these ancient instruments in different museums which show this to have been the case.

To trace the gradual development of instruments of the double reed family through successive ages is beyond the scope of this Catalogue; suffice it to say that for a long time the principal instrument makers were Italians, and the art of instrument making had as early as the 13th century risen to a very high standard.

The reeds used in these early times were generally rather hard and difficult to manage. To render them more manageable they were placed in a sort of case, called *pirouette,* which covered the lower part of the reed; and this, when the lips were pressed against it, assured that the reed was inserted the proper distance into the mouth. The use of the pirouette was not, however, universal, and probably depended to a great extent upon the capability of the player. And it is curious to note that contrivances of a somewhat similar kind are found in the primitive oboes of China, India, and Arabia. The reeds were usually wider and shorter than is now the case, and it was not until the 16th century, when instruments of this family were adopted into the orchestra, that the construction of the reed became the subject of serious study; and the delicate reed of the present day offers a curious contrast even to the reed of the last century.

In the 12th and following centuries the double reed was frequently placed within a box, and the lips were therefore unable to control its vibrations. One family of instruments thus sounded was usually known by the name of *cromorne* or *tournebout* from the fact of the lower end being turned vertically upwards. As, however, a cylindrical bore was applied to them, they will be noticed more particularly in a subsequent place. The *Hautbois de Poitou*, of conical bore, of which Mersenne speaks, were sounded in a very similar manner. There was a complete family of them; they differed from the ordinary schalmeys merely in the construction of the reed, and by the coarseness of their tone. They were chiefly used as out-of-door instruments, the bass being supplied by a *cornemuse* or species of bagpipe.

As was the custom during the 14th, 15th, and 16th centuries, instruments with double reeds were constructed in various sizes so as to form a complete family. An instrument called *schalmei*, (or *bombart* when of larger size than the *schalmei*) is mentioned by Virdung (*Musica Getutscht*, 1511), and again by Luscinius, who translates Virdung's text and reproduces his engravings. From these it would appear that the *schalmei* and *bombart* were pierced with five or six open finger-holes, and that the existence of the double finger-hole near the bell was even in those early days common. In the *bombarts* there was a key, working within a wooden envelope, and by which the compass of the instrument could be extended downwards.

These instruments do not seem to have undergone many changes, for Prætorius, writing in 1616, gives a minute description of the whole family. It consisted of—

(i.) The *little schalmey*, which measured some 17 inches in length, and of which the lowest note was *a'*. It was used but rarely.

E

(ii.) The *discant schalmey*, of which the lowest note was *d'*, and the length about 26 inches.

(iii.) The *alto pommer*, the lowest note of which was *g*, and the length about 30½ inches.

(iv.) The *tenor pommer*, which measured 4 feet 6 inches in length. It was pierced with six finger-holes; four keys enabled the compass to be extended thus:—

(v.) The *bass pommer*, which was 6 feet long, and resembled the tenor; there were four keys, which gave:—

(vi.) The *great double quint pommer*, which was 9 feet 8 inches in length. It had four keys, which carried its compass down thus:—

All these instruments had a compass of two octaves, and the chromatic intervals were obtained both by half stopping and by cross-fingering. They were all made with six open finger-holes; the two smaller varieties had, in addition, a double hole for the little finger at the lower end. There were also two holes pierced in the bell, and which were not stopped by the fingers, but occasionally by the knee, so as to extend the compass of the instrument downwards.

Towards the latter end of the 16th century, when Mersenne wrote, the larger pommers had been replaced by the bassoon or fagotto, then a comparatively recent invention. And the family then consisted of (i.) the *schalmey;* (ii.) the *dessus*, or *discant schalmey*, which did not differ from that described by Prætorius; (iii.) the *taille* or *tenor;* and (iv.) the *basse*.

The discant schalmey became the oboe. The oboe, properly so called, assumed its present shape early in the 17th century; and was, according to M. Chouquet, first employed in the orchestra of the opera, in Cambert's "Pomone," in 1659. The two lower keys for *c'* and *e'*♭ came into use at the end of the 17th century; the double hole, for the little finger, near the bell disappeared, and in 1727 the instrument maker Gerhard Hofmann, of Rastenberg, added two keys for *g'*♯ and *a'*♯. Shortly afterwards the instrument was further improved by the brothers Bessozi, the most celebrated oboe players of the time; and a speaker or octave key was added, which increased the previous compass of the instrument by an octave upwards. Still the usual form of oboe, up till about 1790, had but three keys; and the third and fourth finger-holes were made double in order to allow of the production of semitones. The proportions of the bore had been considerably improved by the clever maker Delusse, and the position of the keys was made more accessible. The principal improvements are, nevertheless, the result of the present century. With the more general use of the instrument other keys came to be gradually added, and a *Method* by Sellner, published in 1825, at Vienna, shows that the instrument had then keys producing *c'*, *c'*♯, *d'*♯, *f'*, *f'*♯, *g'*♯, *a'*♯, *c''*, and also an octave key. The octave key was placed upon the upper side of the instrument, and still retains this position.

The experiments made by Boehm in perfecting the flute led to the adoption, by the maker Buffet, of rings upon the oboe; and further ingenious applications of mechanism were designed by the oboe player Brod, who was also a maker, about 1846, and by lengthening the instrument the lower notes were rendered better and more full. The Austrian maker Uhlmann, of Vienna, had about this time brought out a mechanism somewhat similar to the present Barret action, but which was so delicate and expensive that its use was never general. Turning his attention to the proportion of the bore, and the correct position of the holes, the late M. Lavigne produced, after many experiments, an instrument wonderfully perfect in intonation; but which had, nevertheless, a tone-quality differing somewhat from the ordinary oboe, and on that account never came into general use. Shortly afterwards Triebert, the clever Parisian maker, following up the ideas of Brod and Lavigne succeeded in producing a model almost perfect, and too well known to need a detailed description here. Latterly further improvements made by Barret, and resulting in the Barret oboe of the present day, have raised the instrument from its once humble position to that of the most delicate and perfect reed instrument that is made.

The alto pommer appears to have developed into the *cor anglais* or *oboe di caccia*, which was at first made straight; but, according to Fetis, the bells of these instruments were curved back. The principal improvements, however, were made by an oboe player of Bergamo, Jean Ferlendis by name, who was resident at Strasburg in 1760, and the idea of constructing the instrument with a bend or curve was due to him. The name *cor anglais* would appear, according to Mr. Galpin, to be a corruption of *cor anglé*, by which name it was first known on account of its peculiar shape. The instrument has in the present century been reconstructed by Triebert about 1854, and by Brod. The cor anglais, first introduced into the orchestra by Gluck in the Italian score of "Alcestis," was recognised by subsequent composers, and for special effects is a most valuable acquisition. Of the *oboe di caccia* in *f*, and *oboe d'amore* in *a*, it is hardly necessary to mention more than that both instruments were employed by J. S. Bach, and that within the last few years the latter has been reconstructed by M. Mahillon, of Brussels, first for the Bach Choir in London, and more recently for the Brussels *Conservatoire*.

The tenor pommer became in course of time the *basset oboe*, an octave below the ordinary instrument, and was in general use in England throughout the last century. Attempts to re-introduce the basset oboe, or baryton, have been from time to time made within the present century, and the maker Triebert constructed an instrument of the kind for the celebrated player Vogt in 1825. Triebert's son, who succeeded to his father's business, made several more. At the Paris Exhibition in 1889 a baryton oboe, the work of M. Lorée, was to be seen. The *timbre* of this instrument was singularly sweet and delicate, and it is to be hoped that composers will recognise its value, and not allow the baryton to fall into oblivion. And so we see that, even in this 19th century, the oboe family may yet be said to remain complete, consisting as it does of the oboe in *c'*, the oboe d'amore in *a*, the cor anglais in *f*, and the baryton in *c*.

From the unmanageable size of the 15th and 16th century bass pommers, and from their defective intonation, various endeavours to produce a more compact and reliable bass were made. This led to the doubling of the tube of the pommer, which then became the *fagotto*. The invention is usually ascribed to Afranio, a canon of Pavia, and the earliest description is contained in a work entitled *Introductio in Chaldaicam Linguam, auctore Theseo Ambrosio*, Pavia, 1539. The first instrument was constructed by Bavilius, of Ferrara, to Afranio's design. Superior to the old bass pommers, the fagotto, as it was called from its peculiar shape, became generally adopted, and was improved upon by Sigismond Schweitzer, of Nuremberg. A complete family of these instruments soon came into existence, and are described particularly by Prætorius. The smaller varieties were never much used, but the fagottino in *F* and the fagotto in *C* have lasted until now. The instrument, described by Prætorius, had only two keys, which gave *F* and *D*. According to M. de Pontécoulant (*Organographie*, 1861) the bassoon, like the oboe, first appeared in the orchestra in Cambert's opera "Pomone" in 1659. The compass had been then extended downwards by the addition of a key, which gave *B*,♭. This necessitated a prolongation of the bell; and the long form of the bassoon, as distinguished from the earlier *fagotto*, dates from that time. The fourth key, for *G*♯, appeared in the early part of the 18th century; and the bassoon in general use in 1751 seems to have had but four keys (*L'Encyclopédie*, MM. Diderot and d'Alembert, 1751–1780). Additional keys were added later by the makers, Kusder, Wood, Preston, and Key in England, and by Portheaux and Adler in Paris. The instrument was finally perfected by the well-known maker Savary, who, indeed, became to the bassoon what Stradivari was to the violin; and Savary bassoons are at the present day scarce and highly prized by players and collectors; and the peculiar singing quality of tone of these instruments has never been excelled in bassoons by other makers, before or since.

Early in the present century attempts to construct the bassoon according to more correct acoustical principles, were made by Simiot of Lyons, and by Almenräder in Germany. And Adolphe Sax, in 1840, produced instruments in which the holes were placed in their proper positions along the bore, and were all closed by keys; the idea was that of Sax père of Brussels, in 1830, but the first application of it was made by Adolphe Sax.

In 1850 Cornelius Ward took out a patent for a bassoon which was constructed in four joints; the "wing joint" was dispensed with, and the two tubes were connected by a U-shaped crook of metal at the butt, the "double piece" no longer existing. In Ward's bassoon all the holes (23 in number) were covered by keys, and, the bore being truly conical, the scale was rendered more regular throughout. As, however, players disliked the novelty of Ward's invention, it soon became disused, and the old Savary models have been since generally followed. The principal improvements of late years have been the work of Morton in England, and of Triebert and Jancourt in Paris; and an ingenious application of ebonite, in place of wood, for the wing joints, has been recently made by Mr. Henry Carte.

The attempts of Sax and Ward have led to the construction of bassoons of *brass*, but the only successful invention has been the Sarrusophone, invented in 1863 by M. Sarrus, and described subsequently in this work. A somewhat similar application of metal for a contra-bassoon had been introduced by Schöllnast of Presburg as early as 1839, and the idea was afterwards improved upon by M. Cerveny and by M. Victor Mahillon, both of whom had been working independently to secure the same result; and a metal contra-bassoon, of an entirely different form, the design of M. Martin Thibouville, was exhibited in the Paris Exhibition of 1889. The tone, however, of all is greatly inferior to that of the wooden contra-fagotto or double-bassoon, which has been perfected by Dr. W. H. Stone in recent years, and is described particularly in another place.

And here might be mentioned a singular application of a kind of double reed, consisting of two clarinet reeds placed face to face

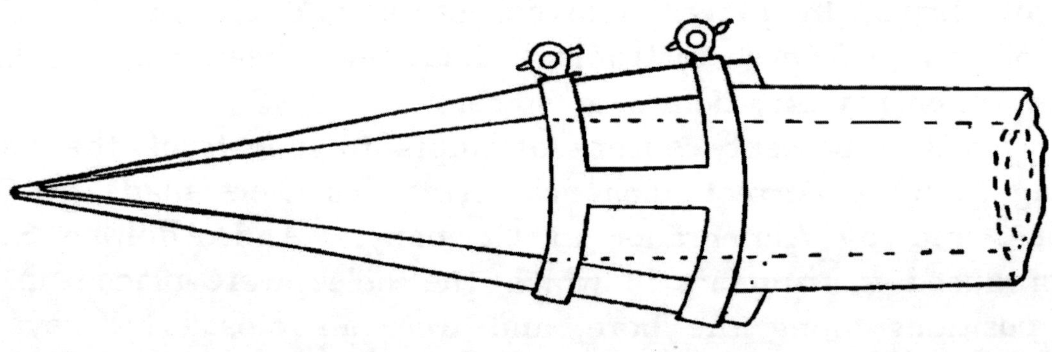

upon a clarinet mouthpiece having a double *lay*. This arrangement was designed and patented in France, in 1858, by M. Bornibus, in conjunction with the well-known instrument maker Gustav Besson. The woodcut is a facsimile of that in their patent specification. The invention was called *Neorgane*, and the inventors' idea was to apply it both to ordinary reed instruments, as well as to keyed and valved brass instruments, such as the ophicleide or tuba.

139.

DISCANT SCHALMEY, in *d'*. This instrument is made of light brown wood, and has been so ingeniously repaired that it is now in perfect condition. The finger-holes give the following notes:—

The lowest finger-hole is made double, to accommodate a right or left handed player. The reed is placed within a *pirouette*. Length, including reed and crook, 26 inches. 16th century. Plate III., fig. B.

Lent by the *Conservatoire Royal de Musique*, Brussels.

140.

ALTO POMMER, in *f*. This is an exact reproduction of an instrument now in the *Grossherzogliches Museum* at Darmstadt. There are six finger-holes, and one open key, with right and left handed touch-pieces, and working within a perforated wooden envelope; the key gives *f* when closed. The reed is placed within a *pirouette* as in the preceding specimen. Plate III., fig. C.

Lent by the *Conservatoire Royal de Musique*, Brussels.

141.

TENOR POMMER, in *c*. This is a facsimile of an instrument now in the *Hotel de Ville* at Middleburg. The lowest note on the instrument is

There are six finger-holes, and a key with right and left handed

touch-pieces for the low note. The intonation produced by finger-holes and key are as follows:—

Length, including reed, 53½ inches. Plate III., fig. A.

Lent by the *Conservatoire Royal de Musique*, Brussels.

142.

Bass Pommer, in *C*. This is an original instrument, probably of the 16th century. It is stamped "G. Strehl" within a scroll, and belonged originally to a Venetian collection. There are six finger-holes and four keys. Two of the keys are disposed in front, and have left and right handed touch-pieces. Two of the keys are worked by the thumb, and are placed at the back. All four keys work within a perforated wooden envelope. The crook is of brass, and bent downwards for the convenience of the player. The successive opening of the keys and holes gives the following series of notes:—

Length, including crook and reed, 8 feet ½ inch. Plate III., fig. D.

Lent by the *Conservatoire Royal de Musique*, Brussels.

143.

Contra-bass Pommer, in *G,*. This instrument is a facsimile of an old 16th century instrument, now in the Museum of the *Hoch Schule für Musik* at Berlin. In general construction it resembles the bass pommer just described, differing merely in size. The successive opening of the keys and holes gives the following fundamental series of notes:—

Length, including crook and reed, 10 feet.

Lent by the *Conservatoire Royal de Musique*, Brussels.

144.

Alto Pommer, in *f*. This is a beautiful specimen, and in good preservation. The key works within a perforated wooden envelope, and in general construction the instrument differs little from the alto pommer previously described. As the key did not close the hole properly the exact pitch could not be ascertained, but from a comparison with the other instrument there was little doubt that the pitch was intended to be *f*. 16th or 17th century.

Lent by the *Grossherzogliches Museum*, Darmstadt.

145.

Bass Musette. This is an exact reproduction of a 16th or early 17th century instrument in the *National Museum* at Munich. The conical bore enlarges rapidly downwards, and the reed is mounted upon a curved brass crook. The position of the keys shows an early attempt to place the holes at their correct acoustical intervals along the bore; the tone is, however, exceedingly rough and strident. The successive opening of keys and holes produces the following series of notes:—

Length 52 inches. Plate III., fig. L.

Lent by the *Conservatoire Royal de Musique*, Brussels.

146.

Schalmey. This instrument is very beautifully made, and the proportions of the bore more nearly resemble those of the modern oboe. It is stamped "R. Haka." There are six finger-holes, and there has been a key working within a perforated wooden envelope; the key, however, has been removed. The instrument gives the following series of notes:—

Length, including reed, 38 inches. Plate VI., fig. A. 17th century.

Lent by M. César Snoeck.

147.

Fagotto, in *C*. This curious instrument, probably one of the earliest specimens in existence, is made of stained wood. The two tubes are bored parallel in the same block of wood. There are six finger-holes upon the front of the instrument; they are disposed in threes, as in the old pommers, there being a gap between the upper and lower set of holes. One brass key, with double touch-pieces, is placed at the lower end. There are two holes for the thumb behind, also a key placed at the lower end. The two keys give

The keys both work inside perforated brass boxes. The crook is of brass, the bend not being curved as much as in the later bassoons. The lowest note is

Total length 3 feet 2½ inches. 17th century.

Lent by the *Conservatoire Royal de Musique*, Brussels.

148.

Fagottino, in *G* (a fifth higher than the bassoon). This unique little instrument, probably of the same date, and in every way similar to the larger instrument preceding, is made of reddish wood. It is made entirely from a single block, the crook at the butt being protected by a shoe of brass. There are two brass keys, working within boxes of perforated brass, and giving *F* and the *D* below. The *D* key is made with two touch-pieces, to suit either right or left handed players. The compass of this specimen is from

 to 

the chromatic intervals being obtained as much as possible by cross-fingerings. Length 25½ inches. Plate V., fig. C. 17th century.

Lent by the *Conservatoire Royal de Musique*, Brussels.

149.

FAGOTTO, in *C*. This is an exact reproduction of an instrument in the *Gesellschaft der Musik-freund*, at Vienna. It is in general appearance similar to the specimens previously described, differing chiefly in the fact that there are four keys. The additional keys are made for the purpose of closing the thumb-holes, which are therefore able to be made of larger diameter, and also placed in their correct positions. All four are open keys; the flap of the *D* key, closing over that of the *E*, when depressed shuts the latter automatically. The lowest note obtainable is *C*. Length 3 feet $2\frac{3}{4}$ inches. 17th century.

Lent by the *Conservatoire Royal de Musique*, Brussels.

150.

BASSOON. With four brass keys of very early pattern. This instrument is made with a wing-joint, and in general shape resembles the bassoon of the present day. There is no maker's name. The keys give

Length 4 feet $\frac{1}{2}$ inch. Early 18th century.

Lent by Messrs. G. Potter and Co.

151.

BASSOON. Of maplewood. This very beautiful specimen probably represents the acme of perfection to which the instrument had been brought at the period when it was made. It is beautifully mounted with bands of brass. There are four flat brass keys upon saddles, giving the same notes as those of the instrument described above. It is stamped "Stanesby, Junior, London, 1747," also with the word "Muracus." The brass mounts are engraved with a coat of arms, and with the inscription "Ex dono R. Jenison, Armiger, 1747."

Lent by the Rev. F. W. Galpin, M.A., F.L.S.

152.

TENOROON, in *F*. With four brass keys on saddles. The keys give *G*♯, *F*, *D*, *B*♭. Stamped with the sign of a harp and the name "Blockley," but the shape of the keys and of the bell leads to the supposition, by comparison with Nos. 151 and 169, that it was made by Stanesby. Length 32¾ inches. 18th century.

Lent by the Rev. F. W. Galpin, M.A., F.L.S.

153.

BASSOON. Of maplewood, with four brass keys. The keys give the same intervals as those of the foregoing specimen. Stamped "Caleb Gedney." Length 4 feet. 18th century.

Lent by Messrs. Rudall, Carte and Co.

154.

BASSOON. Of dark wood, probably maple. Stamped "Küsder, London." There are five brass keys, of the pattern of the period, giving the same notes as described previously; the additional key is for the production of *D*♯. Length 4 feet. 18th century.

Lent by G. Miller, Esq., L.R.A.M.

155.

BASSOON. This instrument was formerly the property of the 42nd Royal Highlanders (Black Watch), and its present owners believe it to have been used during the 1815 campaign. It is in extremely good condition, and is fitted with six brass keys on saddles, giving the following notes:—

Stamped "Preston, London." Length 4 feet. 18th century.

Lent by Messrs. J. and R. Glen.

156.

Bassoon. With six brass keys working upon saddles. Two of the keys are now deficient. The instrument is very much out of order, but the keys were evidently intended to produce the same intervals as those of the specimen No. 155. Stamped "Millhouse, Newark." Length 3 feet ½ inch. 18th century.

Lent by Messrs. H. Potter and Co.

157.

Dulcian, in *c*. An octave above the bassoon. With seven brass keys on saddles, and bound with brass. The keys give *c*♯, *G*♯, *F*♯, *F*, *D*♯, *D*. There is also an octave key in addition. Stamped "George Wood, late James Wood and Son, Maker, 50, New Compton Street, Soho, London. Invented by William Meikle." 18th century. Length 21¾ inches. The bell is rather curiously shaped, and more nearly resembles that of the earlier fagottino. Plate VI., fig. H.

Lent by Messrs. J. and R. Glen.

158.

Dulcian, in *c*. An octave above the bassoon. Of stained box-wood, bound with brass, and with seven cup-shaped keys of brass on saddles, giving the same intervals as in the preceding instrument. Stamped "Wood and Ivy, late George Wood, 50, New Compton Street, Soho, London." The bell is slightly contracted internally, but outwardly resembles that of the former specimen. Length 21½ inches. 18th century.

Lent by the Rev. F. W. Galpin, M.A., F.L.S.

159.

Dulcian, in *c*. An octave above the bassoon. Of stained wood, with six flat brass keys, of early pattern, on saddles. The keys give *G*♯, *F*♯, *F*, *D*♯, *D*, *B*,♭. No maker's name. Length 24½ inches 18th century.

Lent by Messrs. Rudall, Carte and Co.

160.

Bassoon. Of stained wood, with nine flat circular keys of brass. The pattern of the keys is evidently that of a much later period than any of the previous specimens. The nine keys give

the *c*♯ key being placed at the back. There are also two keys for the production of

Stamped "Wood and Ivy, late George Wood, 50, New Compton Street, Soho." Length 4 feet ½ inch. 18th century.

Lent by S. A. Chappell, Esq.

161.

Bassoon. Of maplewood, with nine brass keys. The keys produce the same notes as those of the specimen described above; the pattern is, however, that of an earlier date. Stamped "Cramer and Key, London, Pall Mall." Length 4 feet ½ inch. Late 18th or early 19th century.

Lent by Messrs. Rudall, Carte and Co.

162.

Tenoroon, in *F*. Of stained boxwood, and with ten flat brass keys on saddles. The keys give the following series of notes *b*, *a*, *c*♯, *G*♯, *F*♯, *F*, *D*, and *B*,♭. No maker's name. Length 35½ inches. Late 18th or early 19th century.

Lent by Messrs. Boosey and Co.

163.

Bassoon. This beautiful instrument is of maplewood, bound with brass, and is stamped upon every joint "Savary, jeune, à Paris." There are fifteen brass keys, and the scale is that of the modern bassoon. This instrument belonged formerly to Dr. W. H. Stone, F.R.S.

Lent by Cyril Spottiswoode, Esq.

164.

TENOROON, in *F*. This beautiful instrument is of maplewood, bound with brass. There are fifteen brass keys giving the scale of the ordinary bassoon. It is stamped upon each joint "Savary, jeune, à Paris." Length 37¾ inches.

Lent by Cyril Spottiswoode, Esq.

165.

TENOROON, in *F*, French pitch. This instrument is almost identical with the former, and is stamped upon every joint "Savary, jeune, à Paris." This and the instrument previously described are believed to be the only tenoroons in existence made by this great maker; both specimens belonged formerly to Dr. W. H. Stone, F.R.S. The workmanship of both is very fine, and the tone curiously soft and mellow. There are but fourteen keys to this instrument. Length 38½ inches.

Lent by Cyril Spottiswoode, Esq.

166.

BASSOON. This specimen more nearly resembles the Boehm system in the arrangement of the keys. There are no open finger-holes, but there is an elaborate mechanism of keys and levers which closes 28 holes in all, bored at their correct acoustical intervals. Hence the intonation is absolutely correct, but the instrument lacks the peculiar quality characteristic of the bassoon. This specimen is constructed of two separate conical tubes of rosewood, the lower ends of which are connected by a U-shaped tube of German silver, fastened by a spring. The instrument is stamped with the maker's name, "A. Marzoli, à Paris."

The application of the Boehm system to the bassoon was originally due to Triebert, but experiments in the same direction had been made by Cornelius Ward in this country. This particular specimen once belonged to the band of one of the battalions of the 60th Rifles, but the extreme difficulty of keeping so complicated a mechanism in order, and its necessarily high initial cost, would alone render such

MODERN BASSOON, WITH 17 KEYS.

an instrument for military purposes of little practical value. It probably dates from about 1850, and its length is 52 inches.

Lent by the Rev. F. W. Galpin, M.A., F.L.S.

167.

BASSOON. Modern. Of maple-wood, with ebonite wing-joint and 17 German silver keys. By Rudall, Carte and Co. 1890.

Lent by Messrs. Rudall, Carte and Co.

168.

BASSOON. Similar to the above, but made entirely of ebonite, and by the same makers.

Lent by Messrs. Rudall, Carte and Co.

169.

CONTRA-BASSOON. An octave below the bassoon. This instrument resembles in general appearance the ordinary bassoon. The holes for the right and left hands are so wide apart that considerable inconvenience must have been caused to the player. There are four brass keys, working upon saddles, and giving

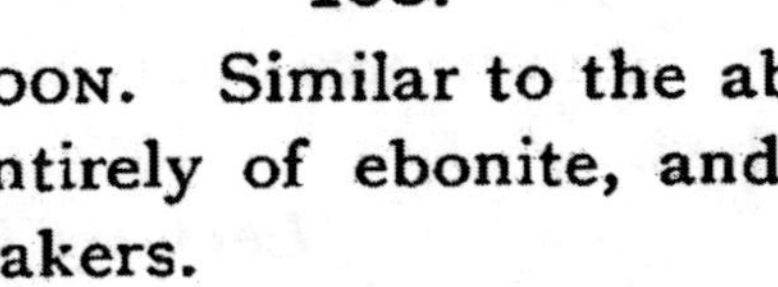

but, in real sounds, an octave lower. The instrument, as regards arrangement of keys, and the disposition of the finger-holes, does not differ from the bassoon of that time. It is stamped "Stanesby, junior"; and is the original instrument made by this maker for the composer Handel, and played by J. F. Lampe at the Marylebone Gardens in 1739. Length 8 feet 4 inches.

Lent by W. Ringrose Atkins, Esq., F.C.A.

170.

CONTRA-BASSOON. Of stained wood, with eight cup-shaped keys of brass upon pillars, giving (in real sounds, an octave lower):—

In shape it resembles an ordinary bassoon, but the bell-joint is of brass entirely. The lowest note upon the instrument is an octave below the *C* of the ordinary bassoon. Stamped "Stehle formals Kuss, Wien," and engraved "Kaiser K. Hof, Capellen Instrument." It probably dates from about 1820. Length 6 feet 6 inches.

Lent by the Rev. F. W. Galpin, M.A., F.L.S.

171.

CONTRA-BASSOON. This is the original instrument designed by Dr. W. H. Stone, F.R.S., and made under his immediate superintendence by Haseneier of Coblentz. This instrument is considerably less fatiguing to blow than the contra-bassoon as previously made, and which in shape resembled an ordinary bassoon. The air column measures 16 feet in length, and the bore is truly conical, enlarging from $\frac{1}{4}$ inch diameter at the reed to 4 inches at the bell. As the tubing is curved four times upon itself, the outside length of the instrument is much the same as that of the ordinary bassoon. The compass of the instrument is as follows:—

 to 

including all the chromatic intervals. The instrument has nineteen keys, those for the first three fingers of each hand being saddle-shaped; those for the little fingers and thumbs are of the usual shape. This ingenious difference of shape enables the player to distinguish "open" and "closed" holes; and, therefore, it is easy for any bassoon player to adapt himself to this instrument. From $C_{,}$ to $F_{,}$ a single sound only is obtained by each key. From $F_{,}$ to f, the same fingering produces two sounds, an octave apart, by change of lip and greater pressure; from $f\sharp$ to c' the scale is continued by means of the twelfth, using the fingering of b, and again increasing the pressure of wind. Plate VIII., fig. B.

Lent by Cyril Spottiswoode, Esq.

172.

CONTRA-BASSOON. Of wood, and in every respect similar to that described above. This instrument was made by Mr. Alfred Morton, who followed the design of Dr. W. H. Stone, F.R.S., the inventor of this form of contra-bassoon. The construction of the instrument is similar to that shown in Plate VIII., fig. B.

Lent by Messrs. Besson & Co.

173.

CONTRA-BASSOON, in $F_{,}$. This instrument in design is identical with those previously described, but is a fourth higher in pitch. It was made by Mr. Alfred Morton, for Sir Arthur Sullivan, for use in the orchestra of the Savoy Theatre.

Lent by Sir Arthur Sullivan.

174.

CONTRA-BASSOON. Made entirely of brass, by Mahillon and Co. This instrument consists of a conical tube 15 feet 3 inches in length, curved round itself four times and a half. Fifteen keys, connected by rods to touch-pieces that are placed conveniently for the player's fingers to manipulate, open lateral holes pierced at intervals acoustically correct along the bore. By the successive opening of these fifteen keys a complete chromatic scale is obtained, of the following range :—

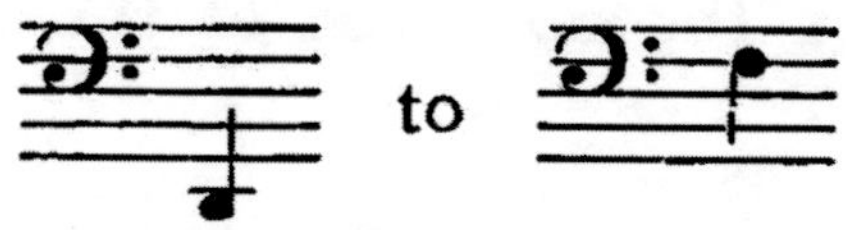

in real sounds 8vo. lower.

Owing to the length of the bore, and its large calibre, the octave

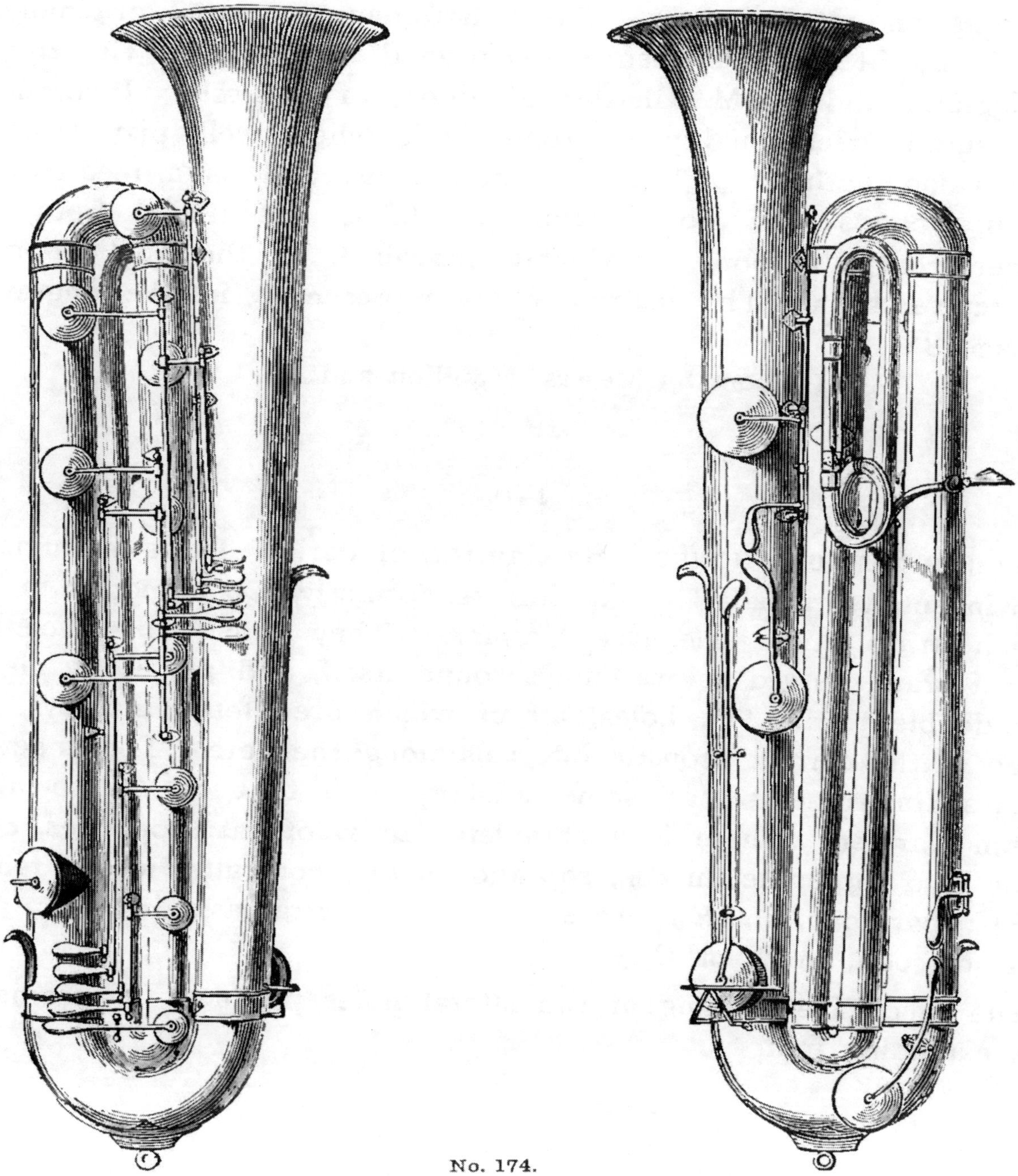

No. 174.

Contra-Bassoon of Metal.

harmonic only can be obtained. Hence there are two octave keys, the use of which enables the compass of the instrument to be carried chromatically up to

sounding an octave lower. This instrument, invented originally in Austria by Stehle, has been reconstructed both by M. Cerveny, of Königgratz, and by M. Charles Mahillon, of Brussels. It produces a singularly rich quality of tone, and, when well played, is of great value, both in orchestral combinations, and as a reed-bass in military bands. In construction it differs essentially from the wooden contra-bassoons, previously described, in the application of the octave keys. The instrument is represented in the engraving on page 83.

Lent by Messrs. Mahillon and Co.

175.

THREE SARRUSOPHONES. By Gautrot, of Paris. These instruments were invented originally by M. Sarruss, formerly a bandmaster in the French army under the last Empire. They consist of a conical tube of brass, curved several times round itself, and played by means of a double reed. The holes, all of which are closed by keys, are placed at the correct acoustic intervals along the bore. The fingering of these instruments has some analogy with that of the so-called Boehm clarinet. There is a complete family of sarrusophones, consisting of a sopranino, in *e'*♭; soprano, in *b*♭; contralto, in *e*♭; tenor, in *B*♭; barytone, in *E*♭; bass, in *B,*♭; contra-bass, in *E,*♭; and contra-bassoon, in *C,* or *B,,*♭.

The successive opening of the lateral holes produces a chromatic scale extending from

 to 

By means of an octave key, and greater pressure, this scale can be extended chromatically upwards to

The higher sounds are formed by the third or fourth harmonics thus:

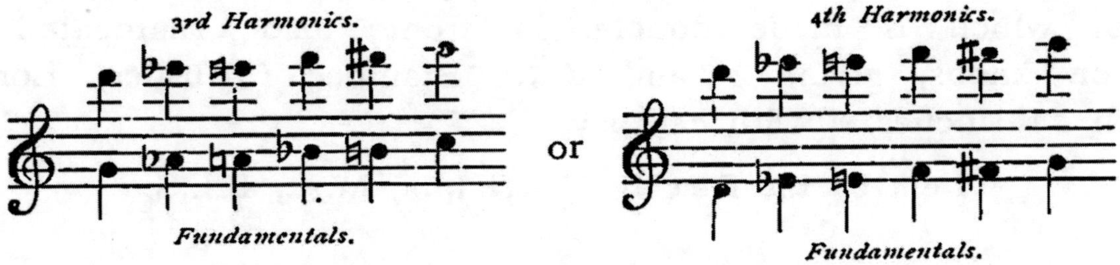

The manner of writing for these instruments is similar to that employed for the saxophone. The inventor's idea was to replace by their use oboes and bassoons in military bands. But the *timbre* being so different, the invention was not largely adopted. They are nevertheless of great use when sparingly employed for special effects in the orchestra. Massenet, in the score of "Esclarmonde," produces, by the use of a contra-bass instrument of this kind, an effect almost electrifying.

Lent by Messrs. Besson and Co.

176.

OBOE. Of light wood, with two silver keys mounted upon knobs, giving *d'*♯ and *c'*; the *d'*♯ key is made right or left handed. There is a hole in the bell, not closed by the fingers, and double holes for the third finger on the top joint, and for the first finger on the middle joint. Stamped "W. Millhouse, London."

Lent by M. Césare Snoeck.

177.

OBOE. Of boxwood, with two silver keys on knobs, giving *d'*♯ and *c'*. There is a hole in the bell left not covered, and double holes for the third finger on the top joint, and for the first finger on the middle joint. The instrument is tipped with ivory, and stamped "Cahusac, London." 18th century.

Lent by Messrs. Rudall, Carte and Co.

178.

OBOE. Of boxwood, tipped with ivory. There are six finger-holes, one of which is made double; in front; also ornamented silver keys on knobs, giving *c'* and *d'*♯. Stamped "Küsder, London." Length 22½ inches. 18th century.

Lent by the Rev. F. W. Galpin, M.A., F.L.S.

179.

OBOE. Of maple, with ivory tips. There are two silver keys on knobs, giving *d'*♯ and *c'*, and a double hole for the third finger on the top joint. There is a hole in the bell left uncovered. Stamped "Küsder, London." Length 23 inches. 18th century. Plate VI., fig. G.

Lent by Mrs. Zoeller.

180.

OBOE. Of boxwood, with ivory tips, with two flat square-flapped brass keys on knobs, giving *d'*♯ and *c'*. There is a hole in the bell left uncovered, and a double hole for the third finger on the top joint. Stamped "Clementi and Broderip." Length 22½ inches. Probably about the end of 18th century.

Lent by S. A. Chappell, Esq.

181.

OBOE. Boxwood, with two silver keys on knobs, giving *d'*♯ and *c'*. There is a hole in the bell left uncovered, and double holes for the third finger on the top joint, and for the first finger on the lower joint. Stamped "Millhouse, London." 18th century.

Lent by D. M. Carmichael, Esq.

182.

OBOE. Boxwood, and ivory tipped, with two keys giving $d'\sharp$ and c', and a double hole for the third finger on the top joint. Stamped "Norman, London." Length 23 inches. 18th century.

Lent by Rev. H. F. Armfield, F.S.A.

183.

OBOE. Of ebony, with beautifully carved tips of ivory. There are three silver keys on knobs, giving $d'\sharp$ and c', the $d'\sharp$ key being in duplicate. There are double holes for the third finger on the top joint, and for the first finger on the lower. There is a hole in the bell left uncovered. Stamped "E. Terton." Length $22\frac{5}{8}$ inches.

Lent by M. Césare Snoeck.

184.

OBOE. Of boxwood, with two flat brass keys on knobs, giving $d'\sharp$ and c'. The hole in the bell is left uncovered and gives c'; and there is a double hole for the third finger on the top joint. Stamped "Goulding, London." This instrument was formerly the standard working model for Goulding's maker. Length 23 inches. Early present century.

Lent by Messrs. Boosey and Co.

185.

OBOE. This instrument is made of ebony and ornamented with ivory. There are six finger-holes, one of which is made double, in front; also two ivory keys, which give c' and $d'\sharp$. There is also an additional top joint for change of pitch. Stamped "Fornari, a Venezia, 1815." The model is, however, that of a much earlier period; with it is a Venetian reed of the time, measuring across the top $\frac{7}{16}$ inch. The reed used at the present day is much narrower, being only $\frac{5}{16}$ inch. Length, with shorter joint, 22 inches; with longer joint $22\frac{1}{4}$ inches.

Lent by the Rev. F. W. Galpin, M.A., F.L.S.

186.

Oboe. There are six finger-holes, two of which are doubled; also three silver keys on knobs, giving *c′*, *c′*♯, and *d′*♯. The long *c′*♯ key, for the little finger of the left hand, is apparently an addition of a subsequent date. During the early part of the 18th century the *c′*♯ was made merely by half closing the *c′* key. The *c′*♯ key first appeared in 1751. An old reed, of the early part of the present century, is attached; width across the top $\frac{3}{8}$ inch. Length of the instrument 22½ inches. Stamped "W. Millhouse, London."

Lent by the Rev. F. W. Galpin, M.A., F.L.S.

187.

Oboe. Of boxwood, with five brass keys on knobs, giving every semitone from *d′*♯ to *b′*♭. There is a speaker key, in addition, placed on the top, and worked with a rocking motion of the first finger; there are also double holes for the third finger upon the top joint, and for the first finger upon the lower joint. The bell resembles that of the oboe d'amore. Stamped "P. Power, London, Inventor." Plate VI., fig. B.

Lent by Messrs Rudall, Carte and Co.

188.

Oboe. Boxwood, with ivory tips. There are six silver keys on knobs, which give

There are double holes for the third finger on the top joint, and for the first finger on the lower. As compared with No. 187, it has no speaker key, but has the cross *f′* and *b′*♭ keys (4 and 6), as in instruments of the present day. Stamped "W. Millhouse, London." Length 22½ inches. Early present century.

Lent by Thomas Bryant, Esq.

189.

OBOE. Made by Mr. Alfred Morton at the conclusion of his apprenticeship to Joseph Uhlmann and Sons, of Vienna, in 1847. This instrument is very beautifully made in boxwood, and is fitted with a tuning slide. It is one of the best models of the period when it was made; the only innovations made consist in rather a different shape of bell and lower joint, also the open *f'*♯ key (which till then had not been used), and also the connection of the *d'*♯ key to close the *f'*♯ key for the notes *d''*, *d''*♯, and *c''*♯. In the Viennese oboes made at that period, the *d'*♯ key had been used for these notes. The instrument is beautifully in tune. Mr. Alfred Morton's name, since he commenced business in England, has become well known as that of a maker of double reed instruments.

Lent by Mr. Morton.

190.

MODELS OF LAVIGNE'S OBOES. Models of oboes, principally experiments, but serving to show various devices imagined by Mr. Lavigne before he designed the model finally adopted and called by his name. These models passed after the death of Mr. Lavigne into the hands of their present possessor.

Lent by J. W. Eagles, Esq.

191.

OBOE. Large bore, Boehm system, with modifications. Formerly the property of the late Mr. Lavigne, the celebrated oboe-player. The lowest note upon the instrument is *b*♮. Length 20⅝ inches.

Lent by Messrs. Boosey and Co.

192.

MUSETTE, OR SMALL OBOE. Of rosewood, by Triebert. Formerly the property of the late Mr. Lavigne. "Boehm" system, with 11 keys and three rings. Length 13½ inches.

Lent by Messrs. Boosey and Co.

193.

Oboe. Rosewood. Part-made model of instrument finally adopted by Mr. Lavigne, to whom this specimen formerly belonged. This instrument was designed in accordance with the Boehm system of fingering. The conical bore enlarges rapidly, and the pad and finger-holes are unusually large. Its lowest note is

Lent by Messrs. Boosey and Co.

194.

Boring Bit, in wooden sheath. Formerly the property of the late Mr. Lavigne. Total length $27\frac{1}{2}$ inches, length of cutting portion $24\frac{1}{2}$ inches. A specimen of a good tool of its kind. Evidently made for the production of the instrument shown by the model No. 193.

Lent by Messrs. Boosey and Co.

195.

Oboe. Of cocuswood. 17 German-silver keys, rings and thumb-plate, descending to *b*♮. By Boosey and Co., 1890.

Lent by Messrs. Boosey and Co.

196.

Oboe. Of rosewood, to *b*♭. 17 German-silver keys, rings and thumb-plate, going down to *b*♭. By Rudall, Carte and Co., 1890.

Lent by Messrs. Rudall, Carte and Co.

197.

Oboe. Of ebonite, to *b*♭. 17 German-silver keys, rings and thumb-plate, going down to *b*♭. By Rudall, Carte and Co., 1890.

Lent by Messrs. Rudall, Carte and Co.

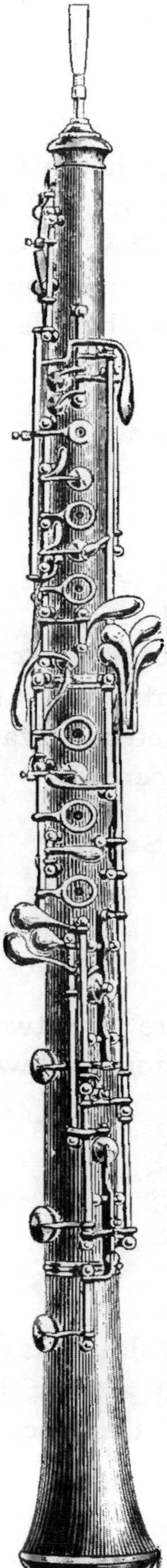

No. 199. Oboe. Barret's System.

198.

Oboe. Of rosewood. By Rudall, Carte and Co., 1890. 17-keyed fingering, with double-action *g′*♯ and octave keys, and automatic half-hole action, going down to *b*♭.

Lent by Messrs. Rudall, Carte and Co.

199.

Oboe. Barret's system. Of rosewood. By Rudall, Carte and Co. This instrument has double-action octave keys to make the transition from one to the other automatic; also a thumb-plate to close the *c″*, and *b′*♭ holes; a lever by which the first, second, or third fingers of the right hand or the fourth finger (by means of the key heads making *c″* or *c″*♯) can work the thumb-plate action; double action *g′*♯, *d′*♯, and cross *f′*♮ keys, and a lever for the fourth finger of the left hand to open the *f′*♮ hole.

Lent by Messrs. Rudall, Carte and Co.

200.

Schalmey, in *g′*. Of dark wood, with six finger-holes, and an additional hole for the little finger, in front, and a thumb-hole at the back. The bell expands slightly at the mouth, and outwardly more nearly resembles that of the clarinet. German. 19th century.

This instrument is the Piffero Pastorale of the Italian shepherds, and is still used in the Austrian Tyrol. Sometimes it is known as the musette.

Lent by the Rev. F. W. Galpin, M.A., F.L.S.

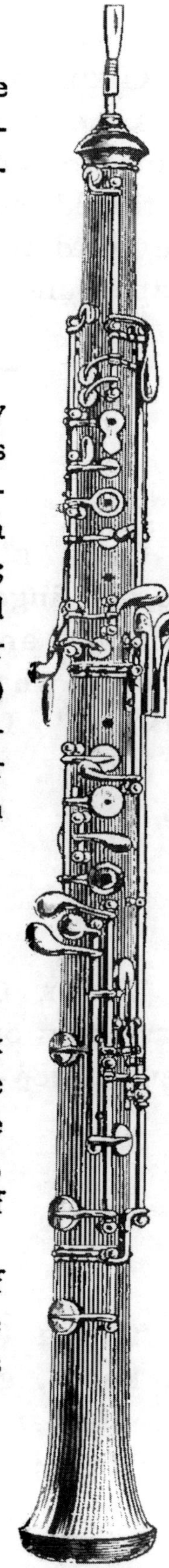

No. 198.

201.

Oboe d'Amore, in *a*. Boxwood, with three square-flapped brass keys mounted upon knobs. The keys give *d'*♯ and *c'*; the *d'*♯ key is made to suit either a right or left handed player. The instrument is tipped with horn, and stamped "P. Wolravpier." The hole for the third finger on the top joint is made double; the bell is pear-shaped and contracted at the mouth. 18th century.

Lent by the *Conservatoire Royal de Musique*, Brussels.

202.

Oboe d'Amore, in *a*. Of light wood, tipped with ivory. There are six finger-holes, two of which are doubled; also two silver keys, giving *c'* and *d'*♯. The bell is pear-shaped and contracted at the mouth, where it measures only 1⅜ inches in diameter. Stamped "Bizey." Length, including staple, 26½ inches. 18th century.

Lent by the Rev. F. W. Galpin, M.A., F.L.S.

203.

Tenor Oboe, in *f*. Of stained rosewood. There are two flat brass keys on knobs, giving *c'* and *d'*♯. Stamped "Millhouse, Newark." Length 28½ inches. 18th century.

Lent by the Rev. F. W. Galpin, M.A., F.L.S.

204.

Tenor Oboe, in *f*. Of stained boxwood, with two flat brass keys on knobs, giving *d'*♯ and *c'*. This instrument stands a fifth below the ordinary oboe of the present day. Stamped "Caleb Gedney." Length 34 inches. Early 18th century.

Lent by the Rev. F. W. Galpin, M.A., F.L.S.

205.

Oboe, in *a*. An old English watchman's waight or hoboy, of the latter part of the 17th century. Of light wood, with six finger-holes, two of which are doubled, and three engraved silver keys giving *c'*♯ and *d'*♯; the *d'*♯ key is in duplicate to suit a right or left handed player. The ivory tips, with which this specimen is ornamented, are peculiarly large and heavy. The tone of this instrument resembles, in many respects, that of the more ancient schalmey, discarded in the previous century. Length, including crook, 25¾ inches.

Lent by the Rev. F. W. Galpin, M.A., F.L.S.

206.

Basset Oboe or Baryton, in *c*. An octave below the ordinary oboe. Of rosewood, with four brass keys (including a speaker key), giving *d'*♯, *c'*♯, and *c'*♮. From the shape of the keys this instrument would appear to be of the early middle part of the 18th century. There is no maker's name. Length 39½ inches.

Lent by the Rev. F. W. Galpin, M.A., F.L.S.

207.

Tenor Oboe, in *f*. Of boxwood, with three flat brass keys. The keys give *c'* and *d'*♯, the *d'*♯ key being in duplicate, for either right or left handed players. Stamped "Lindner." Length 33½ inches.

Lent by Mr. Césare Snoeck.

208.

Cor Anglais, in *f*. Of stained wood, with nine capped brass keys on knobs. The keys give *c''*, *b'*♭, *g'*♯, *f'*♯ (in conjunction with hole), *f'*, *d'*♯, *c'*♯, *c'*, and *b*. The body of the instrument is bent in the middle at an angle of 120°, and the joint is of ivory. Stamped "Kuss, Wien." Length 31 inches.

Lent by E. Renton, Esq.

209.

Tenor Oboe, in *f*. Of stained boxwood, mounted with ivory, and three brass keys on knobs. The *d'*♯ key is in duplicate; the other key gives *c'*. Two of the finger-holes are doubled, as in the oboes described previously. The bell is very much contracted. Stamped "John Georg. Eisenmergen." Length 34 inches.

Lent by the *Conservatoire Royal de Musique*, Brussels.

210.

Cor Anglais, in *f*. Curved form, covered with leather; stamped "Fornari, Venetzia." This instrument seems to have only been repaired by Fornari. There are five keys, of which two are on saddles, and are evidently additions; the original keys are upon knobs. The keys give *b'*♭, *a'*♭, *d'*♯, *c'*♯, *c'*. Length 30¾ inches.

Lent by the Rev. F. W. Galpin, M.A., F.L.S.

211.

Cor Anglais, in *f*. Curved form, covered with leather; stamped "Fornari, Venetzia." There are eight German-silver keys, three of them having double levers; they give *c''*, *b'*♭, *a'*♭, *f'*, *d'*♯, *c'*♯, *c'*, and *b*. There are two rings, which appear to have been added subsequently; also a speaker key. Length 30¾ inches.

Lent by the Rev. F. W. Galpin, M.A., F.L.S.

212.

Cor Anglais, in *f*. With 12 cupped silver keys on pillars. Stamped "Brod, à Paris." The keys give *c''*, *b'*♭, *a'*♭, *f'*, *d'*♯, *c'*♯, *c'*, and *b*. There are two extension keys for the *c'*♯ and *f'*♯ holes, also an additional key to correct the *f'*♯. Length 27½ inches.

This was the instrument used by Brod himself, who was better known, perhaps, as a player than as a maker.

Lent by G. Case, Esq.

213.

Cor Anglais, in *f*. Rosewood, with 12 German-silver keys and five rings. Boehm system. Marked "A. Buffet, Jne., Paris." Formerly the property of the late M. Lavigne.

Lent by Messrs. Boosey and Co.

214.

Cor Anglais, in *f*. With 15 keys, rings and thumb-plate. By Mahillon and Co. The compass of this instrument descends to the *b*♮ of its scale. The mechanism is similar to that of the ordinary oboe, and will be best understood from the annexed woodcut. This instrument is very fine; and the intonation leaves little to be desired.

Lent by Messrs. Mahillon and Co.

215.

Oboe d'Amore, in *a*. By Mahillon and Co. This instrument has been recently re-constructed for the Brussels *Conservatoire* by M. Charles Mahillon. In general appearance it differs little from the cor anglais previously described, while in *timbre* it is singularly sweet and mellow.

Lent by Messrs. Mahillon and Co.

No. 214.
Cor Anglais in *f*.

V.

CLASS—REED INSTRUMENTS.

FAMILY: *Double reeds, (β) with cylindrical bore.*

THE combination of a double reed with a cylindrical bore, although of great antiquity, presents certain theoretical difficulties which have led to its disuse. The subject presents an acoustical problem of too complex a nature to be discussed at length here, but has been fully treated of by various acousticians at different times.

That the use of the double reed, in conjunction with a cylindrical bore, was discarded in favour of the single, or *arghoul*, reed by the ancient nations is tolerably certain. And unless the bore is of small section, association with a double reed is hardly practicable.

During the 14th, 15th, and 16th centuries instruments thus constructed were in common use. Those most generally met with were the *krumhorn*, or *cromorne;* the *racket* or *cervelas;* the *musette;* and the *sourdine.* Of these the *cromorne* was generally played in sets, and the family consisted of four instruments, the respective compass of each being

The krumhorn is described by Virdung, who also mentions an instrument of very similar form, and which he calls *Platerspill.* And in a MS. of the 13th century at Madrid (*Cantigas de Santa Maria*), there is a representation of an instrument apparently of this nature. But Hans Burgmair, a pupil of the celebrated Albert Dürer, gives (*Triumph of the Emperor Maximilien,* Vienna, 1516) a representation of two cromornes, the identity of which cannot be disputed. The instrument is mentioned by Prætorius, and, according to him, the larger varieties had some keys which enabled the compass to be extended downwards. The reed was placed within a cap, and hence was beyond control of the player's lips. The cromorne is again described by Mersenne, who states the best of the kind were made in

England, where it was no uncommon thing to find pieces written for these instruments in four, five, or even six parts. From the fact of the bell being turned up at the end, the cromorne was known in France as *tournebout.* And from the numerous representations of these instruments, contained in old works upon pageantry, their popularity and general use all over Europe is evident.

The racket, or cervelas, was a sort of bassoon, the bore of which was pierced in a sort of zig-zag fashion, in order to shorten the outside length of the instrument. The racket is described by Prætorius, who mentions the existence of a whole family of these singular instruments, and gives engravings of them all. Their compasses were, he states, as follows:—

This instrument is described also by Mersenne, who calls it *cervelat,* a word signifying "a sausage." The larger varieties of them appear to have been furnished with keys, and specimens thus constructed are to be seen in the museum of the *Conservatoire* at Paris. Their intonation must necessarily have left much to be desired; indeed, it is difficult to understand how they could have been played at all. During the last century an interesting attempt to reconstruct the racket was made, but with no success, by the celebrated instrument maker, Stanesby. Sir John Hawkins (*History of Music,* vol. iv., p. 139) thus describes the circumstance:—"Stanesby, who was a diligent peruser both of Mersenne and Kircher, and in the making of instruments adhered as closely to the directions of the former as possible, constructed a short bassoon or cervelat for the late Earl of Abercorn, then Lord Paisley, and a disciple of Dr. Pepusch, but it did not answer expectations; by reason of its closeness, the interior parts imbibed, and retained, the moisture of the breath, the ducts dilated, and broke. In short, the whole blew up."

The sourdine had, like the racket, a cylindrical bore, but the wind-passage had but one bend, and the intonation was consequently better. A family of these instruments is described by Prætorius, who states that they were the work of one Lodovico Zacconi, and that in quality of tone they resembled the cornemuse, but were softer than the krumhorn. The compasses of these instruments were usually:—

An instrument of apparently similar construction is described by Mersenne, who calls it *courtaut*, by reason of its shortness. It had eleven holes, the vent being at the back, precisely as in the two specimens described presently.

The cornemuse, although in a sense belonging to this family, was sounded from a reservoir of air, and has therefore been described particularly in the section of this work devoted to bagpipes.

216.

SOURDINE. A bass instrument having a cylindrical bore. The wind-passage is of very small diameter, and is constructed of two parallel channels, which communicate at the lower end, and are cut in the same block of wood. The total length of the column of air thus formed is 44 inches, inclusive of crook and reed. The crook is of brass, and the reed resembles that of a bassoon. There are six open finger-holes of very small diameter, and a number of brass keys which work within wooden boxes, the tops of which are made to slide off, to allow access to the keys. The instrument measures, outside, 33 inches; and the lower portion is made to serve the double purpose of a box for spare reeds, and for a rest. The successive opening of the keys and finger-holes produces the following series:—

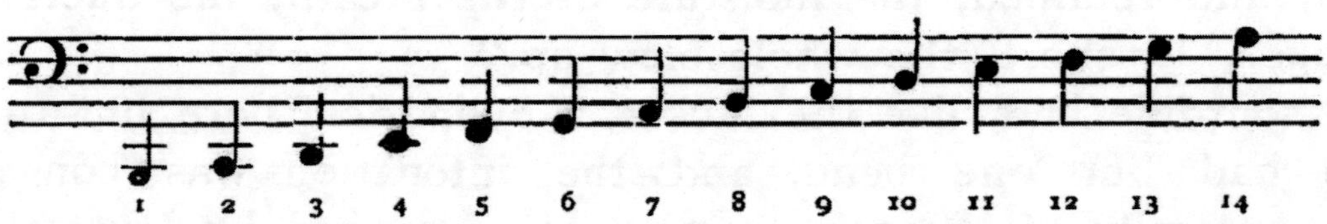

This specimen is a facsimile of an instrument in the *Ambroser*

Sammlung at Vienna, and which formerly belonged to the band of the Emperor Maximilien I. at Insprück. Plate III., fig. I.

Lent by the *Conservatoire Royal de Musique*, Brussels.

217.

SOURDINE. This instrument resembles the specimen previously described in appearance, but is apparently a contra-bass. It is a reproduction of an instrument now in the *Ambroser Sammlung* at Vienna, and which belonged to the band of the Emperor Maximilien I. at Insprück.

The successive opening of the keys and finger-holes produces the following series:—

The length of the air-column is 74 inches, inclusive of crook and reed. The outside length of the instrument itself is $47\frac{1}{2}$ inches. Plate III., fig. K.

Lent by the *Conservatoire Royal de Musique*, Brussels.

218.

CROMORNE. This instrument is played with a double reed, placed within a cap, and hence beyond the control of the player's lips. The lower end is turned vertically upwards and the bell is contracted at the mouth. There are six open finger-holes, and an additional hole for the little finger of the right hand, made double to accommodate right or left handed players. The pitch-note of the instrument is $e'\flat$; but as the crook was not in proper order, the compass of the instrument could not be correctly ascertained. The bore was rather larger than that of the sourdine, and the tone harsher, and somewhat resembling that of the Highland pipes. The total length of the bore is 2 feet $1\frac{3}{4}$ inches; including the reed it is 2 feet $5\frac{1}{2}$ inches; and including the cap it is 2 feet $7\frac{1}{2}$ inches. The instrument is a facsimile of one in the *Ambroser Sammlung* at Vienna. Plate IV., fig. E.

Lent by the *Conservatoire Royal de Musique*, Brussels.

219.

RACKET. This beautiful instrument is constructed in the form of an ivory cylinder, and it is played by means of a rather large double reed placed within a *pirouette*. The bore is of extremely small diameter and is cylindrical throughout. The instrument, not including the reed and crook, measures only $4\frac{3}{4}$ inches in length; with reed and crook, nine inches; and it is two inches in diameter. The bore consists of nine channels, parallel to each other, and which communicate so as to form a single length of wind-passage. The finger-holes open out on to the circumference of the cylinder, and are bored obliquely, as in the bassoon. The front of the instrument is shown in Plate IX. fig. B. There are three finger-holes for the left hand; and three, with an additional hole for the little finger, for the right hand. There are three holes at the back: one for the thumb of the left hand, and two for that of the right hand, one being covered by the first joint, the other by the ball, of the thumb. The vent, for there is no bell, is also at the back. The compass descends to

This instrument is an exact reproduction of one in the *Ambroser Sammlung* at Vienna, and which formerly belonged to the private band of the Emperor Maximilien I.

Lent by the *Conservatoire Royal de Musique*, Brussels.

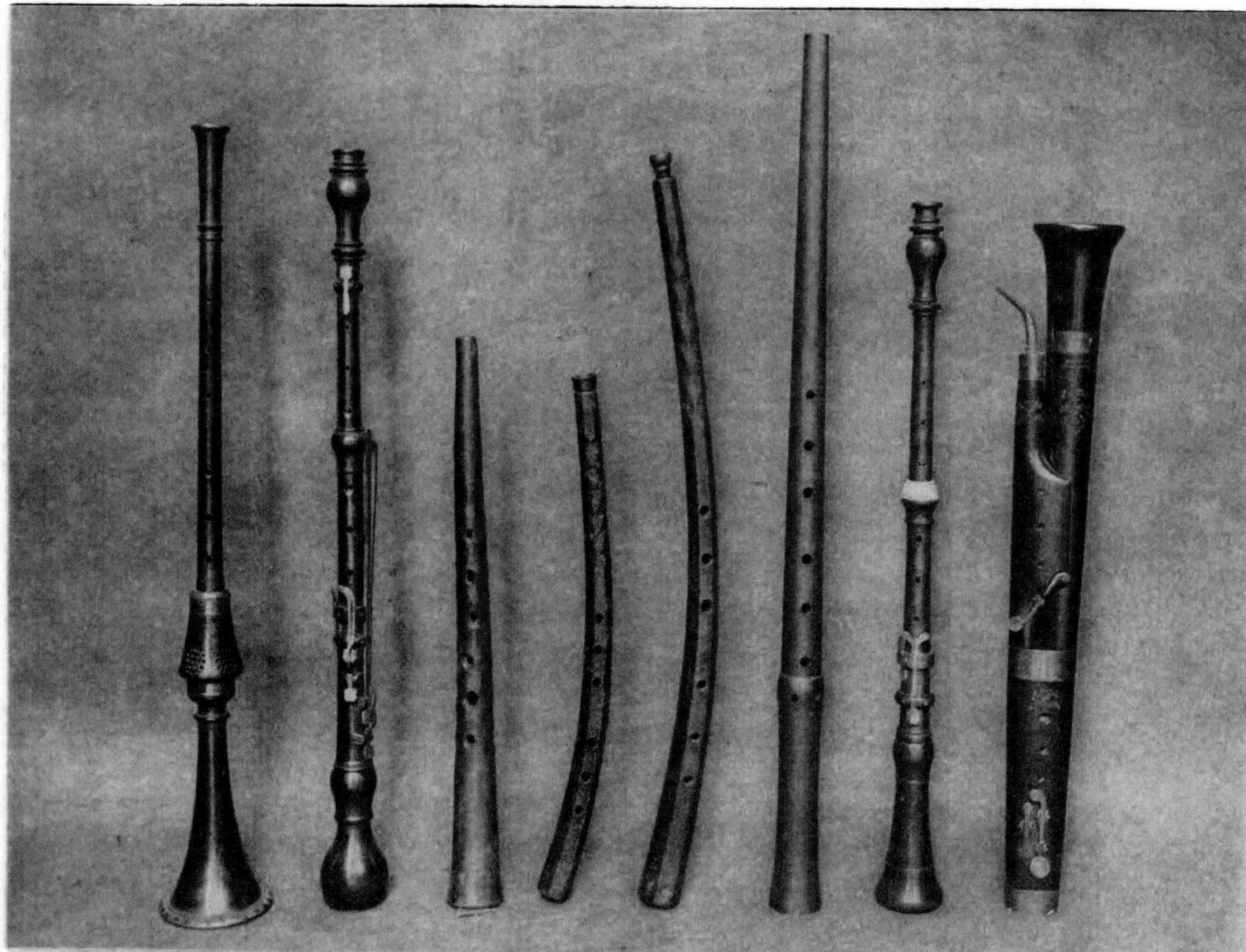

A B C D E F G H

VI.

CLASS—REED INSTRUMENTS.

Family: *Single reeds (α) with cylindrical bore.*

INSTRUMENTS sounded by means of a single-beating reed are of great antiquity, and though almost unknown among the ancient Aryans, were in common use in the early civilization of Egypt; and there have been latterly exhibited before the Musical Association some specimens of very ancient Egyptian instruments, recently discovered by Mr. Flinders Petrie, and which were thus sounded. The single reed is found still in the Arabian and Egyptian *Arghoul*, and its use among the Greeks and Romans was probably borrowed from Egypt. Fragments of ancient *tibiæ* discovered at Pompeii, show the application of this species of reed, and that its use was popular appears to be beyond doubt. Reed instruments of this kind were, however, in their early stages of development, inferior to those of the double reed families; they lacked the delicacy and quality of tone of the latter, and were capable of little expression. Their use was, therefore, confined to musicians of a lower social status. The single *free* reed appears to have been known from time immemorial in China, where it is found in the "Cheng," the prototype of the elaborate reed organ of the present day. Instruments of the free reed type are, however, rarely sounded except from a reservoir of air, and, therefore, need no more than passing notice here.

The *beating* reed, applied so commonly to different kinds of *tibiæ* by the Romans, eventually found its way to Germany; and instruments thus sounded were frequently known as Shalmei, or, in France, Chalumeaux; but the word was sometimes applied to double reed instruments, and its use, therefore, is liable to lead to confusion. The chalumeau of the 13th century was usually a single tube, cylindrical in section, pierced with some nine finger-holes, and sounded by means of a reed, the tongue of which was placed upon the upper side. The tongue of the reed was generally cut from the same wood as the instrument, and shaved down to the required thickness. In course of time the instrument came to be better constructed, and a key was added. About the end of the 17th century Johann Christopher Denner, of Nuremberg, made some experiments upon the chalumeau of that date, and produced the first clarinet. The principle discovered by him was that by opening a key placed at the back of the instrument, the sounds produced by the successive opening of the finger-holes rose a twelfth higher in pitch. The primitive chalumeau, pierced with eight holes, gave the following series of fundamental sounds:—

0 1 2 ‡ 3 4 ‡ 5 ‡ 6 ‡ 7 8

The sounds marked ‡ were obtained by cross-fingering. A second key giving *a'* was invented by Denner, and when this was employed in conjunction with the twelfth key, it gave *b'*♭. In this state the instrument remained for a number of years; a lower key giving *c*♮ and its corresponding twelfth was added at a later date by Denner, and was worked by the thumb of the right hand. This key was placed upon the bell-joint, which was so arranged that it could be turned to either side so as to suit a right or left handed player. But still the instrument was frequently made with a double hole, near the bell, for this purpose; and the duplicate hole not used was stopped with wax, as in the case of the *flûte douce* of the same period.

The mouthpieces of the earlier clarinets were placed with the reed uppermost, and this custom was continued during the 18th century; it is uncertain when, or how, the present downward position of the reed came first into use: and many players in Italy and Spain even now use the reed uppermost.

According to Welcker von Gontershausen (*Magazin Musicalische Tonwerkzeuge*, Frankfurt, 1855), two keys which gave

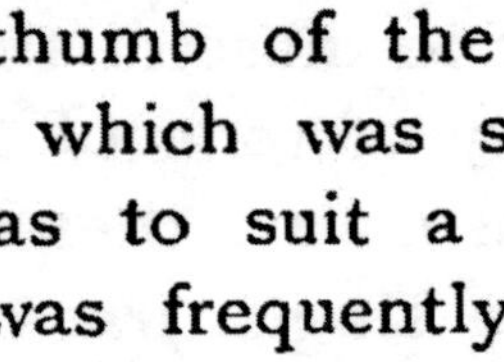

were added to the clarinet by Barthold Fritz, a clever instrument maker of Brunswick, about the middle of the last century. Some years later a sixth key which produced

was invented by the clarinet player Lefèvre, who was one of the professors at the Paris *Conservatoire* about 1790. The clarinet with five keys was, however, in general use at the beginning of the present century.

About the year 1800 the clarinettist Ivan Muller, who had been long studying the defects of the instrument, and the best methods of remedying them, succeeded after many experiments in producing a clarinet which to a great extent has held its own even to the present day. In this new instrument the number of keys was increased to 13, which gave the following sounds:—

The intonation of this clarinet was truer than that of the old five or six keyed instruments, and a great number of shakes were made possible. The fingering, however, became changed, and owing to the antagonism of various makers and professors, the new instrument was adopted but slowly. Owing to the imperfection of the old instruments, they had been made in various keys, and the employment of alternative joints of different pitch (*corps de rechange*) was general. The use, therefore, of so many different instruments was, by the adoption of Muller's clarinet, rendered unnecessary. This possibly influenced players in rejecting the new invention, for they feared that they would lose in quality of tone what they gained by purity of intonation. To render the fingering more easy, rollers were invented in 1804 by Jansen, a clarinet player at the Opera in Paris, and were applied to the keys worked by the little finger of the left hand. The use of rollers was afterwards applied to both the flute and the bassoon.

The clarinet has during the present century undergone various improvements, and has received many additional keys, by which the intonation of several notes has been rendered more true. How Simiot, of Lyons, increased the number of keys to 19 is well known, and needs no more than passing mention here. It is due to Adolphe Sax, the well-known maker of Paris, that the principal alterations in the instrument were made. Seeking for a more regular way of placing the holes, and making a greater use of key-work, he managed to construct a clarinet almost perfect in intonation, and of which the mechanism left little to be desired. Somewhat later, an endeavour was made by the clarinet player Klosé to adapt a system to the instruments somewhat like that of Boehm for the flute. And about 1844 the maker Buffet, of Paris, following Klosé's design, produced the instrument now so generally, but wrongly, called the Boehm clarinet, and which is generally adopted in French orchestras. Of the relative merits of the Boehm system it is not intended to speak, suffice it to say that with instruments of this construction much can be done that is impossible with the 13-keyed clarinet; but whether this is not accomplished somewhat at the expense of intonation is a matter of opinion upon which authorities differ. The 13-keyed instrument underwent considerable improvement at the hands of MM. Buffet-Crampon, of Paris, about 1843, and the first adoption of rings is due to them. In England the clarinet has been considerably improved, first by Cornelius Ward, and afterwards by Mr. Richard Carte. The speaker key, which had invariably been placed at the back of the instrument, was carried round to the front about 1845 by a German called Wehl; and this practice has since been followed generally. Upon the Boehm system instruments the speaker key is almost invariably at the back; and, strange to say, Mr. George Clinton, the well known player, is again reverting to this position of the key.

In 1858 Mr. Richard Carte took a patent for an improved clarinet which really carried out Boehm's principle of placing the holes at regular intervals and venting the notes by open holes below, principles which the so-called "Boehm clarinet" carried out only partially. In this instrument the inventor attacked the great difficulties in the clarinet, *i.e.* the necessity of closing a hole and working a key with the thumb of the left hand; and the management of the *a'* key by

Boehm System Clarinet.

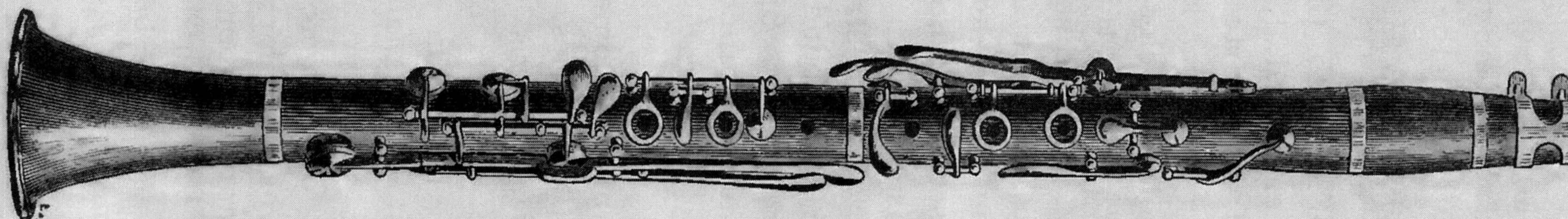

No. 256 (a).
Mr. Carte's Clarinet (*First Modification*).

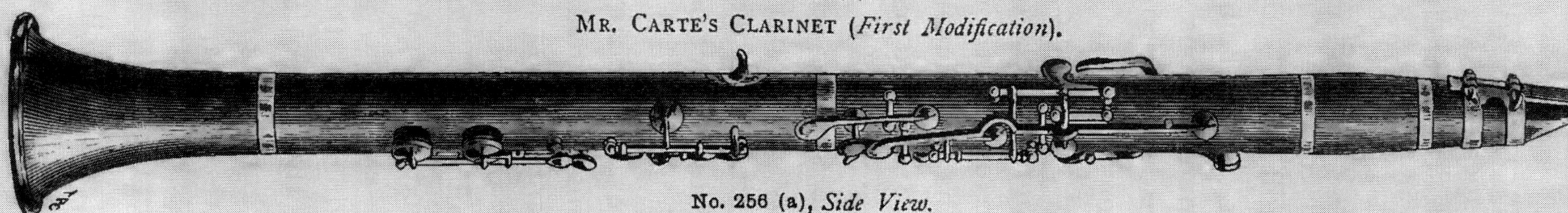

No. 256 (a), *Side View*.

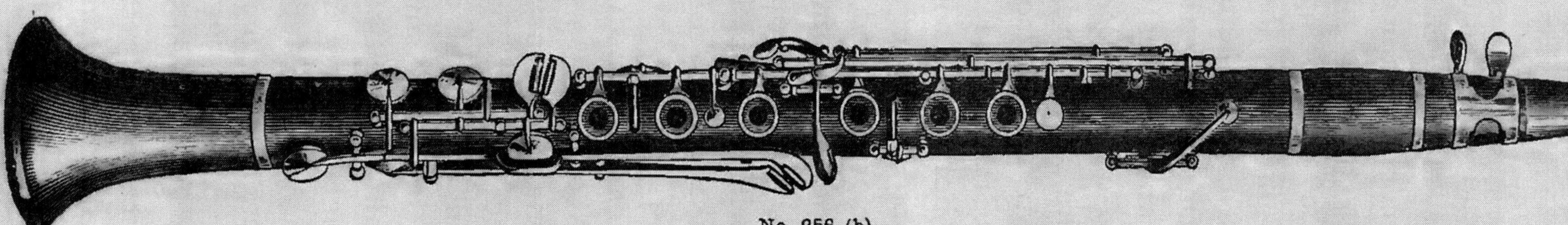

No. 256 (b).
Mr. Carte's Patent of 1858 (*Second Modification*).

the first finger. The instrument was made at first with an open instead of a closed speaker key. Mr. Carte made several modifications of this clarinet, the principal one being that known as the "Second Modification" (page 105), on which the *a'* is made by putting down the third finger of the left hand, a lever holding down the *a'*♭ and *a'* cups being raised by a ring action. The *a'*♭ is made by the first finger of the right hand, together with the third finger of the left; a double-action *g''*♯ key being employed.

On one of the modifications of Mr. Carte's patent clarinet, the *g'*♯ and *a'* holes instead of being *open* and *shut* keys, as just described, were ordinary *open* keys. The *a'* hole was closed by the first finger of the right hand, and the *a'* and *a'*♭ by the third finger of the left.

Mr. Carte also designed a clarinet with ordinary fingering, a thumb-plate taking the place of the thumb-hole; but though the instrument can be played with the old fingering, a ring action for the first and second fingers of the left hand closes the *g'* hole, and the player is therefore enabled, if he wishes, to dispense with the use of the thumb except for opening the speaker key. This instrument (page 105) has been rather extensively used, and will be found described elsewhere; as will also an instrument designed by Mr. Spencer, that has met with approval. Recent improvements in France have been made by Messrs. Evette and Schæffer, and by M. Paradis, a clarinet player in the band of the Garde Républicaine.

About 1853 a Spaniard, named Antonio Romero y Andria, invented an elaborate instrument pierced with 28 holes, and which was produced about 1862 by the maker Bié, of Paris. The mechanism was based upon that of Buffet and Klosé, and was extremely complicated. The invention simplified the fingering of certain passages, and removed certain difficulties of execution, but unfortunately caused a radical change in the fingering. So that, although adopted by the *Conservatoire* of Madrid, the invention of Romero never entered into general use. A mechanism somewhat similar to that of Romero was patented in Paris by M. André Thibouville in 1886. The very great improvements, both in the method of boring and the application of the mechanism, that have been brought out by M. Albert, of Brussels, are so well known that they need only passing allusion here.

The clarinet, although invented in 1700, appears to have made but slow progress in England, and Grassineau's *Musical Dictionary* (1740) makes no mention of it, although describing particularly other wind instruments then in use. The chalumeau appears in the scores of Gluck, and this name possibly applied to the earlier forms of clarinet. The first composer who seems to have made much use of the clarinet is Mozart, although Haydn had used it sparingly before.

The desire which prevailed during the 16th and 17th centuries to arrange music for complete families of instruments, led to the construction of deeper toned clarinets, but it was not until about 1777 that any of these experiments met with success. According to M. Lavoix (*Histoire de l'Instrumentation*), a maker named Horn invented at Passau an instrument which became to the clarinet what the cor anglais or "taille" was to the oboe. This instrument took the name of its inventor, and was known as the *Basset Horn*. By a singular misnomer it became known in France as the *cor de basset*, and in Italy the *corno di bassetto*. The instrument after undergoing some modifications at the hands of Lotz, of Presbourg, in 1782, was employed by Mozart in "Die Zauberflöte," and other operas. Its adoption in England and in France was not general until some fifty or sixty years ago, when it became known as the alto clarinet. The difference, however, between the alto clarinet and basset horn of the present day, consists in the extension of the scale of the latter chromatically from *e* to *c*, by means of four keys worked by the thumb of the right hand.

The invention of the bass clarinet followed rapidly upon that of the basset horn, and the first instrument of the kind was made by Grenser, of Dresden, in 1793; and an instrument made by this maker, in the shape of a bassoon, probably as an experiment, was to be seen in this Exhibition. The difficulty of bringing the finger-holes together, so that they could be conveniently covered, was from want of properly constructed key-work very great, and numerous endeavours were made to overcome it. Sometimes the bore was made in a serpentine shape, and instruments thus constructed were introduced by the Italian maker Piana, of Bologna. About 1807 a jeweller named Dumas brought out a bass clarinet with 13 keys, but which met with small success. A later attempt was made by Streitwolf, of Göttingen, in

1828; and his instrument was constructed in the shape of the basset horn, and had 17 keys. It sounded an octave below the *c'* clarinet. The maker Halary, of Paris, produced bass clarinets in brass, and this metal was for some time employed by Adolphe Sax. Following up the attempts of Streitwolf, Buffet succeeded in constructing a fairly reliable

CONTRA-BASS CLARINET.

bass clarinet in *c*, an octave below the ordinary *c'* instrument, and which was employed by Meyerbeer in "Les Huguenots." This instrument underwent further improvements at the hands of Sax, and a contra-bass upon the same principles was brought out, but with small success. The German musician Wieprecht had been working in the same direction, and an instrument, designed by him and called the *Batyphone*, was made shortly afterwards by the German maker Skorra. Not answering the expectations of the inventor it was afterwards discarded. Of late years, acting upon the advice of M. Poncellet, of the Brussels *Conservatoire*, M. Albert, of Brussels, has succeeded in constructing a contra-bass clarinet in *F*, an octave below the alto instrument. And last year an instrument of the same nature, but in design entirely new, was brought out under the auspices of M. Fontaine Besson, of Paris. This last contra-bass clarinet, constructed in *B*,♭, an octave below the ordinary bass clarinet, possesses a chromatic scale as follows:—

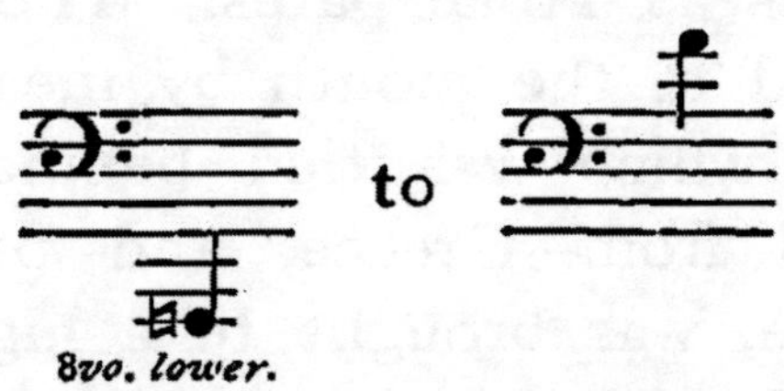

The arrangement of the tubing is ingenious, and can be best understood from the woodcut upon the opposite page. The arrangement of the keys is very simple, and the illustration, since it shows them all, needs therefore little explanation. The method of boring is peculiar, and consists of an ingenious combination of both cylinder and cone; and the tone produced by this novel instrument, resembling in quality that of the organ, will be probably found of great service, as a reed bass, in the orchestra.

220.

Tibia. Greek or Roman, facsimile. Length 1 foot 8¾ inches without reed, with reed 1 foot 11 inches. This is an exact reproduction of one of four instruments of this kind discovered, in 1876, at Pompeii, and now preserved in the Museum at Naples. This instrument is made of ivory, cased with silver or bronze. It has a cylindrical bore, and is pierced with eleven lateral holes. Fitting over the holes are eleven sliding sockets or shutters, any one of which can be closed, and thereby cut off communication with the air column inside the pipe. Small rings are soldered on to these shutters, and served probably to facilitate their use. These shutters were evidently used as a means for putting the instrument in the *mode* desired by the instrumentalist.

The instrument was probably played by means of a single reed, like the Egyptian arghoul. With this kind of reed the following scale is produced :—

Instruments of this kind were frequently played in pairs, and were known to the Romans as Tibiæ pares. The reeds fitted into a sort of stock, which was held to the mouth by means of a strap or bandage, called *capistrum*, and which was tied behind the player's neck. The art of music derived from Greece, and practised in the early days of the Roman empire, was brought to a high state of perfection, and has been fully treated of by various writers in the 17th century, such as Meibom and Dr. Wallis. Through their efforts the remaining treatises have been collected; and the learned commentaries of these writers are indispensable to all students of ancient music. Plate IV., fig. C.

Lent by the *Conservatoire Royal de Musique*, Brussels.

221.

CHALUMEAU, in g', French pitch. This instrument consists of a tube of cane open at the lower end, the upper being closed by the natural joint of the cane. The tube is covered with red leather; and the reed consists of a small tongue detached from the cane itself, and shaved down to the required thickness. It is worthy of note that in this instrument the reed is placed upon the upper side, unlike the arrangement in the clarinets of the present day, and, therefore, the lips could have exercised but little control over the vibrations of the tongue. There are six finger-holes upon the upper side, with a seventh or thumb-hole below. The bell note is g'. The tone of the chalumeau is not unlike that of its successor the modern clarinet. Length $8\frac{1}{4}$ inches, diameter ·6 inch. Plate IV., fig. A. 16th or 17th century.

Lent by M. Césare Snoeck.

222.

Clarinet, in *a*, French pitch. Said to be by C. Denner, but stamped "Lindner." Of maple or sycamore wood, with three brass keys, with square flaps of very early pattern. The low *f*—c'' key is made as a thumb key, and placed upon the under side; hence, it does not show in the plate. The

hole is duplicated, so that it can be used for either a right or left handed player. The keys give the following:—

The lowest note is *f*, and the bore is nearly identical with that at present in use. The design of the instrument is beautifully modelled, and is a very good example of the careful workmanship of the period. Length 2 feet 11¼ inches. Plate IV., fig. D. Late 17th or early 18th century.

Lent by the *Conservatoire Royal de Musique*, Brussels.

223.

Small Clarinet, in g', French pitch. Stamped "J. B. Willems." An instrument of boxwood, with two brass keys on knobs, with square flaps, giving

It is difficult to assign any date for this instrument, but according to the *Indicateur de Bruxelles*, 1765, there were resident there at that date six instrument makers, viz.: "M. Snoeck, Luthier de la Cour; G. A. Rottenburgh, rue de l'Hôpital; Willems, près des Bons Secours; J. H. Rottenburgh, près de St. Jean; Bouwens, rue de l'Évêche; et Boon, au Plattensteen." Length 1 foot 5 inches. 18th century.

Lent by the *Conservatoire Royal de Musique*, Brussels.

224.

Small Clarinet, in *d'*, French pitch. Stamped "G. A. Rottenburgh." Of stained wood, with two brass keys of very early pattern upon knobs, and giving *b'*♭ and *a'*. The bell-joint is made sufficiently long to include the lowest finger-hole upon the instrument, and this can be turned to either side, so as to accommodate a right or left handed player. The maker was living at Brussels in 1765, and there are many of his instruments in existence. Length 1 foot 9 inches. 18th century.

Lent by the *Conservatoire Royal de Musique*, Brussels.

225.

Clarinet d'Amour, in *a*, French pitch. Stamped "Deginan." With four keys, with square flaps on knobs, and horn tips. The four keys give

The mouthpiece is mounted upon a metal crook, and the bell is pear-shaped, and contracted at the mouth in order to produce a veiled sound. Length 2 feet 2 inches. 18th century.

Lent by M. Césare Snoeck.

226.

Clarinet, in *c'*, French pitch. Stamped "J. B. Willems." With four keys. This instrument is interesting, since it shows the *b*♮ key for the little finger of the left hand; so that, henceforth, it became impossible to construct clarinets that could be played either right or left handed, as was the case with the earlier models. Length 1 foot 10 inches. Plate IV., fig. G. 18th century.

Lent by M. Césare Snoeck.

227.

Clarinet, in *c*. Of French make. It is of boxwood and tipped with black horn; the mouthpiece is fixed upon a bent crook of brass.

The bell, resembling that of the clarinet d'amour, is pear-shaped and contracted at the mouth. There are five square-flapped keys of brass working upon knobs, and giving *c*, *f*♯, and *g*♯, with their corresponding twelfths; also *a'* and *b'*♭. Length 1 foot 11 inches. 18th century.

Lent by M. Césare Snoeck.

228.

Clarinet, in *a*. Of boxwood, tipped with ivory, and with five silver keys upon knobs, giving *e*, *f*♯, *g*♯, and their corresponding twelfths above; also *a'* and *b'*♭. Stamped "A. Bland and Weller, No. 23, Oxford Street." Length 27¼ inches. 18th century.

Lent by the Rev. F. W. Galpin, M.A., F.L.S.

229.

Clarinet, in *f'*. Of boxwood, with ivory tip upon bell. Five brass keys on knobs, producing the same notes as in the instruments described above. Stamped "H. Grenser, Dresden." Probably about the end of last century. Length, without mouthpiece, 1 foot 4 inches.

Lent by the *Grossherzogliches Museum*, Darmstadt.

230.

Clarinet, in *c'*. Stamped "Astor and Co., London." Of boxwood, with five keys, and with ivory tips. Length 1 foot 11½ inches. 18th century.

Lent by Corporal Roberts, 4th Hussars.

231.

Clarinet, in *b*♭. Boxwood, with six flat brass keys on knobs, giving *e*, *f*♯, *g*♯, and their corresponding twelfths above, and *a'*, *b'*♭; also a shake upon *a'*. The bell is in one piece with the lowest joint. Stamped "H. C. Tölcke, Bronsvig." Late 18th century. Length 26¼ inches.

Lent by the Rev. F. W. Galpin, M.A., F.L.S.

232.

CLARINET, in *e′♭*. Of stained boxwood, ivory mounted. There are six flat brass keys, with square flaps, working upon knobs. The keys give the same intervals as those of No. 231 described above. It is stamped "Goulding, 45, Pall Mall, London." Length 19¼ inches. Late 18th century.

Lent by the Rev. F. W. Galpin, M.A., F.L.S.

233.

CLARINET, in *c′*. Stamped "Pask." Of boxwood, with five brass keys on knobs, and with ivory tips. A sixth key on pillars has been added, evidently at a later date. Length 1 foot 11 inches. Late 18th century.

Lent by E. Hooker, Esq.

234.

CLARINET, in *c′*. Of boxwood, stained and spotted. It is tipped with ivory, and furnished with eight flat circular keys of brass working upon knobs. The keys give *e*, *f*♯, *g*♯, with their corresponding twelfths; also *a′* and *b′*♭. Of the other keys, one is intended to correct the *b′*♮, the other being a shake upon *a′*. Stamped "D'Almaine and Co., late Goulding and D'Almaine, Soho Square, London." Length 23 inches. Early 19th century.

Lent by the Rev. F. W. Galpin, M.A., F.L.S.

235.

CLARINET, in *b*♭. With five brass keys on knobs, and with ivory tips. Stamped "Cramer, London." Early 19th century. This instrument has a socket and mouthpiece, evidently modern. Length 2 feet 2 inches.

Lent by Messrs. Rudall, Carte and Co.

236.

CLARINET, in *c′*. Boxwood, with six brass keys, having square flaps, mounted upon knobs, and with ivory tips. The keys give the same intervals as those of No. 234 described above. Stamped "Otten, London." Length 1 foot 11¼ inches. Early 19th century.

Lent by Messrs. Boosey and Co.

237.

CLARINET in *c'*. Of boxwood, with ivory tips. There are six brass keys, mounted in the usual way upon knobs, giving the same sounds as those previously described. Stamped "Astor." Length 1 foot 7½ inches. 18th century.

Lent by Messrs. Rudall, Carte and Co.

238.

CLARINET, in *b♭*. Of boxwood, with six square-flapped brass keys upon knobs. The instrument is tipped with ivory, and does not differ materially from any of the foregoing types. It is stamped "J. Astor, London," and measures 2 feet 2¼ inches in length. 18th century.

Lent by Messrs. Rudall, Carte and Co.

239.

CLARINET, in *b♭*. Of boxwood, with six brass keys, having square flaps, working upon knobs. The instrument is tipped with ivory, and is marked with the name "D'Almaine and Co., London." Length 2 feet 2 inches. Early 19th century.

Lent by E. Hooker, Esq.

240.

CLARINET, in *b♭*. Of boxwood. There are six circular flat brass keys upon knobs. The instrument is stamped "Cramer," but was probably not of his make. The mouthpiece is fitted over a ring, a rather late pattern. It was probably made about 1840, as an instrument of moderate cost, and without the improvements of the time. Length 2 feet.

Lent by Messrs. Rudall, Carte and Co.

241.

Clarinet, in *b*♭. With eight circular flat keys on knobs, with ivory tips. The mouthpiece has a long pin for tuning in place of socket. The eight keys give the same notes as in the instruments previously mentioned, with the addition of two for

Stamped with the maker's name, "Monzani." Length 2 feet 1$\frac{3}{4}$ inches. Early 19th century.

Lent by George Butler, Esq.

242.

Clarinet, in *c′*. Boxwood. There are eight brass keys on knobs, giving the same notes as before mentioned. The mouthpiece is made to fit over the pin in the socket, instead of into it. Stamped "Key, London." Length 1 foot 11$\frac{1}{4}$ inches. Early 19th century.

Lent by Messrs. Rudall, Carte and Co.

243.

Soprano Clarinet, in *g′*. Of brass; skeleton model, with eleven German-silver keys on pillars. Engraved "Wünnenberg, Cöln." Length 15$\frac{1}{8}$ inches. 19th century.

Lent by Messrs. Boosey and Co.

244.

Clarinet, in *c′*. By Key. Formerly the property of Sir W. Sterndale Bennett, and given by him to Mr. George Case. This instrument belonged to a clarinet player in the band of the 1st Guards, and is believed to have been used during the 1815 campaign. There are 11 brass keys with square flaps, on knobs, giving

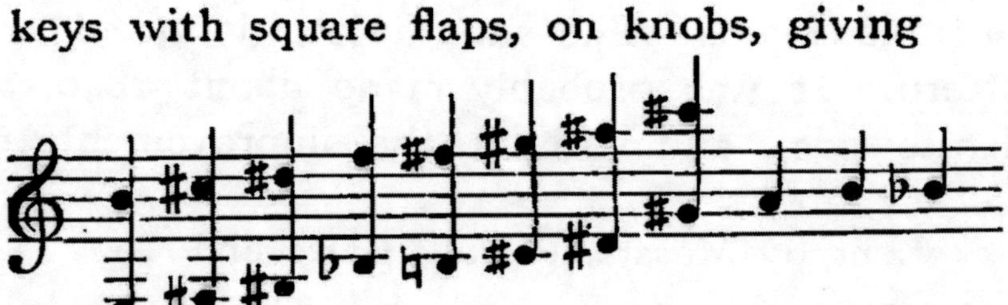

An *f* key has apparently been planned, but has never been put in. The key for *g'*♯ appears for the first time here; it was invented by James Wood in the year 1800, and formed the subject of a patent. Length 1 foot 11⅛ inches.

Lent by G. Case, Esq.

245.

CLARINET, in *c'*. Of boxwood. There are 13 brass keys mounted upon knobs; the keys are all cup-shaped and very carefully made. There is a roller upon the *c''*♯ key. The 13 keys give the same notes as described under No. 244. There is, however, a duplicate key for the *b*♮ and its corresponding twelfth; also an additional key, giving

The instrument is stamped "George Wood's Patent." The patent is apparently that of James, and not George, Wood, and consists in "placing the fingering parts of the long keys *b'*♮ and *c''*♯ in one line, and that in a direction parallel to the length of the instrument, so that the finger of the performer has only to move slightly forward in the direction of the length of the instrument to operate upon the said two keys, and thereby the fingering of the said two keys is much facilitated." The two keys in question had been rather differently placed before this; this arrangement, patented in 1819 by Jas. Wood, is practically similar to that now used. Length 1 foot 11 inches.

Lent by Messrs. Köhler and Son.

246.

CLARINET, in *b*♭. Of boxwood, made by Key in 1825. This instrument has now 12 keys, several of them evidently having been added at a late date. This clarinet formerly belonged to Mr. John Blizzard, then first clarinet player in the band of the 1st Life Guards, and afterwards Bandmaster of the Duke of York's School. Mr. Blizzard played upon this instrument up till the year 1838, when it became the property of its present owner.

Lent by Henry Lazarus, Esq.

247.

CLARINET, in *a*. By Key, of Charing Cross. This instrument is of stained boxwood, and has ten keys working upon knobs; an addition of two rings was made subsequently. This clarinet was played upon by Mr. Henry Lazarus, in the orchestras of Her Majesty's and Royal Italian Operas, under Sir Michael Costa, from 1843 to 1855, in which year Mr. Lazarus changed to an instrument of another English maker (Fieldhouse).

Lent by Henry Lazarus, Esq.

248.

CLARINET, in *a*. Made by Fieldhouse. This instrument has an improved bore "medium," suggested by Mr. Henry Lazarus as being between that of the old English clarinets and that of the more modern Belgian instruments. This clarinet was played upon by Mr. Henry Lazarus from 1855 to 1865, when he changed to the Belgian instrument made by M. Albert, of Brussels, and which he still uses.

Lent by Henry Lazarus, Esq.

249.

CLARINET, in *b*♭. Boxwood. Thirteen silver keys upon pillars, and very richly chased, as are also the silver tips with which this instrument is mounted. By C. Boosè, London. This clarinet was exhibited at the 1851 Exhibition, London, and is remarkable, as it is the earliest specimen in this collection which has the speaker key carried round to the top of the instrument; in all the preceding clarinets it was placed below, which must have affected the tone considerably. The *f*♯ key is worked with the third finger of the right hand, in lieu of the ring arrangement which is in use at the present day. Length 2 feet 1½ inches.

Lent by Messrs. Boosey and Co.

250.

CLARINET, in *b*♭. Boxwood, with 14 brass keys. In reality this is a 13-keyed instrument, the 14th key merely being a side *b'*♭ shake. The keys are mounted upon knobs, and the thumb rest is cut, as a knob, from the same block of wood as the instrument itself. The maker's name is not stamped upon this clarinet, but it is known to have been made by EULEZ, of Frankfurt, probably about 1850. Length 2 feet 1½ inches.

Lent by Messrs. Boosey and Co.

251.

CLARINET, in *b*♭. This instrument has the usual 13-keyed fingering, but is provided with a key, worked by the fourth finger of the right hand, and giving the note *e*♭. This key was designed by Adolphe Sax with the idea of rendering the use of the *a* clarinet unnecessary, the *e*♭ upon the *b*♭ instrument producing the same note in real sounds as the *e*♮ of the *a* clarinet. The quality of the note is, however, rather different; and the inventor's idea was never generally adopted. This instrument was made by Sax, and gained a prize medal in the International Exhibition in 1862.

Lent by W. Hugh Spottiswoode, Esq.

252.

A SET OF FOUR CLARINETS, in *e'*♭, *c'*, *b*♭, and *a*. Modern instruments, with 13 keys upon pillars. By Rudall, Carte and Co.

Lent by Messrs. Rudall, Carte and Co.

253.

A SET OF FOUR CLARINETS, in *e'*, *c'*, *b*♭, and *a*, with 14 keys, and rings upon the lower joint. By Buffet-Crampon, Paris. Good specimens of modern French instruments.

Lent by W. Hugh Spottiswoode, Esq.

254.

A SET OF FOUR CLARINETS, in *e'*♭, *c'*, *b*♭, and *a*. By Rudall, Carte and Co. Modern instruments of cocus-wood; all having 15 keys of German silver, the double action *g''*♯, and six rollers upon the keys, worked by the third and fourth fingers of each hand.

Lent by Messrs. Rudall, Carte and Co.

255.

A Set of Four Clarinets, in *e′♭*, *c′*, *b♭*, and *a*. Similar instruments to the previous set, but made entirely of ebonite. By Rudall, Carte and Co.

Lent by Messrs. Rudall, Carte and Co.

256.

Clarinet, in *b♭*. Of ebonite. By Rudall, Carte and Co. Designed by Mr. Richard Carte. Two modifications of this instrument are shown. In No. 256 (**a**) the *g′* hole is placed towards the front and closed by a thumb lever, or with a ring action by the first and second fingers of the left hand, thus leaving the thumb free to work the speaker key only. In the second modification, No. 256 (**b**), the ordinary keys for *a′♭* and *a′*, worked by the first and second fingers of the left hand, are dispensed with; the *a′* is made by the third finger of the left hand, and the *a′♭* by the addition of the first finger of the right hand. This arrangement much facilitates the playing of passages in which *a′♭*, *a′*, and *b′♭* occur, besides rendering the shake *g′♯*, *a′* satisfactory. The instrument has also the double action *g″♯* key, and is fitted with rollers upon the keys worked by the third and fourth fingers of each hand. An engraving of these instruments will be found upon page 105.

Lent by Messrs. Rudall, Carte and Co.

257.

Clarinet, in *b♭*. This instrument was designed by Mr. A. Clinton to give equal facility for every scale and shake, and was made by Boosey and Co.

This clarinet has several keys and fingerings in addition to those on the Spencer model described (No. 260). There are in all 20 keys and five rings, but the details of all the fingerings cannot be clearly described without handling the instrument.

Lent by Messrs. Boosey and Co.

258.

Clarinet, in *b♭*. Ebonite, special model. By Boosey and Co. In addition to the usual keys, this instrument has the "Barret" action

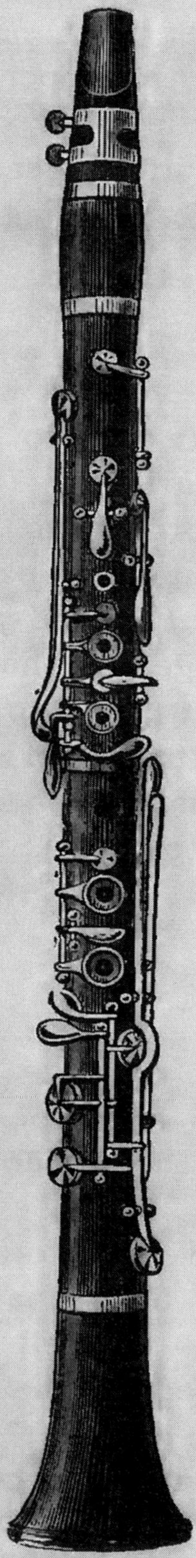

No. 258.

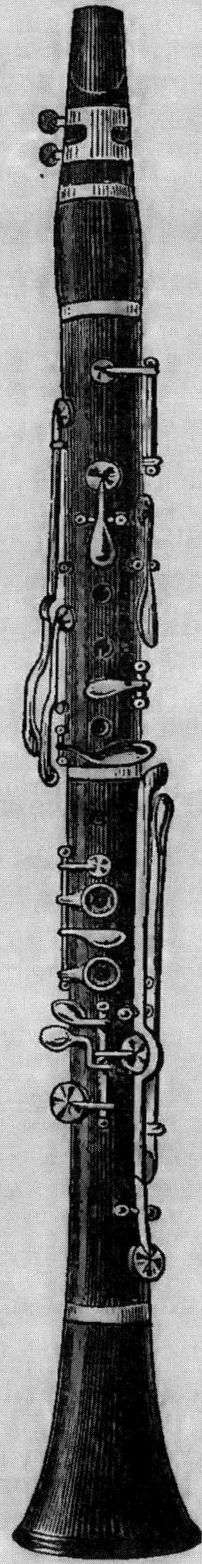

13-KEYED CLARINET,
WITH RINGS ON LOWER JOINT
(as usually employed).

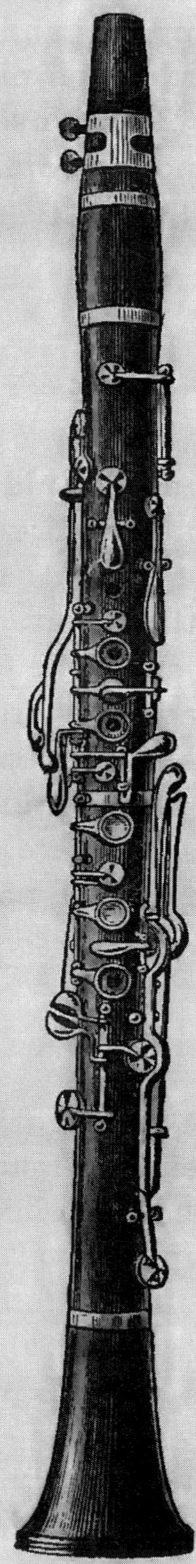

No. 260.
MR. SPENCER'S
CLARINET.

on the upper, and the "extra c''♯ key" on the lower joint. It has also extra touch-pieces to the keys for c'♯ and a'♭ on the upper joint, enabling the player to use these keys either with the right or left hand, and a duplicate key for a'♮, taken with the first finger, right hand. There are 10 rollers to the keys to facilitate the fingering.

Lent by Messrs. Boosey and Co.

259.

Clarinet, in *b*♭. Boehm system. By Rudall, Carte and Co. This instrument should properly be called the Klosé clarinet. It was designed by Klosé to carry out the principles according to which Boehm planned the flute bearing his name, but it only partially carries them out. In the middle register it has the *f''*♯ and *f''*♮ of Boehm, and the *b''*♭ as also made by the first finger of the right hand and the first finger and thumb of the left. It has also alternative keys to make *c''* and *b'*, with the fourth finger of either hand. In addition to the ordinary keys for the first finger of the right hand there is a key for shaking from *b'*♭ to *c''*. See the engraving upon page 105.

Lent by Messrs. Rudall, Carte and Co.

260.

Clarinet, in *b*♭. Spencer's model. By Boosey and Co. This instrument is made with the "Barret" action on the upper joint, and with the following further additions, viz.:—

A duplicate *f''*♮ key on the lower joint to improve the fork *f''*♮, making it as full-toned and good a note as that from the cross *f''*♮ key. The *b*♭, a twelfth below, is also brought out well by it, and this note is not playable on the ordinary 13-keyed clarinet as a fork note.

The *c'*♯—*g''*♯ key is placed in its proper position; as good and full a note is therefore obtained from it as any on the instrument. It can be fingered either in the usual way, or with the first finger, right hand; this alternative fingering gives certain advantages in extreme keys.

An extra key on the top joint, giving a perfect *b'*♭, and which is useful for the shakes,

Lent by Messrs. Boosey and Co.

261.

Bass Clarinet, in *B*♭. Of German make. This instrument is of German make, and is in all probability one of the earliest bass clarinets in existence. It is made of wood, covered with leather, and has a brass crook and bell, which is turned up at an acute angle. The wooden body is flat, and about an inch in thickness, the finger-holes, which slant upwards through the thickness of the wood, are brought near enough for the fingers to cover them. There are three brass keys on saddles, producing in actual sounds *A*♭, *G*, and the low *D*. Outside length 3 feet 1½ inches. Plate V., fig. A.

Lent by the *Conservatoire Royal de Musique*, Brussels.

262.

Bass Clarinet, in *B*♭. Stamped "Nicola Papolini, Inventore." This curious instrument is made of pear wood, and is carved out of two separate slabs, which are fitted together with wooden pins. There are in all 19 finger-holes, numbered in succession upwards from the bell. The holes 2, 3, 4, 18, and 19 are covered by keys, which work on knobs. The first hole does not appear to have been covered at all by either fingers or keys. The keys are all of brass, with square flaps. The instrument is made in three joints, and is tipped with horn. The socket joint has a curve so as to get increased length of tubing. In the middle joint the bore takes a serpentine shape, probably to shorten the length of the instrument; and the bell joint is made of wood entirely. Outside length 2 feet 3½ inches. See Plate V., fig. B.

Lent by the *Conservatoire Royal de Musique*, Brussels.

263.

Bass Clarinet, in *B♭*. Stamped "Widerman, à Paris." This instrument is doubled at the butt into a semi-circular brass bend, at about half its total length. The bore is very large, and measures 1¼ inches. There are 20 brass keys on pillars; but as the pads do not stop the holes, and the instrument is out of order, it is impossible to examine it in detail. Length 27 inches.

Lent by M. Césare Snoeck.

264.

Batyphone, in *E♭*. This is a sort of contra-bass clarinet, and was one of Wieprecht's endeavours to produce a reed contra-bass. It is a fifth below the ordinary bass clarinet, and therefore of the same pitch as the *E♭* tuba of the present day. There are 18 brass keys, some of which stand open. The thumb of the left hand manipulates the keys 15, 16, and 18; the fingers of the same hand taking Nos. 9, 10, 11, 12, 13, 14, and 17; the thumb of the right hand takes the keys 1, 2, and 4; the remainder 3, 5, 6, 7, 8, being taken by the fingers of the right hand. The first key is of course the bell key. The whole instrument is made of wood, in one piece, the bore being doubled near its centre. The crook and bell are of metal, the latter being engraved "W. Wieprecht and E. Skorra, Patentirte Erfinde." Outside length 3 feet 3½ inches, diameter of bore 1·33 inches.

Wieprecht has given the following description of this invention in a MS. treatise upon Instrumentation, which is now in the possession of Herr Otto Lessmann:—

"This is an invention of our own in conjunction with Sporra, the Court instrument manufacturer of Berlin; it was completed in 1839, and patented for ten successive years throughout the Prussian Monarchy. The demand for a contra-bass wind instrument bearing technical resemblance to the clarionet, flute, oboe, and bassoon, induced us, after many experiments, to construct this instrument. We made it to a scale twice the size of that of the *c'* clarionet, the divisions of the chromatic scale being arranged according to acoustical principles. Those holes which were too far apart to be covered by the fingers, were made accessible by means of so-called crank or swivel-keys (similar to those of the keyed contra-bassoon). This instrument was made of maple, and had a deep-toned clarionet mouthpiece of suitable size. Between the mouthpiece and the instrument there was a cylindrical  shaped crook of brass, of proportionate size, as in the bassoon. To ensure portability the instrument was constructed of two upright cylindrical tubes, and the mouth was provided with a brass bell. The quality of its tone was somewhat like that of the lower notes on the manual of an organ, pleasant and full, but not sufficiently powerful to take the place of the contra-bass in a military band; and, further, it could be played with facility only in its nearly related keys. It sounds two octaves lower than the *c'* clarionet, and possesses the same compass, but was played by means of keys. The easiest keys for this instrument were *G* and *F* major; and the farther one went from these keys, the more difficult it became."

The invention, however, does not seem to have been of much practical use, and was abandoned. A somewhat similar attempt to produce a contra-bass clarinet was made by Adolphe Sax, of Paris, in 1843. Sax made an instrument of brass, with a cylindrical bore, somewhat differing in outward appearance from the Batyphone, and gave it the name of Saxophone, a word which he afterwards applied to a class of instruments totally different.

Lent by M. Césare Snoeck.

265.

Glicibarifono, in *B*♭. This instrument is a kind of bass clarinet with a vertical bell, and in shape somewhat resembling the bassoon. About 1838 the instrument maker, Catterino Cotterini, of Bologna, produced instruments of this description. This particular specimen is however stamped "P. Maino, Milano," and has 17 brass keys fitted on studs, which work in grooves cut in the thickness of the keys.

Lent by the *Conservatoire Royal de Musique*, Brussels.

266.

Bass Clarinet, in *C*, made in the form of a bassoon. This instrument is made of light wood, and has nine square-flapped brass keys working on knobs. The keys give *B*♭, *A*, *G*♯, *F*♯, *F*♮; there is also a speaker key. There was originally a crook, which had a key working upon it, but this has since been lost, and the whole instrument is very much out of order. It is stamped with "L," and below "A. Grenser, Dresden." So that it is evidently one of the earliest instruments of this shape in existence, as this maker was the inventor of the bass clarinet.

Lent by the *Grossherzogliches Museum*, Darmstadt.

267.

BASS CLARINET, in *B*♭. Of stained boxwood, with four finger-holes in front and a thumb-hole behind. There are 20 German-silver keys on pillars, which give the *a* shake, speaker key, *a*, *g*♯, *f* (in duplicate), *e*♭, *c*♯, *c*, *B* (in duplicate), *B*♭, *A*♭, *F*♯, *F*, *E*, with all of their respective twelfths, and in the lowest register *E*♭, *D*, *C*♯, and *C*. The lower joint is curved back, thereby resembling the bassoon; this admits of the extension of the scale from the *E* to the lowest *C* below the lines of the bass clef, and giving of course the *B*♭ lower in real sounds. Total length, including crook and mouthpiece, 42½ inches.

Lent by the Rev. F. W. Galpin, M.A., F.L.S.

268.

CLARINET D'AMOUR, in *g*, French pitch. The instrument is made of boxwood, and is tipped with bone. The bell is pear-shaped and much contracted at the mouth. There are five brass keys on knobs, which give

The instrument is stamped "P. Piana, a Milano." Total length 2 feet 9 inches.

Lent by the *Conservatoire Royal de Musique*, Brussels.

269.

ALTO CLARINET, in *g*. This instrument is made in a curved form, much like that of the cor anglais. It is of stained boxwood, and has eight brass keys with square flaps on knobs. The tone much resembles that of the basset horn, but the bore is very much smaller; like the basset horn, the compass of this instrument extends to the *C* of its scale. There is no maker's name. Total length 2 feet 10½ inches.

Lent by M. Césare Snoeck.

270.

Tenor Clarinet, in *f*. This might be called appropriately enough a clarinet d'amour, alto, in *f*, since it has a pear-shaped contracted bell. The bore, too, is rather smaller than that of a basset horn, though a trifle larger than the ordinary tenor clarinet. The instrument only goes down to the *e*, and not the *c*, of its scale. There are 12 brass keys with square flaps on knobs. It is stamped "Cramer & Son, London, No. 20, Pall Mall." Length 3 feet 1 inch.

Lent by Messrs. J. and R. Glen.

271.

Basset Horn, in *f*. Of stained wood, with 13 brass keys on knobs, and with ivory tips. Some of the keys are mounted upon saddles, and appear to have been subsequent additions. The keys give a complete chromatic scale. The instrument is stamped "Key, London." Length 3 feet.

Lent by Messrs. Rudall, Carte and Co.

272.

Basset Horn, in *f*. This curious instrument is in shape almost unique. It is of boxwood, with ivory mounts and mouthpiece. There are 10 keys of plated metal, with square flaps, working upon knobs. The bore of the instrument is bent at an angle of about 120 degrees near its centre. The bell is globular and very much contracted at the mouth, and is turned back towards the player at right-angles to the lower joint of the instrument. It is stamped "Strobach, Carlsbad," and its total length is 3 feet 7 inches.

Lent by M. Césare Snoeck.

273.

Basset Horn, in *f*. This interesting instrument is made of stained boxwood, and is tipped with brass and ivory. It has six finger-holes in front, and a thumb-hole at the back. There are 16 flat brass keys on saddles, which give the following series:

The instrument is bent about the middle of the bore at an angle of 40 degrees. There is a wooden block at the bottom of the lower joint just above the bell. Inside this block the bore is reflexed, and then curved down again, ending in a bell of brass, and of an oval shape. The peculiarity of the basset horn consists in the extension of its scale to *c*, which in real sounds of course gives *f*. This instrument is stamped "H. Grenser, S. Wiesner, Dresden." Length 40½ inches.

Lent by the Rev. F. W. Galpin, M.A., F.L.S.

274.

Basset Horn, in *f*. Of stained boxwood, with 17 keys and two rings, mounted upon pillars. This instrument is tipped with brass, and possesses a complete chromatic scale, with the exception of the two lowest keys, which give only intervals of a whole tone. It is stamped "Heckel, Biebrich." Length 3 feet 4½ inches.

Lent by H. A. Smith, Esq.

275.

Basset Horn, in *f*, by C. Mahillon, of Brussels. A modern instrument of beautiful workmanship and tone. The bell is in a straight line with the body, and not turned vertically upwards.

Lent by W. Hugh Spottiswoode, Esq.

Modern Bass Clarinet.

276.

TENOR CLARINET, in *e♭*. Shown as a type of the modern instrument used in military bands. With 14 German-silver keys. By Rudall, Carte and Co. Made entirely of ebonite.

Lent by Messrs. Rudall, Carte and Co.

277.

BASS CLARINET, in *B♭*. Shown as a type of the modern instrument used in military bands. Of ebonite. By Rudall, Carte and Co. A similar instrument to the tenor clarinet above.

Lent by Messrs. Rudall, Carte and Co.

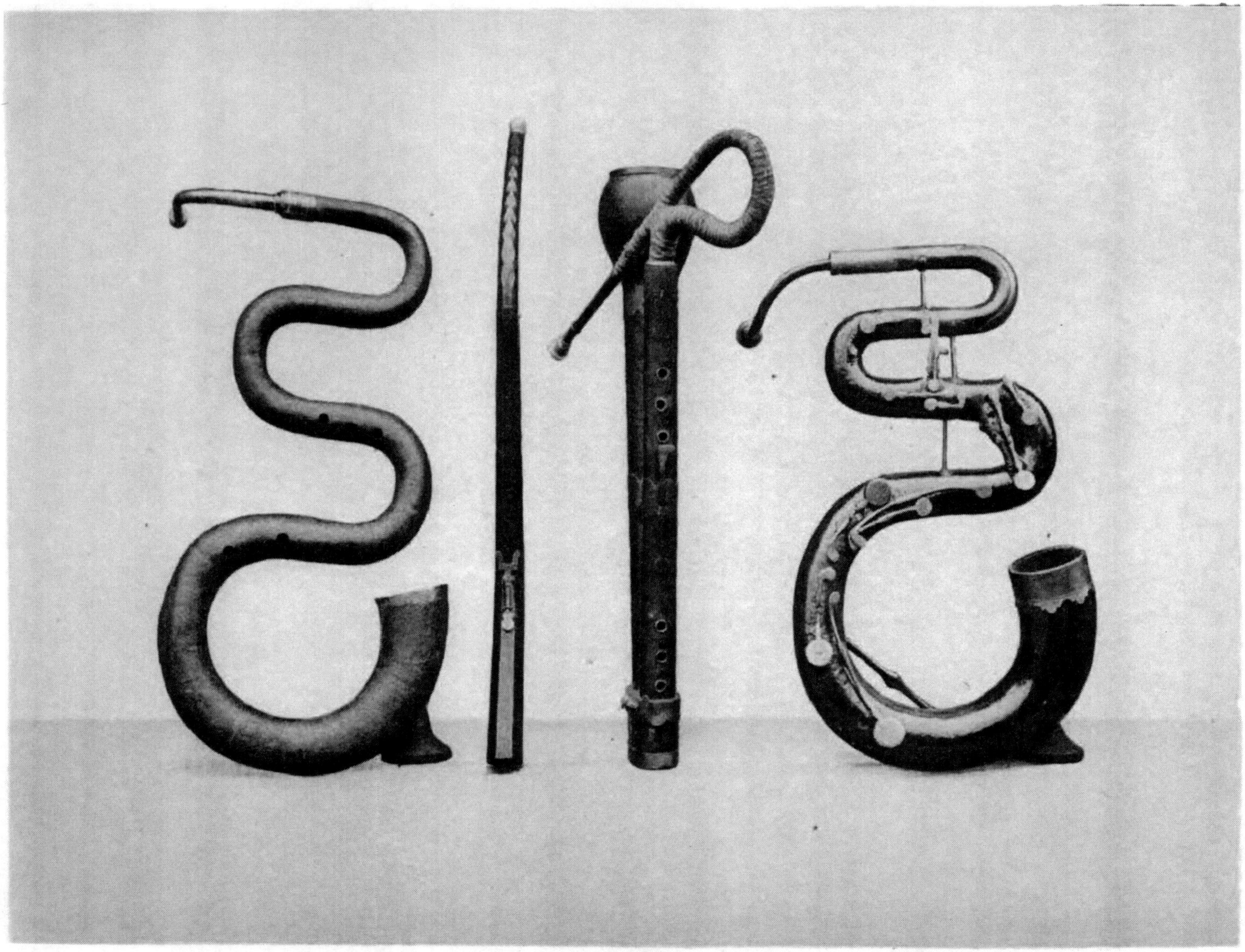

A B C D

VII.

CLASS—REED INSTRUMENTS.

FAMILY: *Single reeds (β) with conical bore.*

THE application of the single-beating reed to a conical tube has been usually attributed to Adolphe Sax. There is, however, reason to believe that experiments in this direction had been made at the commencement of the century; and a curious wooden clarinet, having a conical bore, and bearing the name of "Desfontenelles, Lisieux, 1807," is to be seen in the Museum of the Paris *Conservatoire*. This interesting instrument is all the more remarkable since it has not only a conical bore, but also the bell turned vertically upwards, and 12 keys. The maker was a clockmaker, of Lisieux, and it has been urged that he suggested to Ivan Muller many of the improvements, in the ordinary clarinet, since attributed to Muller himself. The priority of the invention of the saxophone is, then, due to Desfontenelles. According to M. Lavoix (*Histoire de l'Instrumentation*), it was probably in endeavouring to construct a clarinet which should overblow the octave, instead of the twelfth, that Sax invented, in 1840, the instrument to which he gave the name of Saxophone. Whatever may be the real origin of this invention, it is, nevertheless, certain that the credit of having introduced and perfected the instrument belongs rightly to Sax.

The saxophone consists essentially of a conical brass tube furnished with some 20 lateral orifices covered by keys, and with six touch-pieces for the first three fingers of each hand. The saxophone, therefore, becomes, as regards brass instruments, what the clarinet is as regards wood.

Comparatively little used in England and Germany, the saxophone, introduced first in 1846 into military bands in France, completely superseded the clarinet. French makers have, therefore, from time to time introduced various improvements. The maker Goumas, in 1879, adding an additional fingering for *b'*♭, rendered it possible for certain passages, hitherto of difficult execution, to be played with ease. An improvement upon this, with further changes, was, some years later, effected by the "Association Générale des Ouvriers," and patented by them. In 1887 the instrument was again improved by MM. Evette and Schæffer, and by M. Millereau; the exact nature of the improvements formed the subject of patents in France, and is of too technical a nature to be described at length here. Of late years several additional fingerings, and improved mechanism, have been effected by M. Fontaine Besson. In Belgium, as in France, the saxophone is in common use, and the Belgian makers M. Albert and M. Charles Mahillon, of Brussels, keeping pace with recent improvements, produce large numbers of these instruments.

With application of the so-called Boehm system to the clarinet by Klosé, came the desire to apply a fingering somewhat similar to the saxophone; and the first makers who succeeded in producing instruments thus constructed were MM. Lecomte. As, however, Boehm's invention related principally to the division of the bore, and the position and size of the lateral holes, the name "Boehm-saxophone" seems hardly correct; the proportion of the bore and disposition of the holes remaining the same, the alterations being only as regards mechanism and fingering. The saxophone, though inferior to the clarinet both as regards compass, quality of tone, and articulation, is, nevertheless, of considerable value in military bands; and it has recently been adopted at the Royal Military School of Music. Up to the present time it has not been received as an integral part of any military band in England.

There is a complete family of these instruments formed as follows:

I.	II.
Sopranino in *f′*.	Sopranino in *c′*♭.
Soprano in *c′*.	Soprano in *b*♭.
Contralto in *f*.	Contralto in *e*♭.
Tenor in *c*.	Tenor in *B*♭.
Baryton in *F*.	Baryton in *E*♭.
Bass in *C*.	Bass in *B,*♭.

I. are intended for use in the orchestra; II. in military bands.

In France the use of four or five of the varieties of these instruments is common. In Belgium those most employed are the contralto, tenor, and baryton.

In the orchestra, for the production of special effects, or for solo playing the saxophone is of great value. First introduced in 1844 by M. Kastner in "Le dernier Roi de Juda," it was afterwards employed by Limnander in the opera of "Barbe Bleue." Meyerbeer, Massenet, and Ambroise Thomas have made use of the instrument. And in the last named composer's opera of "Hamlet," the value of the contralto saxophone, as a solo instrument, accompanied first by strings, and afterwards by three trombones and the bass saxophone, is especially evident. In the scene on the platform, in the same opera, when the spectre appears, the baryton saxophone, in combination with the cor anglais, produces an effect as weird as it is novel and appropriate to the surrounding scene.

278.

Soprano Saxophone, in *b♭*. By Mahillon and Co. This instrument is constructed of brass, and is furnished with 20 keys and touch-pieces. There are also two octave keys. The compass of the instrument is, in real sounds,

 to 

including all the chromatic intervals.

Lent by Messrs. Mahillon and Co.

279.

Contralto Saxophone, in *e♭*. By Mahillon and Co. Of brass, with 20 keys and touch-pieces. There are also two octave keys. The compass of the instrument is, in real sounds,

 to 

with all the chromatic intervals.

As the contralto saxophone is the instrument in most general use, it is thought best to describe it rather than any of the others which, in point of construction, do not differ materially. The saxophone is written for invariably in the clef, whatever may be the real sounds produced. The lowest note upon the instrument is written *b*, sounding *e*♭. By the successive opening of the lateral holes the following fundamental sounds (using the notation adopted for the instrument) are obtained:

By means of the octave keys the following sounds are obtained:

SAXOPHONE IN *e*♭.

Hence the use of the second harmonics of the first three fundamental sounds is rendered unnecessary. The compass of the instrument is completed by the notes

which are produced by four keys conveniently placed in the upper part of the instrument; the notes thus produced are the *second* harmonics of the sounds

The instrument is represented in the annexed woodcut.

Lent by Messrs. Mahillon and Co.

280.

TENOR SAXOPHONE, in *B*♭. By Mahillon and Co. The compass of this instrument is, in real sounds,

 to 

with all the chromatic intervals. It is written for in the  clef.

The instrument does not differ in construction from the contralto saxophone in *e*♭, already described.

Lent by Messrs. Mahillon and Co.

281.

BARYTON SAXOPHONE, in *E*♭. By Mahillon and Co. The compass of this instrument is, in real sounds,

 to 

with all the chromatic intervals. It is written for in the  clef.

The construction of the instrument resembles that of the contralto saxophone, already described.

Lent by Messrs. Mahillon and Co.

VIII.

CLASS—INSTRUMENTS WITH CUP-SHAPED MOUTHPIECES.

FAMILY: *Tubes of fixed length.*

THE antiquity of instruments sounded by means of a cup-shaped mouthpiece is very great. The lips, pressed against the cup, vibrate as a reed; the pressure upon the cup determines the rapidity of the vibrations, and this, in conjunction with the length of the tube, determines the pitch of the sounds produced.

Instruments thus sounded can be traced back to prehistoric times; they were known in the ancient Assyrian civilisation, and figure frequently upon various sculptures that remain. The principle was also recognised in China; and the descriptions contained in early Sanskrit musical treatises prove the existence in India of such instruments from periods equally remote. Many of the carvings and frescos remaining in India upon ancient temples and caves, such as those at Ellora and Ajanta, show the use of horns and trumpets, and in many of these the cup-shaped mouthpieces can be distinguished. The importance of the trumpet as an emblem of royalty, in connexion with religious ceremonies or for military purposes, appears to have been early recognised. The voice of the trumpet was heard from mount Sinai during the wanderings of the children of Israel, it was used by Saul and David, and is frequently mentioned in the Bible. Adopted by the Romans, in common with other ancient nations, for military purposes, the trumpet retains its place in the armies of most countries to this day.

Instruments of this kind consist of two classes, viz., those, such as the horn or trumpet, in which the upper harmonics (from the 3rd or 4th to the 12th or 16th) are mostly employed; and those in which the lower harmonics (from the 2nd to the 6th or 8th) are generally used, such as the bugle or post horn.

The trumpet, as we know it now, consists of a cylindrical tube, slightly expanding at the bell, and sounded by a mouthpiece, the cup of which is almost hemispherical, and the orifice small and angular.

The bore is usually turned once or twice round itself. The bending of the tube has frequently been attributed to a Frenchman called Maurin, about 1400; but this construction was known in the East centuries before: that instruments so made were employed in Italy is proved from the bas reliefs of Luca della Robbia, which were intended to ornament the organ chamber in the Cathedral of Florence.

Three kinds of trumpets are cited by Virdung (*Musica getutscht und auszgezogen*, 1511), and called by him *felttrumet, clareta*, and *thurner horn*. The engravings given by Virdung are so indistinct that it is difficult to understand in what the differences between these instruments consisted. M. Victor Mahillon, of the Brussels *Conservatoire*, is, however, of opinion that the felttrummet was used for military purposes, and that the clareta resembled the clarino, a form of trumpet which will be presently described, the thurner horn being used by watchmen and guards.

Prætorius (*Syntagma*, 1618) mentions only the *trummet* and the *jäger trummet*. Of these the *trummet* was in *D*, and by the aid of a crook could be put in *C*. The *jäger trummet* was a *cor de chasse*. The same writer takes notice of the Alp horn, which he describes as the *hölzern trummet*. The *D* trumpet he tells us had a compass, which, by a really good player, could thus be extended upwards:—

And Bach, in his cantata "Der Himmel lacht," writes the trumpet part up to the 20th harmonic! The trumpet parts at the end of the 17th and beginning of the 18th centuries were generally divided into three, and called by the following:—

Principal.—Embracing from the 5th to the 10th harmonic sounds.

Clarino I.—Embracing from the 8th harmonic sound upwards to the extreme high limit, according to the capability of the player.

Clarino II.—Embracing from the 6th to the 12th harmonic sounds.

To these a fourth part called toccato was sometimes added.

The mouthpieces used for clarino parts were necessarily very small; the intonation, therefore, especially of the lower and middle notes, left much to be desired, and the players endeavoured to correct faults by means of what is technically termed "pinching." It is probable also that trumpets which were intended for clarino parts were of a smaller bore; and such a trumpet is now in the possession of Mr. Harper. Parts thus written were found up to the middle of the 18th century, when, as a means of remedying the defective intonation of certain notes, the use of crooks or *tons de rechange* came to be largely employed. Trumpets then came to be used in *F* instead of in *D*, and with shanks for *E*, *E*♭, *D*, *D*♭, *C*, *B*, *B*♭, and even for *A*; and by means of employing several trumpets crooked in different keys it was made possible to enrich the harmonies, and to make almost every harmonic progression possible, provided of course that the band was numerous enough. Here then we see the starting point of the so called "brass" band.

The horn, developed from the *jäger trummet* mentioned by Prætorius, at first did not differ much in quality of tone from the trumpet; its tubing was differently disposed for the sake of portability, and it was played with a shallow mouthpiece somewhat like that of the trumpet. Of French or German origin, it superseded the oliphant, or ivory hunting horn, which was akin to the modern bugle; and being improved by French makers, and a conical bore substituted for the cylindrical, the musical quality of the *cor de chasse* rapidly became evident; and it was introduced into the wind bands of the period in combination with trumpets and trombones. The instrument was perfected by the maker Raoux, of Paris, and horns of his make are greatly prized by players.

Used principally in the hunting field for signals and calls, of which there were a very great number, the use of which is utterly unintelligible to an Englishman, the horn was adopted into the orchestra in France by Campra in the opera "Achille et Déidamie" produced in 1735. There is reason for believing that the *cor de chasse* was employed previously by Lulli in "La Princesse d'Elide." It had, however, been employed in England as early as 1720 by Handel in his opera "Radamisto"; and its use in Germany dates from about the same period.

The completion of the scale of the horn by means of what are termed *bouché* sounds, produced by the introduction of the hand into the bell, is attributed to a player named Hampl, of Dresden, about 1770. Attempting to produce a softer tone by the introduction of a pad or "mute" of cotton wool, he found the pitch became lowered by a semitone; and then, employing his hand, instead of the mute, he discovered the method by which intervals between the open notes, or natural harmonics, could be, to a great extent, bridged over.

The same principle was applied to the trumpet in 1780 by Wögel, of Rastadt, and his instrument was known in Germany as the *invention horn*. An instrument very similar, and called *stopftrompete*, was for a short time in use, but achieved but small success, the true trumpet quality being lost.

282.

RAMSHORN TRUMPET. The Jewish Shofar. Polish. The natural horn is partially straightened and flattened by heat, and the small end is formed into a mouthpiece. Length of outside curve, 20½ inches. The harmonics available are the 2nd, 3rd, and 4th, sounding—

The fundamental sound *d*♭ could not be obtained from a tube of this length. Indeed, the proper tones of such a tube as the shofar are not harmonics in the true sense. It seems more rational to regard *d'*♭ as the fundamental, and the *a'*♭ and *d''*♭ as, owing to the irregular form of the tube, *disturbed* harmonics. The subject, however, is of too complicated a nature to discuss here.

In the Bible, *keren, shofar, and khatsotsrah* are the Hebrew names for instruments of the trumpet kind. The keren and shofar are sometimes used synonymously. The shofar appears to have been in common use as a military instrument, and was used by Saul (1 Sam. 13. 3) to rouse the people against their enemies. The shofar was also used in pageants or processions, and is several times mentioned in the Psalms.

The shofar is of especial interest as being the only Jewish instrument whose use for ritual purposes has been retained to the present day. When the shofar is blown in the Synagogue, as it is on New Year's Day and the Day of Atonement, greater attention is paid to the rhythm or tongueing of the notes than to their actual sounds. Hence by some players the octave harmonics are blown, by others the fifth and octave.

The following signals are sounded in the Western Synagogue, St. Alban's Place, Haymarket:—

The Roman lituus, which was used by the sacred augurs as well as by the cavalry, probably took its shape from the shofar or a similar horn.

Lent by the Rev. F. W. Galpin, M.A., F.L.S.

283.

Buccina, in *G*. This instrument is a facsimile of one found at Pompeii, and now preserved in the National Museum at Naples. The instrument is curved in a semicircular form, and the bell rests upon the shoulder of the player like that of the modern circular valved bass. The pitch is *G*, and the following series of notes can be produced:—

By reason of the small size of the mouthpiece and the proportions of the tube, the fundamental *G* cannot be produced. In quality the tone resembles that of the bugle. The buccina, sometimes called cornu, was employed in the Roman armies. In what the distinction between the two consisted is not certain; but it is probable that the cornu was somewhat smaller. That the cornu and buccina were both employed, is proved by Vegecius, who states (III. v.) that calls were sounded by the tuba, cornu, and buccina. The historian Pollux mentions a curved trumpet (σάλπιγξ), and M. Gevaert inclines to the belief that this referred to the buccina. Each legion of the Roman army, Vegecius tells us, had its tubicines, cornicines, and buccinatores; and he describes certain duties peculiar to each.

Lent by the *Conservatoire Royal de Musique*, Brussels.

284.

Lituus, in *g*. This instrument is a facsimile of a lituus discovered in 1827 at Cervetri, the ancient Caera of the Etruscans, and now preserved in the palace of the Vatican at Rome. Trumpets of this kind were in use in the Roman cavalry. The Roman lituus, the shape of which was probably derived at some remote period from the sacrificial ramshorn trumpet, similar to the Jewish shofar, was essentially the emblem of the Augurs, and was borne by them as a staff. From the sacred lituus, the cavalry trumpet, somewhat similar in shape, took its name, and was probably of smaller size and convenient for a mounted trumpeter to sound. The bore of this specimen is cylindrical, expanding at the bell end, which is turned vertically upwards; the instrument therefore is shaped J. The pitch is *g*, in unison with the *g* trumpet, which in quality of tone this lituus resembles. The lituus was made in different sizes, and many specimens, both small and large, have been from time to time discovered.

Lent by the *Conservatoire Royal de Musique*, Brussels.

285.

Ancient War Trumpet. Of bronze. The shape resembles . The total length is 56 inches; inside width across the bell 4 inches; outside diameter of tube at mouth and below mouthpiece ½ inch. The mouthpiece being fixed upon the tube prevents the inside of the bore being measured. There are four metal bosses or bands disposed at regular intervals, two of which are mounted with rings.

The following intervals are furnished by this instrument:—

The cup of the mouthpiece is very shallow, and the orifice small and angular. With a somewhat larger mouthpiece the fundamental sound (*A*) could probably be produced.

This instrument formerly belonged to the late Mr. John Davidson, F.R.S.

Lent by T. Davidson, Esq.

286.

Ancient Ship's Trumpet. 14th century. Of thin sheet brass, with beautifully ornamented and embossed bands of bronze round the bell and upper part of the tube. There is also an embossed ferrule and boss, of the same metal, at half the length of the trumpet. The pitch appears to be a rather flat *F*. The workmanship was evidently executed with great care, the metal joints being beautifully dovetailed together the whole length of the tube. Length 5 feet 5 inches.

A representation of a trumpet, very similar to this, is to be seen engraved upon the official seal of the Corporation of the town of Hythe, Kent.

Lent by H. Mackeson, Esq.

287.

Oliphant (Ivory). Portuguese, 15th century. This unique and beautiful oliphant measures 1 foot 10¾ inches in length, and is of ivory. There are three raised bands of ornamental work, and above the upper of these there are carved figures of men and crocodiles. From the style of the ornamentation this instrument is evidently of the 15th century. It is sounded by means of a horn mouthpiece, carved, and without doubt of the same date. Plate II., fig. A.

Lent by G. Donaldson, Esq.

288.

Oliphant, or Ivory Hunting Horn. Richly carved with representations of scenes in the chase, and the conversion of St. Hubert (after Dürer). Length (including mouthpiece) 3 feet 5 inches. It is in the key of *F*, giving in real sounds:—

It is strengthened by a metal tube internally. German, 17th century.

Lent by the Rev. F. W. Galpin, M.A., F.L.S.

289.

Silvered Horn. This horn is somewhat like a modern hunting horn, but is ornamented with embossed designs, and is evidently of French manufacture. Probably about the middle of the 17th century. Length 1 foot 7 inches.

Lent by G. Donaldson, Esq.

290.

Trumpet, in *e′♭*. Of brass, with figures of cherubim embossed upon the bell. The bosses, or ferrules, on the instrument are beautifully worked, and are good examples of the work of that day. This trumpet has evidently been carefully restored at some later date. Engraved "Iohann. Wilhelm. Haas. In Nürnberg." 17th century. Length 2 feet 2 inches. Plate X., fig. D.

Lent by the *Conservatoire Royal de Musique*, Brussels.

291.

Trumpet. With gilt mounts and boss, set with crystals. The bell is ornamented with figures of cherubim, and is engraved "Macht. Iohann. Wilhelm Haas in Nürnberg. 1694."

This instrument is bent in places so as to shorten the length. There are several ornamental turns disposed at regular intervals, and carefully planned for outward appearance. Length 20 inches. Plate X., fig. A.

Lent by the *Conservatoire Royal de Musique*, Brussels.

292.

Trumpet, in *D*. With silver boss and mounts, beautifully worked. The bell is ornamented with figures of cherubim, relieved by floriated designs, and embossed, "William Bvll, Londini, Fecit." The original mouthpiece remains; it can be detached at pleasure; the cup is very shallow and the orifice angular. Probably late 17th century. Length 2 feet 5 inches. Plate X., fig. B.

Lent by Thomas Harper, Esq.

293.

Trumpet, in *D*♭. With one turn, and with a very small bore. The boss and bell are beautifully ornamented. Round the bell is engraved "Iohn Harris, Londini, Fecit." Length 2 feet 5 inches. Early 18th century.

Lent by Thomas Harper, Esq.

294.

Trumpet, in *D*, with Banner. Made in silver, and with engraved boss and beautifully worked rim round the bell. Engraved "Hofmaster, London," also with the arms and crest of the Hellier family. Length 28¼ inches. 18th century.

Lent by Colonel Shaw-Hellier.

295.

Pair of Trumpets, in *D*. Each trumpet has two crooks, for *C* and *B*♭. With ornamented bosses and rims to bells, both engraved "Nicholas Winkings, Maker, London." Length 34 inches.

This pair of instruments was purchased by Sir Samuel Hellier, of the Wodehouse, in 1735, for use in his private band. The original mouthpieces have been lost, but the crooks are the original ones, made at the time.

Lent by Colonel Shaw-Hellier.

296.

Two Bass Trumpets, in *D*. These instruments are of similar make, and were evidently a pair, and by the same maker. The tubing is bent round so as to form one long turn the whole length of the trumpet, and one short turn of about half the length of the instrument. At the further end of the short turn the tuning slide is placed, and this is made to slide with one tube exterior and the other interior. Length 3 feet 3 inches. 18th century.

Lent by Her Majesty the Queen.

297.

TRUMPET. Brass, with two turns, and ornamented mounts and bell. Round the bell is engraved "J. Alexander, 101, Leadenhall Street, London." Length 16½ inches. 18th or early 19th century.

Lent by the Director of Artillery.

298.

TRUMPET, in *E*♭. Of brass, with stamped ferrules and boss. The rim of the bell is engraved "William Shaw, 21, Red Lion Street, Holborn, Lond." Length 2 feet 2 inches. Late 18th or early present century.

Lent by the Director of Artillery.

299.

SIX STATE SILVER TRUMPETS. These State trumpets are all mounted with embossed ferrules and rims to the bells. The earliest, which has a hall-mark of 1803, is engraved "Wm. Shaw, 21, Red Lion Street, Holborn, London." Two, with hall-marks ten years later, appear to have been the property of the 1st Life Guards, being engraved "1st L. Gds, H × S," and "1st L. Gds, D 4" respectively; both bear the maker's name, "Shaw and Son, 21, Red Lion Street, Holborn, London." The rims of the bells are evidently stamped with identically the same die used for the trumpet made ten years before. The other three trumpets are of quite recent date.

Lent by Her Majesty the Queen.

300.

TRUMPET, with three crooks. By Courtois Frères. This trumpet is perfectly straight, and some five feet in length, and it was apparently made for effect in some procession or opera. Trumpets of very similar shape to this are employed by Verdi in the opera "Aida."

Lent by the *Grossherzogliches Museum*, Darmstadt.

301.

TRUMPET, in *E*♭. The tubes are brought together so as to be all grasped in one hand; there are bends or loops at the extremities, in order to prevent sharp turns in the wind-passage. Trumpets of this shape were employed in the Garde Impériale of the late Emperor Napoleon III.

Lent by Messrs. Besson and Co.

302.

WALKING-STICK TRUMPET. Of metal, covered with leather. When used as a trumpet, the ferrule at the lower end is unscrewed and a mouthpiece inserted; the handle also is removed, and replaced by a metal bell. This musical curiosity was invented by the late Mr. T. Harper some forty years ago.

Lent by Messrs. Köhler and Son.

303.

ALP HORN. Made of red willow and bound with white willow. It is mounted with horn and curved upwards at the bell end, this shape being peculiar to the Bernese Oberland. The present specimen was constructed in the woods of Lauterbrunnen by Fritz von Almen, one of the few peasant makers still living. It is in *B*♭. The natural harmonics used are

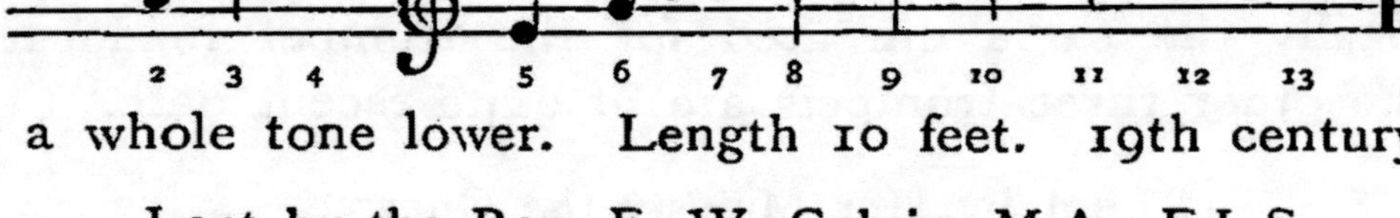

sounding a whole tone lower. Length 10 feet. 19th century.

Lent by the Rev. F. W. Galpin, M.A., F.L.S.

304.

ALP HORN. Of wood, bound with birch bark. The tube of this instrument is bent once round itself, so that in general appearance it somewhat resembles the trumpet. This bending of the tube of the Alp horn is probably of modern introduction, designed to render the instrument less cumbersome. This form of Alp horn is used chiefly in the Cantons of Uri, Unter Walden, and Swyz.

Lent by the *Grossherzogliches Museum*, Darmstadt.

305.

THREE BUGLES. Of paper, plaister of Paris, and gutta percha. Made as experiments, and proving that quality of tone is not dependent upon the material of which an instrument is made, but upon the proportions of the air column.

Lent by Messrs. Besson and Co.

306.

A Collection of DUTY BUGLES and TRUMPETS of all Nations; showing different patterns of these instruments employed at various times.

Lent by Messrs. Besson and Co., Potter and Co., Q. Cecconi, Mahillon and Co., &c.

307.

COR DE CHASSE, in *E♭*. Beautifully made of brass, the rim of the bell being stamped with figures of fleur-de-lys. Width across coils of tubing to exterior edge of bell 15 inches. No maker's name. French. Probably 17th century.

Lent by the *Grossherzogliches Museum*, Darmstadt.

308.

PAIR OF FRENCH HORNS. Complete with crooks. This very interesting pair of horns were purchased by Sir Samuel Hellier in 1735, and are preserved in their original wooden cases. The instruments are, of course, considerably smaller than the horns used in the orchestras of the present day. Their greatest width, measured from the outside of the bell across the coils of tubing, is but 20 inches. The coils of tubing are covered with a strip of felt, wound round, apparently to prevent vibration and to afford an easier grip for the hand. The instruments are, as they stand, in *D*♭, present pitch. The first crook is *B*, the others *B*♭, *A*, and *G*♭. These four crooks are of the same bore and cylindrical throughout, and a rather large mouthpiece is employed with them. There are also two crooks with a tapering bore, and used with a smaller mouthpiece. They give *B*♭ and *G*♭. The smaller of these crooks in all its couplings gives *A*♭, *G*, *G*♭, *E*. The larger gives *E*, *E*♭, *D*, *D*♭. There are some original tuning bits of different sizes. On the bell of each horn is stamped, upon the rim, "IOHN CHRISTOPHER HOFMASTER, IN PICCADILLY, LONDON, 17 ." The two last figures of the date are wanting. Both instruments are in exceedingly good condition, and as specimens of first-rate horns of the period are probably unique.

Lent by Colonel Shaw-Hellier.

309.

COR DE CHASSE, in *G*. By Carlin, Paris, maker to the King. The rim of the bell is ornamented and stamped with figures of fleur-de-lys below a crown. Stamped upon the bell is "FAIT À PARIS, CARLIN, ORDINAIRE DU ROY." Extreme width 20 inches.

Carlin was a celebrated trumpet player, and maker of cors de chasse, during the reigns of Louis XV. and Louis XVI. His business was in the Rue des Petit-Champs, Paris, where he lived till his retirement, just before his death, which occurred about the year 1780.

Lent by the *Conservatoire Royal de Musique*, Brussels.

310.

FRENCH HORN. Complete with crooks. This interesting instrument is thus described by Mr. T. S. Mann, the well-known horn player, and Professor of the instrument at the Royal Military School of Music; and as his views are of great interest, it is thought better to give them in his own words:—

"I have taken some trouble to find out as near as possible the maker's name, and date when made, of the "French" horn exhibited by me, and, thanks to the kindness of Mr. Goodison, one of the very best English makers of brass instruments, have come to the decision that the horn in question is decidedly German, and made in Leipsic by Schmidt. No doubt at the time it was made (about 60 years ago) it was considered a very fine solo horn. It is very complete, having every crook necessary for the different keys, viz., *B♭* alt, *A♮*, *A♭*, *G*, *G♭*, *F*, *E♮*, *E♭*, *D*, *D♭*, *C*, *B♮*, *B♭*, making in all thirteen changes. These changes are made, not by means of crooks, but by removing the slide and substituting a smaller or larger amount of tubing as required for higher or lower keys. It may be interesting to give the length of the different crooks from the high *B♭* alt to the octave *B♭* bass.

B♭ alt Crook	- - -	Length about	1 ft. 6 in.
A♮ ,,	- - -	,, ,,	2 ,, 1 ,,
A♭ ,,	- - -	,, ,,	2 ,, 8 ,,
G ,,	- - -	,, ,,	3 ,, 4 ,,
G♭ ,,	- - -	,, ,,	4 ,, 0 ,,
F ,,	- - -	,, ,,	4 ,, 9 ,,
E♮ ,,	- - -	,, ,,	5 ,, 7 ,,
E♭ ,,	- - -	,, ,,	6 ,, 3 ,,
D♮ ,,	- - -	,, ,,	7 ,, 2 ,,
D♭ ,,	- - -	,, ,,	8 ,, 0 ,,
C ,,	- - -	,, ,,	8 ,, 10 ,,
B♮ ,,	- - -	,, ,,	9 ,, 9 ,,
B♭ bass ,,	- - -	,, ,,	10 ,, 10 ,,

thus making the length of the horn, when crooked in *B♭* bass, about 18 feet of tubing. The fact of every semitone in the chromatic scale being mentioned, and that there is for each a separate crook, gives one some idea of how difficult an instrument it must be for an orchestral performer. Continual changes of key occur in most of the music written for horns. These changes are necessary to enable the composer to avail himself of the open notes which, on all crooks, are so limited; namely, taking the compass of the horn in every key, two octaves, the open notes within the two octaves are limited to twelve, the extreme low and the extreme high being uncertain. Since the introduction of valves (about 1825), which are now attached to the horn, the notes before made by stopping the bell, more or less, can be made equal to the natural notes of the instrument. This fact is now fully appreciated by modern composers, who avail themselves of it by writing such notes as were on the hand horn not likely to be heard, requiring so much stopping. It has been said that the addition of valves destroys the tone of the horn. I differ in opinion on this point most strongly. So much depends upon how the valves are made, for they *can* be added to the instrument without interfering with the tubing of the common horn; then when the valves are not used the instrument remains the same. At the present day the use of valves is indispensable, for passages are written that it would be absurd to attempt to play upon the hand horn. The hand horn is now a thing of the past; the three-valved horn is now in general use throughout Germany, and must become so everywhere. It is very difficult to find a player upon the horn without valves, in the United Kingdom. It seems absurd to say that Beethoven or any composer wrote passages of *hand* notes for effect; when certain notes were written, the only way that they could be produced was by closing the bell with the hand, therefore nothing else could be done."

Lent by T. S. Mann, Esq.

311.

French Horn. With interior of bell elaborately painted. There are no crooks, but with a small modern crook the instrument is in *B*♭. It is stamped on rim of bell "Dubois & Couturier, Lyons." Probably made about 1820. Greatest width 21½ inches. The tone of this instrument is particularly fine.

Lent by Messrs. Besson and Co.

312.

French Horn. Raoux model, with 10 crooks. By Antoine Courtois. Shown as an example of the finest model of French horn procurable, being an exact copy of the instrument as perfected by Raoux.

Lent by S. A. Chappell, Esq.

313.

Cor Russe. Modern reproduction. A short conical tube, the mouthpiece of which is turned almost at right angles to the instrument. Cors Russes form a special family. There is a distinct instrument for each interval of the chromatic scale; and the "horn bands" formed in this manner often embrace as many as a hundred performers. Their use is peculiar to certain districts of Russia.

Lent by Messrs. Besson and Co.

314.

INVENTION HORN, in *E*♭, with *D* crook. The interior of the bell of this instrument is prettily painted. The tubing is wound in an ornamental manner, and the crooks fit into the middle of the instrument, as in the French horn previously described (No. 310). This instrument, however, is in reality a *hand* trumpet. The idea of applying the crooks for changes of key to the middle of the bore, instead of, as previously, to the upper end, is attributed to Michael Wögel, born at Rastadt in 1748. The name of "Invention horn" was given to this instrument in Germany; and it is interesting as showing (excepting the *tortil* described later, see p. 175) the earliest application of the kind suited for crooks of any length. Length 18 inches.

Lent by the *Conservatoire Royal de Musique*, Brussels.

315.

COR OMNITONIQUE. This instrument was invented and constructed by C. Sax, père, of Brussels, in 1824. The bell is engraved with the royal arms of the Netherlands. In this instrument there is no need for the use of crooks. The instrument can be put in any of the keys ordinarily used (*i.e.* *B*♭ (high), *A*, *G*, *F*, *E*, *E*♭, *D*, *C*, and the low *B*♭), by means of a piston which moves in a graduated tube, and which puts the additional lengths of tubing successively into communication with the main windway of the instrument. The interior of the bell of this instrument is beautifully painted. Its greatest width is 23½ inches.

Lent by the *Conservatoire Royal de Musique*, Brussels.

IX.

CLASS—INSTRUMENTS WITH CUP-SHAPED MOUTHPIECES.

FAMILY: *Length varied by means of lateral holes.*

INSTRUMENTS sounded by means of cup-shaped mouthpieces, and whose length is varied by means of lateral holes, can be traced back to a very remote period. The principle involved consists in connecting certain intervals of the harmonic series formed by the open tube, chromatically or otherwise, by means of the successive opening of a number of lateral holes. Whether instruments thus constructed were known to the Romans it is impossible to say, but it appears at all events probable. Their invention is decidedly of European origin, for no trace of them can be found in countries further East, or in India or China.

About the twelfth century the *cornetto* or *Zinck* was in use, and an instrument, presumably the same, appears in a MS. now in the National Library at Madrid (*Cantigas de Santa Maria*). Some few centuries later, when wind bands had assumed a definite design, *Zinken* or *cornetti* became important instruments. Prætorius (*Syntagma*, 1618) mentions that they were, in shape, both straight and curved. There were, he tells us, two kinds of straight cornets. The name *cornetto diretto* was given to an instrument of which the mouthpiece was detachable, and an instrument in which the mouthpiece was made in the same block of wood was called *cornetto muto*, by reason of its softer tone. This latter was also known in Germany as the *stille zinck*.

There were also *cornetti curvi*, which differed only in shape from the straight *cornetti*. They were usually of a coarser and louder quality of tone; and an instrument of this shape, which was often used by town watchmen, received the characteristic name of "Stadtkalb," or "Town Calf"! All these instruments had a compass of 15 notes from *a* to *a''*, and their compass could be extended upwards even to *g'''*, by means of cross-fingering. The *corno*, or *cornetto torto*, called also *cornon*, formed the natural bass to this family. The cornon was a fifth in pitch below the cornetto; it was usually shaped like , and was considered to have a compass of 11 notes only, from *d* or *c* to *d'*. Others, however, treated it in the same manner as the ordinary cornetto, and made use of cross-fingering. Its tone, Prætorius tells us, was unpleasant and harsh, and therefore the use of the trombone became necessary.

Prætorius mentions the employment of small instruments called *cornettini*, standing a fifth higher than the cornetto, and which had the same compass and were not unpleasant in tone. Instruments of this kind were much admired in former days, and, when well played, are capable of much effect. The cornetto is an exceedingly difficult instrument, since it leaves so much to the capability of the performer, as regards both tone and intonation. How far the *cornetti* were used as transposing instruments is rather doubtful; they were written for in various clefs, and were employed by Bach, and later by Gluck; the original scores of "Paride el Elena," "Orpheo," "Alceste," "Armida," have parts for them.

These instruments during the 16th, 17th, and 18th centuries underwent little change. They are described at length by Mersenne (*Harmonie Universelle*), who evidently thought highly of them. The Venetian writer Artusi in his rare work (*Della Imperfettioni della Moderna Musica*, Venetia, 1600) gives a regular method for the cornetto, and much valuable advice regarding the *embouchure* and tongueing of the instrument; the best players he tells us were, in his time, the Cavaliere de Cornetto and Girolamo d'Uldine.

About the end of the 16th century a canon of Auxerre, Edme Guillaume by name, experimenting upon the *cornon*, succeeded in producing the instrument now known as the serpent. The invention of Guillaume is described by the Abbé Lebœuf (*Memoire Concernant l'Histoire Ecclésiastique et Civile d'Auxerre*, Paris, 1743). The serpent is not mentioned by Prætorius, but Père Mersenne describes it in detail, ascribing to it a compass of 17 notes from *E* to *g'*. The best notes of the serpent, he tells us, were from *A* to *g*. At first made with six finger-holes only, of very small diameter, the intonation naturally left much to be desired; during the last century many improvements were made, and the application of keys became general; it thus became possible to place the holes at their proper positions, and to make them of a diameter suitable to the proportion of the bore. The most improved form of the serpent, as made at the commencement of the present century by the English maker Key, had 17 keys, and no open finger-holes, and will be found described in detail subsequently.

About 1780, according to Gerber (*Lexicon der Tonküstler*, Leipzig, 1790), a musician named Rêgibo, of Lille, produced an instrument of the serpent type, but gave it the form of a bassoon, thus rendering it more portable. A few years later Frichot, a refugee from Paris, brought out, in London, an instrument somewhat similar to that of Rêgibo, but made in brass, and called by him the *bass horn* or *basson russe*. The bass horn was soon introduced into military bands, and being carried by the English bands into Belgium in the 1815 campaign, its use rapidly extended, and shortly afterwards became general throughout Europe.

The gradual disuse of the cornetto, owing to the difficulty of procuring efficient players, led eventually to the application of keys to the trumpet. The idea originated about 1770 with Kœlbel, a horn player in the Imperial Guard at St. Petersburg, but it was not generally adopted until about 1795, when the instrument maker Weidinger, of Vienna, succeeded in producing a trumpet which had five keys. The advantages resultant from this construction becoming evident, trumpets thus made were eagerly received into the orchestra; and, throughout Italy, were in general use for a number of years.

In 1810 Joseph Halliday, the bandmaster of the Cavan Militia, patented an invention by which he gave the bugle a compass of 25 tones. This was brought about by the application of five keys, thereby binding together by chromatic degrees the second and third harmonics (*c′* to *g′*). The *key bugle*, called also *Kent bugle* or *cor à clefs*, easy to play, and tolerably certain as regards intonation, imparted a a new colour to wind bands. Its use soon became general, it was received into the orchestra, and was everywhere looked upon with favour. A sixth key (open) was shortly afterwards added; and the instrument thus constructed underwent further improvements at the hands of different makers.

The key bugle, when played by an artist, is capable of far more than is now generally supposed; and in agility and rapid articulation it is still preferable to any piston instrument. Shakes and rapid passages, diatonic or chromatic, can be executed upon it with the greatest precision and ease. The key bugle therefore became, next to the clarinet, the principle solo instrument in military bands from 1820 until 1835, when it began to be superseded by the cornet à piston.

The principle of the key bugle was applied to the bass horn by Jean Hilaire Asté, an instrument maker of Paris, in 1817. This maker is better known as Halary; and according to the *Rapport de l'Académie Royale des Beaux Arts de l'Institut de France* (meeting of July 17, 1817) an application for a patent was made for several new instruments of Halary's invention. The invention of the ophicleide, or keyed serpent, has been generally, but wrongly, attributed to Frichot, but the real credit belongs to Halary. The instruments for which application for a patent was made were called (1) the *clavi-tube;* (2) the *quinti-tube* or *quinti-clave;* (3) the *ophicleide.* Of these the clavi-tube was the key bugle slightly modified, and the quinti-tube was in reality an alto ophicleide. The patent was taken out in Paris in 1822, and from the specification it appears that the ophicleide had nine or ten keys, each key giving a semitone's difference in pitch. By reason of the length and proportions of the tubing the fundamental sounds are employed; the instrument has, therefore, a compass of a little over three octaves (38 semitones) from $B_{,}$ or C to c''.

Of accurate intonation, and of a tone-quality entirely its own, the ophicleide for a time enjoyed great popularity, and in the hands of a good player was deservedly popular. Of late years it has been replaced by the tuba and euphonion, and with the death of its only remaining player, Mr. Samuel Hughes, the artistic value of the ophicleide may be said to have ceased. First introduced into the orchestra of the opera at Paris in 1817 by Spontini, the importance of the ophicleide became recognised by subsequent composers, and it was employed as a bass to the trombones. Among others, Meyerbeer and Mendelssohn both made use of the instrument, and it was not until about 1848 that the use of the tuba, the tone of which was found to blend better with that of the trombones, came to be generally adopted.

The alto ophicleide in $E\flat$, a minor third higher in pitch than the instrument in C, had for some time been in use in military bands, but its employment never entered into the orchestra. This instrument in its turn was, according to M. Lavoix (*Histoire de l'Instrumentation*), replaced, at the suggestion of M. Danays, by the clavicor; which, perhaps less agile, offered fewer difficulties to the performer, and was more reliable as regards intonation.

316.

CORNETTINO RECTO. This curious old specimen is made from an antelope horn, and is straight. It has six finger-holes, rather irregularly placed, and in front. The mouthpiece is in one piece with the instrument. Total length 18 inches. Probably 17th century. Plate VI., fig. C.

This specimen was found in a Norfolk village, where it was known as the "Harvest Horn," and had existed for generations. It is probably one of the oldest instruments of the kind in existence, and does not possess the thumb-hole at the back, as in the later *cornetti*. An instrument almost identical, but with the addition of the thumb-hole at the back, is in the Museum of the *Conservatoire* at Paris. It is described in M. Chouquet's Catalogue as an Italian Chalumeau, but it seems probable that the cap, which holds a *double* reed, has been added at a later period, by mistake.

The compass of the cornettino is

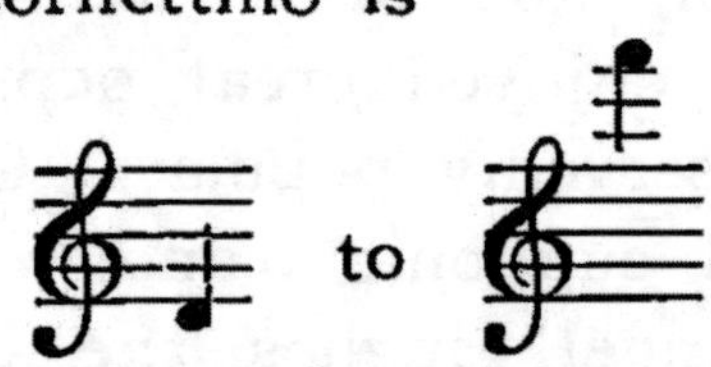

Lent by the Rev. F. W. Galpin, M.A., F.L.S.

317.

CORNETTINO CURVO, in *d'*. This is of wood, covered with leather and stamped with an ornamental pattern. There are six finger-holes upon the upper side, with a seventh for the thumb upon the under side. This instrument is of the curved form, and has a detachable mouthpiece of horn. Its compass is that of the preceding instrument. Length 17 inches. Probably 16th century. Plate VI., fig. D.

Lent by the *Conservatoire Royal de Musique*, Brussels.

318.

CORNETTO CURVO, in *a*. This instrument is made of wood, covered with stamped leather. There are six finger-holes on one side and a thumb-hole upon the other. It possesses also its original mouthpiece of horn, which is detachable. The compass is

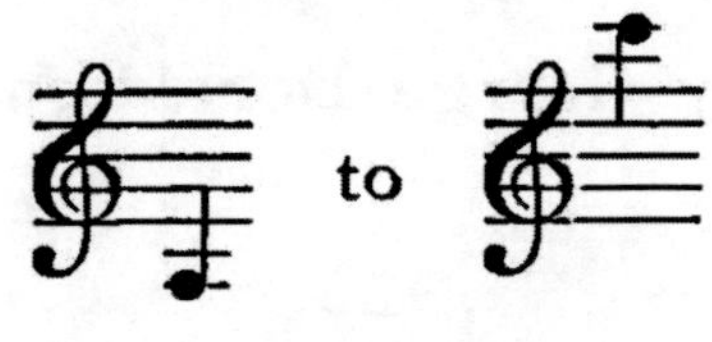

with all the chromatic intervals. Total length, including mouthpiece, 24 inches. Diameter at bell 1 inch, at small end $\frac{1}{4}$ inch. The inside diameter of the mouthpiece is $\frac{9}{16}$ inch. 16th or 17th century. Plate VI., fig. E.

Lent by the Rev. F. W. Galpin, M.A., F.L.S.

319.

CORNETTO CURVO, in *a*. Of wood, covered with stamped leather. There are six finger-holes on one side, with a thumb-hole upon the other. There is a detachable mouthpiece of horn. Total length, including mouthpiece, $23\frac{1}{4}$ inches. 16th or 17th century.

Lent by the *Conservatoire Royal de Musique*, Brussels.

320.

CORNETTO CURVO, in *a*. This instrument is of wood, covered with leather, and has six finger-holes upon one side and a thumb-hole upon the other. The mouthpiece is missing. Total length 23 inches. 16th or 17th century.

Lent by Her Majesty the Queen.

321.

CORNETTO CURVO, in *a*. Of wood, covered with stamped leather. There are six finger-holes on one side and a thumb-hole upon the other. The mouthpiece is detachable. Total length $23\frac{1}{2}$ inches. 16th or 17th century.

Lent by the *Conservatoire Royal de Musique*, Brussels.

322.

CORNETTO CURVO, in *a*. This beautiful specimen is of ivory, and has six finger-holes upon one side, with a thumb-hole on the other. The mouthpiece, which was detachable, is missing. Total length 23 inches. 16th or 17th century. Plate II., fig. G.

Lent by George Donaldson, Esq.

323.

CORNETTO CURVO, in *a*. This instrument is of carved ivory, beautifully decorated, and tipped at each end with bands of engraved brass. There are six finger-holes on one side and a thumb-hole upon the other. The mouthpiece, which was detachable, is now missing. Total length $23\frac{1}{4}$ inches. 16th or 17th century.

Lent by the *Grossherzogliches Museum*, Darmstadt.

324.

CORNETTO CURVO, in *a*. This instrument is of wood, stained black, and polished. There are six finger-holes upon one side and a thumb-hole upon the other. The mouthpiece has been lost. Length 22 inches. 17th or early 18th century.

Lent by Mrs. Zoeller.

325.

CORNETTO MUTO (DIRETTO), in *g*. This instrument is of light wood and perfectly straight. There are six finger-holes upon one side and a thumb-hole upon the other. The mouthpiece is in one piece with the instrument. The compass is

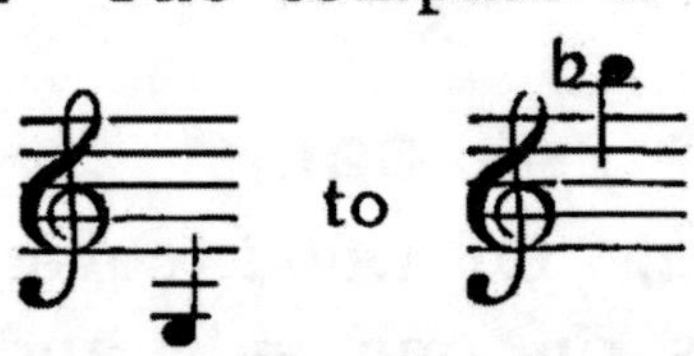

Total length $25\frac{3}{4}$ inches. Diameter of bell $1\frac{1}{8}$ inch, at small end $\frac{1}{4}$ inch. Inside diameter of mouthpiece $\frac{9}{16}$ inch. 17th century.

Straight cornets, with the mouthpiece made upon the instrument, have a rather softer tone than the other varieties. In Germany they were called "stille zincken." The name "diretto," or "gerade," was more generally applied to an instrument of similar shape, but which differed in so far as the mouthpiece was detachable.

Lent by the *Conservatoire Royal de Musique*, Brussels.

326.

CORNETTO MUTO, in *f*. This instrument, like the preceding, is of light wood, and perfectly straight. There are six finger-holes upon one side, with an additional lower hole, made double to accommodate a right or left handed player; also a thumb-hole at back. The mouthpiece is made in one piece with the instrument. The compass is as described for the preceding instrument, but descends a note lower. This lower note is of course given by the double finger-hole, and, in playing, the duplicate hole not required by the performer was stopped with wax or similar substance. 17th century. Plate VII., fig. B.

Lent by the Rev. F. W. Galpin, M.A., F.L.S.

327.

CORNETTO TORTO, or CORNO, in *c*. This is an exact reproduction of an ancient instrument now in the museum at Middleburg. It is made of wood and covered with stamped leather. There are six finger-holes, and a hole for a low note, closed by a brass key, upon the upper side, and also a thumb-hole at the back. The mouthpiece is of ivory, and is detachable. The instrument is curved to resemble , and measures 40 inches in length. Diameter at bell $1\frac{5}{8}$ inch, at small end $\frac{3}{10}$ inch. The inside diameter of the mouthpiece is $\frac{7}{8}$ inch. Plate VII., fig. B. The compass of the cornetto torto is

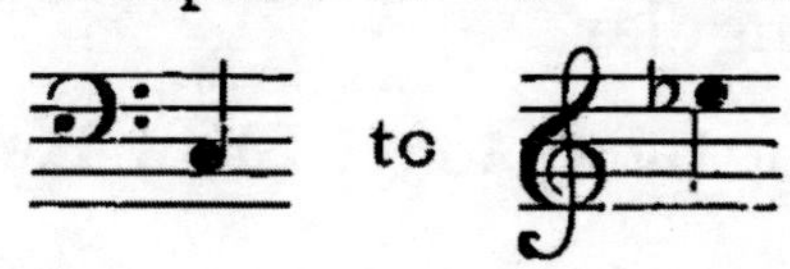

Lent by the *Conservatoire Royal de Musique*, Brussels.

328.

SERPENT. This instrument is in *C*, and is made of wood, covered with leather. There are six finger-holes, not bushed. The mouthpiece is fixed upon a crook of silvered metal, and there is a sliding ring, with a screw, which regulates the insertion of the crook into the instrument. The length *across* the instrument (not the total length of the air column), not including the crook, is 34 inches, and the greatest width 16 inches. The diameter at the bell is $3\frac{5}{8}$ inches, and at the small end $\frac{7}{16}$ inch. 17th century.

The serpent stands an octave below the cornetto torto, and forms the natural bass to this family. The compass, although it depends to a great extent upon the ability of the player, is usually considered from

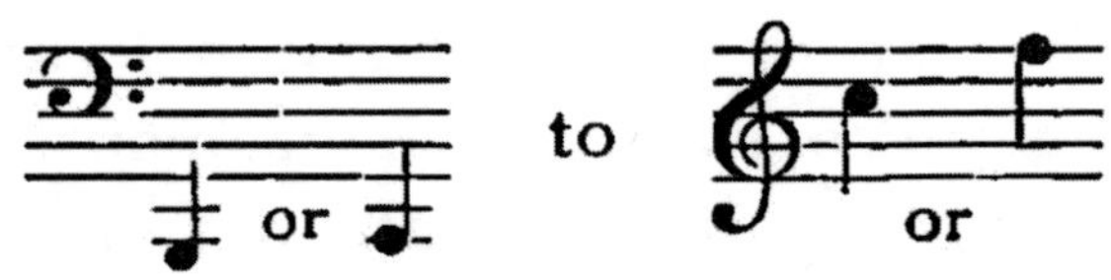

The chromatic intervals were obtained on the serpent without keys by half stopping, and not by cross-fingering.

Lent by the *Conservatoire Royal de Musique*, Brussels.

329.

SERPENT. This remarkably fine specimen is of wood, stained black, and extremely light to handle. It is mounted with silver, and has six finger-holes. The crook is silver-plated, and the original ivory mouthpiece is still upon it. Length across the instrument, not including crook, 33 inches, greatest width 17 inches. Early 18th century. Plate VII., fig. A.

The mouthpiece resembles that of No. 318, but is, of course, larger: it is exceedingly thin, while the cup is shallow, and the central orifice very small and angular.

Lent by Colonel Shaw-Hellier.

330.

SERPENT. Of wood, covered with leather. There are seven finger-holes, bushed with ivory; the extra hole, which is at the back, gives *B*♮. There is a brass crook, also the original mouthpiece of ivory. Length across the instrument, not including crook, 29½ inches. Greatest width 17½ inches. 18th century.

The earlier serpents were all constructed so that the bell lay in the same plane as the bends of the tube. In this instrument the bends are brought more closely together, and this was done in all subsequent instruments.

Lent by C. A. Barry, Esq.

331.

SERPENT. Of wood, and covered with leather. There are six finger-holes, bushed with ivory, and three flat brass keys on saddles, two of which give *B* and *F*♯, and are in front; and one giving *D*♯ is at the back. The crook is of brass, and the mouthpiece of ivory. Greatest length across the instrument, not including crook, 29 inches. Greatest width 17 inches. About the middle 18th century.

Lent by Messrs. G. Potter and Co.

332.

SERPENT. Of wood, covered with leather. There are six finger-holes, bushed with ivory, and three flat brass keys on saddles, two of which, giving *B* and *F*♯, are in front; and one giving *D*♯ is at the back. The crook is of brass, and the mouthpiece of ivory. Length across the instrument 28½ inches. Greatest width 17 inches. Middle 18th century.

Lent by D. L. Isaacs, Esq.

333.

SERPENT. Of wood, covered with leather. There are six finger-holes, bushed with ivory, and three flat brass keys on saddles. The keys give *B*, *F*♯, and *D*♯; the *B* key, as well as the *D*♯, is placed at the back. The crook is of brass, and the mouthpiece of ivory. Greatest length across the instrument 29½ inches. Greatest width 17 inches. 18th century.

Lent by G. Miller, Esq., L.R.A.M.

334.

SERPENT. Of copper, with six finger-holes, bushed with brass, and four flat brass keys on saddles. The keys giving *B* and *F♯* are in front; the keys giving *D♯* and *C♯* are at the back. This instrument has apparently been made for a left-handed player. The crook is of brass, as is also the mouthpiece. Greatest length across instrument 27 inches. Greatest width 17 inches. Late 18th century.

Lent by the *Edinburgh University* (*Chair of Music*).

335.

SERPENT. Of wood, covered with leather. There are six finger-holes, bushed with ivory, and four flat brass keys on saddles. The keys giving *B* and *F♯* are in front; those giving *D♯* and *C♯* are at the back. The crook is of brass, and the mouthpiece of ivory. The bell is turned slightly outwards. Greatest length across instrument 29½ inches. Greatest width 18 inches.

The turning of the bell outwards, in order to give greater freedom for the emission of sound, is said to have been an improvement made at the suggestion of King George III. The serpents made in the 19th century are made almost always after this model.

Lent by Rev. F. W. Galpin, M.A., F.L.S.

336.

SERPENT. Of wood, covered with leather. There are four finger-holes, bushed with ivory, and seven flat brass keys on saddles. The keys give *B*, *F♯*, *F♮* (open key), *D♯*, *C♯*, *C♮* (open key), and *B*, (open key). This last key is intended to facilitate the production of *B*,♮ and *B*,♭ in the lowest register. The keys for *B*, *F♯*, *F*, and *C* are in front, the remainder at the back. Greatest length across the instrument 29 inches. Greatest width 17½ inches. The *B* open key at the bottom of the instrument is found also in the ophicleide, and is intended to facilitate the production of *B* and *B♭*, usually obtained by means of the *C♯* and *C* keys and relaxing the lips. This improvement, however, does not seem to have been generally adopted.

Lent by Messrs. R. Ward and Sons.

337.

SERPENT. Of wood, covered with leather. There are four finger-holes, bushed with ivory, and seven flat brass keys on saddles; the two lowest work upon wooden bars. The keys give *a*, *B*, *F*♯, *F* (open key), *D*♯, *C*♯, and *C* (open key). The keys for *D*♯ and *C*♯ are at the back, the remainder in front; the keys for *C*♯ and *C* are fitted with rollers. The crook is of brass, and the mouthpiece of ivory. Total length across the instrument 29 inches. Greatest width 18 inches.

This instrument was formerly used in Melling Church, near Carnforth, Lancashire.

Lent by the Rev. W. B. Grenside.

338.

SERPENT. Of wood, covered with leather. There are six finger-holes, bushed with ivory, and seven flat brass keys on saddles. The keys give *a'*, in the highest register, *B*, *G*, *F*♯, *E*, *D*♯, and *C*♯ in the middle and lowest register. The first bend of this serpent is made of brass, and is stamped "New Improved, by T. Key, 20, Charing Cross, London." All the keys are closed, those for *E*, *D*♯, and *C*♯ being at the back, the remainder are in front. The crook is brass, and the mouthpiece of ivory. The greatest length across the instrument is 30 inches, and the greatest width 18 inches.

Lent by G. Butler, Esq.

339.

SERPENT. Of wood, covered with leather. There are no open finger-holes, but the holes are closed by 12 flat brass keys on saddles, giving the chromatic scale. The crook is brass, and the mouthpiece of ivory. The *B*, *G*, *F*, *D*♯, *D*, *C* (open), and the *B*♭, *G*♯, and double *F*♯ (closed) keys are in front; the *E* and *C*♯ (closed) keys are at the back. Length across the instrument 29 inches. Greatest width 17 inches.

Lent by Messrs. Boosey and Co.

340.

SERPENT. Of wood, covered with leather. There are 14 flat brass keys on saddles, giving the chromatic scale. The top bend is made entirely of brass to ensure strength. Stamped "New Improved, by T. Key, 20, Charing Cross, London."

The keys give the same as described for the preceding instrument, with the addition of one for *a'*, and a duplicate key for *B*♭. The total length of the tube of this instrument is 8 feet. This instrument shows the highest development at which the serpent arrived. It was then gradually superseded by the perfected bass horn or ophicleide, which in its turn has given place to the valved brass basses of the present day. This instrument was probably made about 1830; its greatest length across is 29½ inches, and greatest width 17½ inches. The diameter of the bell is 3¾ inches, and at the crook end $\frac{9}{16}$ inch. The inside diameter of the mouthpiece is 1⅛ inches.

Lent by Messrs. H. Potter and Co.

341.

SERPENT. Of wood, covered with leather. There are 14 keys, giving the chromatic scale, and arranged as in the preceding instrument. It is stamped "Key, 20, Charing Cross," and is probably of the same date as the serpent mentioned above. Length across the instrument 29 inches. Greatest width 17 inches.

Lent by the Rev. F. W. Galpin, M.A., F.L.S.

342.

SERPENT. Of wood, covered with leather and bound with brass. There are no open finger-holes, but, as in the preceding instruments, 14 brass keys. The upper bend of this serpent is of brass, and by a peculiar twist in the crook the instrument is brought more in front of the player. This instrument was used in the band of the 46th regiment until about 1840, and is in remarkably good playing order. It was probably one of the best of its kind ever made. Length across the instrument 29½ inches. Greatest width 17 inches. Plate VII., fig. D.

Lent by W. Bateson, Esq.

343.

Bass Horn, in *C*. This very curious looking instrument is made of wood, and is stained black and bound with brass. It is made of two separate pieces of conical wooden tubing, which fit into a shallow butt-joint also of wood. There are six finger-holes, bushed with ivory, and three flat brass keys on saddles, giving *B*, *F*♯, and *C*♯. There is a bent crook of brass, and it is played with an ivory mouthpiece. The bell is contracted, and resembles that of the cor anglais, but on a much larger scale. The maker's name has been stamped upon the brass rim of the bell; it is now almost illegible, but is apparently "F. Pace, M"[aker]. Total length $33\frac{1}{2}$ inches. Diameter at bell $3\frac{7}{8}$ inches, diameter at small end $\frac{1}{2}$ inch. Inside diameter of mouthpiece $\frac{7}{8}$ inch. The compass is from

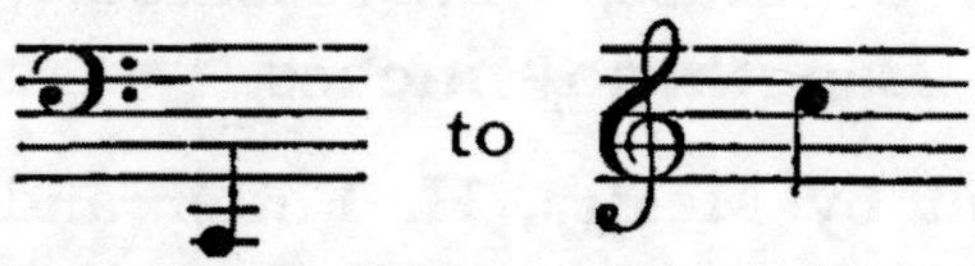

or even *f''*. This instrument dates from the latter end of the 18th century, and is evidently one of the earliest efforts to perfect the serpent by giving it a fresh shape and more regular bore, thereby rendering the scale less capricious. Plate VII., fig. C.

Lent by Mr. Q. Cecconi.

344.

Bass Horn, in *C*. An instrument of wood, covered with leather and painted black. There are six finger-holes and three round brass keys, two on saddles and one on pillars. The instrument is constructed, like that previously described, of two tubes fixed in a short butt-joint. The conical tubes, however, are in this case bored with their axes running parallel, in the same block of wood. The bell is of brass, and is fashioned in the form of a serpent's head. The keys give *F*♯, *E*♭, and *C*♯. The instrument is stamped "Tabard, à Lyons," and has the same compass as that described previously.

Lent by the *Conservatoire Royal de Musique*, Brussels.

345.

Bass Horn, in *C*. This instrument is made of brass, and in shape resembles No. 343, but has a bell more nearly allied to that of an ordinary trumpet. There are six finger-holes, and four flat brass keys on saddles. The keys give *B*, *F*♯, *E*♭, and *C*♯. Stamped, "Made by Fredk. Pace, 15, King Street, Westminster, and sold by W. Howlett, Norwich." Early this century. Length 33½ inches.

Lent by the *Conservatoire Royal de Musique*, Brussels.

346.

Bass Horn, in *C*. There are four flat brass keys to this specimen, giving the same intonations as described for No. 345. The instrument is made entirely of brass, and resembles in most respects that previously described. Length 30½ inches.

Lent by Messrs. H. Potter and Co.

347.

Ophicleide, in *C*, or perfected Bass Horn. This instrument is very beautifully made, and is of wood. It is exceedingly light to handle. The wood is covered with folds of canvas, and, over that, with leather. The bell is of copper. There are nine flat brass keys on pillars; the lowest key stands open. The crook and mouthpiece have unfortunately been lost. The total length of this instrument is 39½ inches. The compass is from

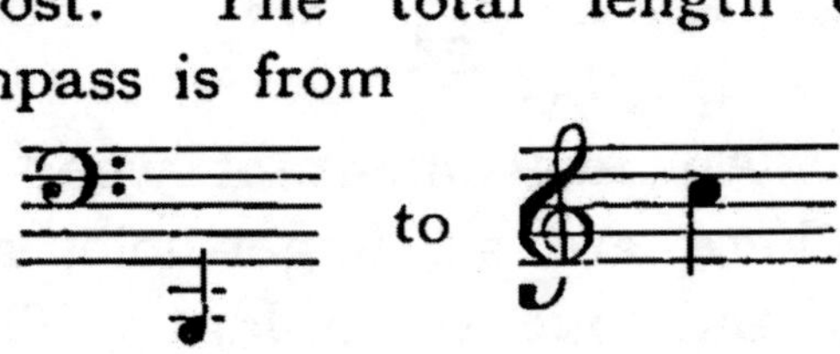

About 1830.

Lent by C. Brock, Esq.

348.

Ophicleide, in *C*. Of brass, with nine flat brass keys on pillars. The lowest key is open. Stamped "Labbaye, Breveté du roi, à Paris." Length 41½ inches.

Lent by the *Conservatoire Royal de Musique*, Brussels.

349.

OPHICLEIDE, in *C*. Of brass, with eleven flat brass keys on pillars, giving the chromatic scale. The lowest key stands open. The two additional keys in this instrument give *F*♯ and *A*♭.

Lent by Messrs. H. Potter and Co.

350.

OPHICLEIDE, in *C*. This very beautiful instrument is made of burnished copper, and has eleven embossed keys of silver, upon pillars, also of silver. The bell is fitted with a deep rim of silver beautifully worked with *repoussé* designs of musical instruments. The bell is engraved "R. J. Ward, 57, St. Thomas Buildings, Liverpool, 1848." This ophicleide was evidently made to order, as there is a silver shield, with armorial bearings, attached to the bell. The mouthpiece is of ivory. Plate VIII., fig. A.

The compass and general design of the instrument are very similar to that of No. 349. Length 42 inches.

Lent by Messrs. Ward and Sons.

351.

OPHICLEIDE, in *C*. Of brass, with eleven flat brass keys on pillars. Stamped "Higham, Maker, Victoria Bridge, Manchester." Length 40 inches.

Lent by Messrs. Besson and Co.

352.

OPHICLEIDE, in *B*,♭. Of brass, with eleven flat brass keys upon pillars, the lowest key being open. Stamped "Besson, 7, Rue des Couronnes, à Paris." Total length 42½ inches.

Lent by Messrs. Besson and Co.

353.

KEYED TRUMPET. This instrument is specially interesting, as it shows the earliest application of keys to brass instruments. It is of brass, and has five flat brass keys on saddles, which give a complete chromatic scale. The notes which the keys give vary of course with the crook or tuning bit employed. The fundamental note

is not employed. The lowest note employed is *g*. When the trumpet was crooked in *D*, which was frequently the case, the keys gave the following intervals, and of course their respective harmonics. The first key is that nearest the bell of the instrument.

Total length 17 inches.

Lent by the *Conservatoire Royal de Musique*, Brussels.

354.

Keyed Trumpet (Bass), in *G*. This instrument is of brass, and has six flat brass keys, on pillars, which complete the chromatic scale. There is also a tuning slide. It is stamped "Picolet et Benoit, à Lyons," and dates from about 1830. The fundamental is

but its compass does not extend below the second harmonic. The instrument therefore is exactly an octave lower than No. 353. The sixth key is required only when the trumpet is crooked in a lower key.

Lent by Messrs. Besson and Co.

355.

Key Bugle, in *c′*. Halliday's model. This interesting specimen is one of the earliest instruments of the kind made, and bears the mark of its inventor. It is of copper, and has six flat brass keys, working upon saddles. It is stamped "Royal patent Kent Bugle. Halliday, Inventor. Made by P. Turton, 5 Wormwood Gate, Dublin." The length of the model is 17 inches. Total length of tubing, including mouthpiece, 50½ inches. Diameter at bell 5¾ inches; diameter at mouthpiece ½ inch. Plate XI., fig. D.

Joseph Halliday, then bandmaster of the Cavan Militia, patented the key bugle in 1810. The patent specification was for a bugle with five keys, which gave 25 notes. The sixth key, which he added afterwards, and which became the first key, gave *b*♮. The harmonics which are available are as follows:—The closing of the first key, which in its normal position is open, produces

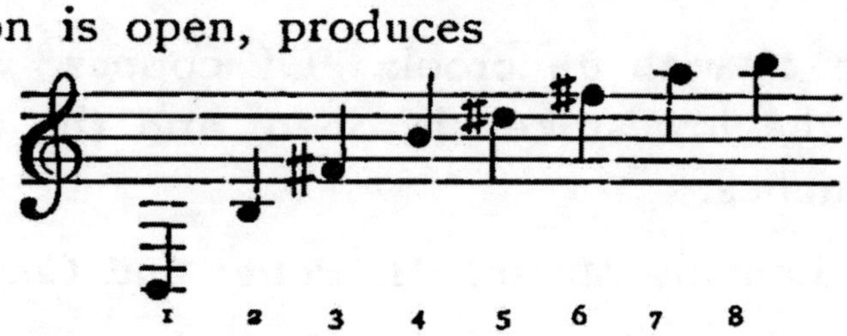

The open notes of the instrument are

The opening of the second key gives

The opening of the third key gives

The fourth key gives only

To complete the chromatic scale of the instrument the notes

are produced by means of the fifth and sixth keys. The numbers below the notes, in each case, refer to the harmonic series. The fundamental sounds, though they could be produced in certain cases, are never used, and the harmonics above the sixth are of very doubtful intonation.

Lent by Colonel Shaw-Hellier.

356.

KEY BUGLE, in *c′*, with *b♭* crook. Of copper, with six flat brass keys, on saddles; the lowest key is open, and the total length of the instrument is 17 inches.

Lent by Messrs. H. Potter and Co.

357.

KEY BUGLE, in *c′*. Of copper, with six flat brass keys, on saddles. There is a brass rim to the bell, engraved "Metzler & Son, London." Length 17 inches.

Lent by the Rev. F. W. Galpin, M.A., F.L.S.

358.

KEY BUGLE, in *c′*. Of copper, with six flat brass keys, upon small saddles; the lowest key is open. Stamped "Improved and made by Charles Pace & Son, 8 John Street, Westminster."

Lent by Messrs. Boosey and Co.

359.

KEY BUGLE, in *c′*, with *b♭* crook. Of copper, with brass rim and six curved brass keys, on saddles. Stamped "T. Harper's Improved Royal Kent Bugle. No. 348. Manufactured solely by Muzio Clementi & Co., 26, Cheapside, London." The shape of the keys is rather peculiar; they are bent so as to adapt themselves the better to the curved surface of the holes. Length 16½ inches.

Lent by Messrs. George Potter and Co.

360.

Key Bugle, in *c'*. Of copper, with six curved brass keys, and patent pads. Stamped "George Smith, Wolverhampton. Fecit." Length 16½ inches.

Lent by Colonel Shaw-Hellier.

361.

Key Bugle, in *c'*, with *b♭* crook. Of copper, with white metal rim to bell, and with six cup-shaped keys of brass, on small saddles. Stamped "F. I. van Engelen, à Lierre, Province d'Anvers." Length 18½ inches.

Lent by the *Conservatoire Royal de Musique*, Brussels.

362.

Key Bugle, in *c'*, with *b♭* crook. Of copper, with a brass rim to the bell, and with seven flat brass keys, on saddles. The seventh key is made to facilitate the production of

Stamped "Royal South Gloucester." Length 19 inches.

Key Bugle, in *c'*, with *b♭* crook. Of copper, with brass rim to the bell, and in every respect similar to that previously described.

These two instruments were formerly in the band of the South Gloucester Militia.

Lent by Colonel Hill, C.B.

363.

Key Bugle (Alto), in *e♭*. This instrument, whose place has now been taken by the valved tenor saxhorn, is made of copper, and bent in a semi-circular form. There are seven flat keys of brass, upon pillars; the lowest key is of course open. The compass of the instrument was much the same as that of the *b♭* keyed bugle. It is stamped "Sarthedebat, Strasburg." The instrument is so much damaged that it was impossible to ascertain its pitch. It was called an "alto" key bugle by its owner, but the measurement of the tubing (*viz.* 44 inches) suggests that it was in reality a soprano key bugle in *e′*♭, instead of an alto in *e*♭.

Lent by M. Césare Snoeck.

364.

Key Bugle (Soprano), in *e′*♭. This instrument is made entirely of brass, and has seven flat keys upon saddles. There is also an ingenious arrangement for lengthening the tuning bit by means of a rack and pinion adjustment. Length 14 inches.

Lent by Messrs. Besson and Co.

365.

Key Bugle (Soprano), in *e′*♭. Of copper, with seven flat keys of white metal, upon saddles. It is stamped "Wigglesworth, Maker, Otley." Length 14¼ inches.

Lent by Messrs. Ward and Sons.

366.

Key Bugle, in *c′*. Of copper, with seven cup-shaped keys of white metal, upon saddles. Stamped "Royal Kent Bugle, Patent." The mouthpiece is of ivory. Length 17½ inches.

Lent by the Rev. F. W. Galpin, M.A., F.L.S.

367.

Key Bugle, in *c′*, with *b*♭ crook. Of copper, with eight flat brass keys, on saddles. The eighth key is worked by the little finger of the left hand, and is intended to facilitate the shake upon

Length 17 inches.

Lent by Mr. Q. Cecconi.

368.

KEY BUGLE, in *b♭*. Of copper, with eight flat brass keys, upon saddles. Stamped "Potter, King Street, Westminster, London." There is also a silver plate inlaid, bearing this inscription, "Presented to the Light Infantry of the Honourable Artillery Company by their attached friend, Samuel Barnard, Captn. 1828." Length 17 inches.

Lent by the *Honourable Artillery Company.*

369.

KEY BUGLE, in *c′*, with *b♭* crook. Of copper, with ten flat brass keys, fitted with patent pads. The two additional keys found here are intended to facilitate the shakes upon

Stamped "Macfarlane's Improved. Manufactured by J. Köhler, Henrietta Street, Covent Garden, London."

The fact of there being three shake keys upon this instrument is remarkable; their employment varies of course with the crook used; for instance, to produce the shake upon *d″*, if the instrument is in *c′*, the higher key would be used, while the lower one would produce the same shake were the *b♭* crook in use. This instrument shows the highest state of perfection to which the key bugle had been brought before it was superseded entirely by the valved cornets-à-piston in use at the present day. Length 18 inches.

Lent by Messrs. Köhler and Son.

X.

CLASS—INSTRUMENTS WITH CUP-SHAPED MOUTHPIECES.

FAMILY: *Length varied by slide.*

INSTRUMENTS of which the length of the air column is varied by means of slides are of great antiquity. The principle appears to have been known in China at a very remote period. Some writers have endeavoured to ascribe the invention to Tyrtæus in 685 B.C. Others have imagined the principle to be of Egyptian origin, and have ascribed its introduction to Osiris. That instruments thus constructed were known to the Romans is, however, certain, and some specimens were discovered at Pompeii in 1738. Neumann, in his *Tutor for the Trombone*, describes the finding of these instruments, and mentions that they were made of bronze, but had mouthpieces of gold. The king of Naples, he states, gave one of these instruments to King George III. This statement was confirmed by the late Mr. William Chappell more than fifty years ago; the whereabouts of the instrument is now unknown, but it is hoped that at some future time it may again be found, and thus an important point regarding the history of musical instruments may be decided. That the Romans made use of instruments thus constructed would seem clear from a passage in the Vulgate, which is there rendered "In tubis ductilibus" (Ps. xcviii. 6); "tubæ ductiles" are mentioned by various classical writers, and Mersenne quotes a passage of Apuleius to the effect that "dexterâ extendente vel retrahente tubæ canales, musicales soni ab eâ edebantur."

Instruments of this family are now known by the generic name of *trombone;* in former days they were known as *sackbut*, or *saqucbut*, a word derived from the Spanish *sacabuche*. There is in an old MS. of the 9th century, at Boulogne, a representation of a sackbut, or rather the slide of one, for the bell itself is not shown; as far as can be seen the form did not then differ materially from that of the modern trombone. The instrument is mentioned by Bonanni (*Gabinetto Armonico*) under the name of *tromba spezzata*. Virdung (*Musica Getutscht*,

1511) calls it *busaune*, and from this word the modern German name of posaune has been derived. In Virdung's work an engraving of the instrument is given, which has been reproduced by Luscinius (Nachtgall) in his *Musurgia*, already spoken of in this work.

The sackbut was for a long time a very popular instrument in England, and the best players upon the Continent were often Englishmen. In the private band of Henry VIII. there were, among other instrumentalists, ten sackbut players; and appreciation of the English artist is shown by the fact that in 1604 King Charles III., of Lorraine, endeavoured to procure sackbut players from England. Of the use of the instrument in Lorraine further account may be found in the beautiful work of M. Jacquot (*La Musique en Lorraine*, Paris, 1886).

In the time of Prætorius (about 1618) the sackbuts formed a complete family, which he thus arranges: (1) *alt* or *discant posaun*, the compass of which was from *B* to *d''*; (2) *gemeine rechte posaun*, having a compass from *E* to *g'*; (3) *quart posaun*, the compass of which was *A*, to *c'*; (4) and the *octav posaun* from *E*, to *a*. Prætorius mentions that the octav posaun was usually of a larger bore than the others, and had a slide double the length of that of the ordinary instrument. This system was an improvement designed by one Hans Schreiber, the octav posaun usually made being slightly different. All the instruments are described at length, and there are drawings which show the details fully. The use of crooks was employed when Prætorius wrote, and they were termed *krümmbügle*, and placed as now, between the instrument itself and the mouthpiece. A form of crook called *tortil* came into use some years later, and is described by Mersenne. The *tortil* was placed in the middle of the instrument, between the bell and the slide, and consisted of a coil of tubing sufficiently long to lower the pitch of the instrument a fourth, in order that it might serve as a bass to concerts of hautboys. And as a bass instrument the trombone was generally used, and had supplanted, as early as 1618, the use of the *cornetto torto*, or bass zinck, the intonation of which was faulty, and the tone harsh and strident.

The theoretical principle upon which the trombone is constructed is simple, and consists merely in lengthening the air column sufficiently to produce the difference of a semitone in pitch. This result is obtained by means of the slide, which is made long enough to allow of seven different *positions* (like the *shifts* employed in the violin). These positions, as practically employed, enable, in the case of the *B*♭ instrument, the execution of the following series:—

The family of trombones consists in the present day of the alto in *e*♭ or *f*, the tenor in *B*♭, and the bass in *G* or *F*. The *F* bass trombone is in constant use in Germany, but unfortunately is little employed in this country.

The trombone has not altered materially the shape which it had in the 16th century. A novel instrument was brought out by the French maker Halary, about 1830, with the view of facilitating the execution of passages requiring a rapid interchange of positions, and also to diminish the length of the slide, which in the larger instruments was very great, and caused a considerable amount of manual labour to the executant. In Halary's instrument the slide was made *double*, and thereby required to be lengthened only half the distance necessary to the ordinary trombone to procure the same result. This application of a double slide has been improved upon by various makers, first by Sax, then by Gustav Besson and Distin, and lastly by Mr. Goodison.

The trombone with double slides becomes, however, a different instrument, and requires a different method. For although the length of the shifts is short, and consequently rapid passages, impossible upon the ordinary trombone, can be executed with comparative ease, yet it must be remembered that new difficulties are presented, and faults of intonation are necessarily increased in proportion. The difficulty of keeping the double slide air-tight is very great.

The application of the slide to the trumpet is believed to have been made during the last century. Accurate information upon this point cannot be obtained; the instrument, nevertheless, is mentioned by Altenburg (*Versuch einer Anleitung zur heroisch-musikalischen Trompeter und Pauken Kunst*, Halle, 1795), and it appears probable that the slide principle was adapted from the trombone at a comparatively late period, and that the slide trumpet supplanted the *Inventions* trumpet (or hand trumpet) of Michael Wögel, an instrument described upon page 151.

The scale of the modern slide trumpet extends from

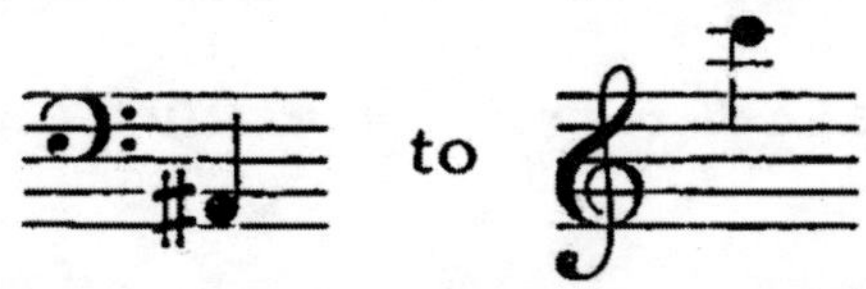

but contains several gaps which cannot be filled. The slide is constructed sufficiently long to allow of four positions, and is kept automatically closed by means of a spring. Within the last year an application of the double slide principle has been made to the trumpet by Mr. W. Wyatt, who has taken out a patent for his improvement. The instrument thus constructed possesses a complete chromatic scale, and loses nothing of the quality of the ordinary slide trumpet. The remarks already made about the double slide are of course equally applicable in this case, for the shifts necessarily being very short require great nicety of manipulation on the part of the player.

370.

TENOR SLIDE TROMBONE. Of brass. The rim of bell is engraved with floriated pattern, and there are winged cherub's heads in raised work at intervals. Inscribed with maker's name as follows: "MACHT. HANNS HAINEE, IN NURNBERG, 1668"; also on rim of bell a cock's head flanked with initials H. H., no doubt Hainee's device or trademark. The stays of both bell and slide are chased and engraved, the slide-stays being, by an ingenious arrangement, detachable. This instrument is a good example of the pre-eminence of the Nuremburg metal art in the Middle Ages. Plate XI., fig. A.

Lent by the *Conservatoire Royal de Musique*, Brussels.

371.

TENOR TROMBONE. With bell shaped to resemble a dragon's head. Probably made about 1800. The shape of the bell is made in imitation of the Latin Buccina. The origin of this shape is no doubt Eastern, but it in no way improves the quality of tone. There are several similar instruments at the present time in H.H. the Khedive's band at Cairo. Trombones of this shape have been used at different times in both English and French military bands. In France these instruments were known as *Buccin*, a word derived from the Latin *Buccina*.

Lent by the *Edinburgh University* (*Chair of Music*).

372.

Tenor Slide Trombone. With bell in shape of a dragon's head. About 1800. An instrument very similar to that preceding.

Lent by the *Conservatoire Royal de Musique*, Brussels.

373.

Slide Trumpet. By Garrett, London. With ornamental mounts and boss. The slide is held in its normal position by means of a watch-spring, placed in a round case. This application of the spring is found in all the earlier slide trumpets. In the later models either a spiral spring, or a piece of elastic is used for the same purpose.

Lent by the *Conservatoire Royal de Musique*, Brussels.

374.

Slide Trumpet. Modern Harper's improved. By Köhler. Shown as an example of a slide trumpet of the present day.

Lent by Messrs Köhler and Son.

375.

Bass Trombone, in *F*. By Boosey and Co. It is for this instrument that all the bass trombone parts in German classical music were written. It is called in Germany *Quart Bass Posaune*, the pitch of the instrument (*F*) being a fourth below the tenor trombone in *B*♭, most usually employed. It is only upon this bass trombone that the *C*♮ below the lines of the bass clef can be played, a note which

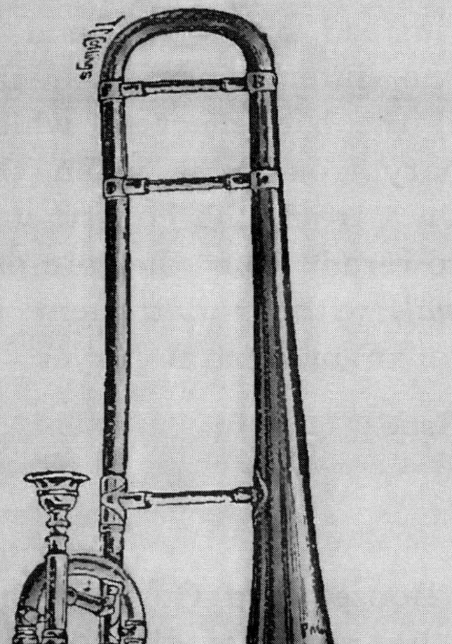

No. 379.
DOUBLE-SLIDE TROMBONE.

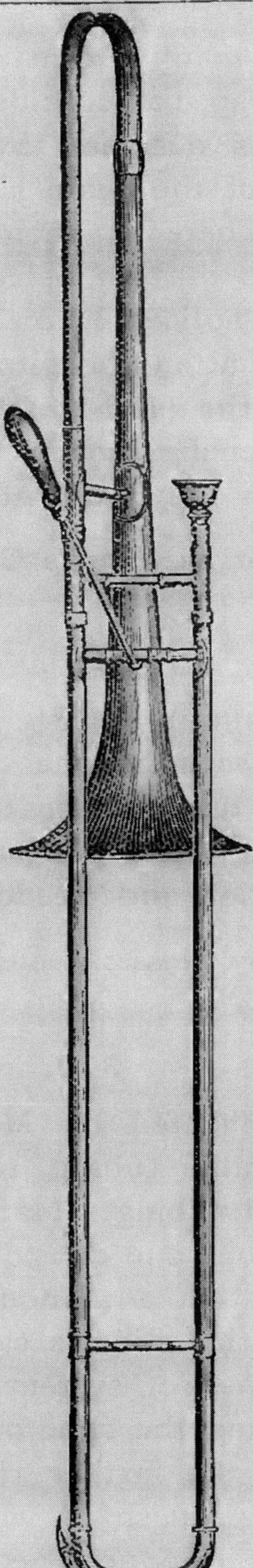

No. 375.
BASS TROMBONE (CASE'S SYSTEM).

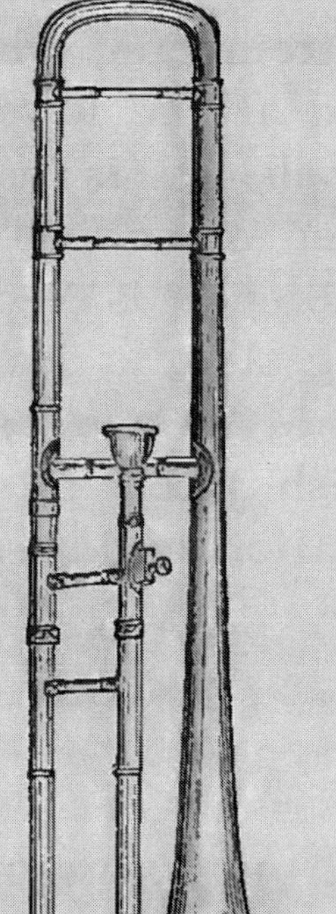

No. 376.
TENOR TROMBONE.

appears in the scores of many German composers, who have written the trombone parts with special consideration for this instrument. In this trombone, which was designed by Mr. Case, the tuning slide is placed at the lower end of the main slides, instead of at the bend in the bell, as is usual. There is therefore no interference with the tapered or conical portion of the instrument, the bad effect of which interference is especially noticeable on ordinary trombones when the tuning slide is drawn to flatten the pitch. On a trombone constructed upon Mr. Case's system the pitch may be lowered from the present English pitch to the French *Diapason Normal*, without detriment to intonation and freedom, a great advantage to an orchestral player.

Lent by George Case, Esq.

376.

SLIDE TROMBONE (TENOR), in *B*♭. By Boosey and Co. In this instrument, as should always be the case, the taper of the bell is carried right through the tuning slides; so that although the exterior of these slides is cylindrical, the interior is conical, as required to give the best results in intonation and freedom.

Lent by Messrs. Boosey and Co.

377.

TROMBONE SLIDE. Invented by Mr. George Case, and so constructed that, of the movable tubing, one leg telescopes outside, and the other inside, the fixed tubing. Made by Messrs. Boosey and Co. This slide is that of a trombone considered as a scientific instrument, that is, in the same way that a monochord is used to determine the harmonics of a string, so this slide is capable of giving, with of course the addition of a bell, a perfect system of tube harmonics. This has been effected by constructing the slide on the telescopic principle, with the great advantage, that the further the slide is extended, so at the same time a corresponding length of wide tubing is added at the end nearest to the bell, where it is most necessary.

Lent by George Case, Esq.

378.

Contra-Bass Trombone, in *B♭*. With double slide, giving all the notes of the *B♭* tenor trombone one octave lower, the lowest chromatic note being therefore

and the pedal *B♭* being

This particular instrument was made by Boosey and Co. for the Inventions and Music Exhibition in 1885, but the model was first introduced at the Crystal Palace Brass Band Contest in July 1861.

Lent by Messrs. Boosey and Co.

379.

Three Patent Double-Slide Trombones, in *B♭* tenor, *E♭* bass, and *G* bass. By Rudall, Carte and Co.

The application of the double slide to the trombone, although invented by Halary about 1830, and adopted by subsequent makers, appears to have fallen into disuse. Whether the principle was previously applied to trombones of all sizes, or only to the bass trombone, is doubtful. It seems to have been re-invented and patented by Mr. Goodison in 1884.

Lent by Messrs. Rudall, Carte and Co.

XI.

CLASS—INSTRUMENTS WITH CUP-SHAPED MOUTHPIECES.

FAMILY: *Length varied by Valves.*

THE first application of valves, now so generally applied to brass instruments, is generally attributed to a horn player named Stölzel, a native of Breslau, at the beginning of the present century. The real credit, however, of the invention is due to the oboe player Blümel, a Silesian, who, according to M. Kastner (*Manuel Général de Musique Militaire*, Paris, 1848), sold the right of his invention to Stölzel, who, improving upon it, took out a patent in Germany for a horn, with three pistons, and by which he secured the right for a period of ten years. And hence Stölzel has frequently been considered as the inventor of the valve. Blümel, nevertheless, in conjunction with the instrument makers Griessling and Schott, took out another German patent, and produced brass instruments of all kinds with valves, but which, owing to their defective intonation, met with little success. Stölzel, by adding tuning slides to the additional lengths of tubing brought into use by the depression of the valves, greatly improved upon Blümel's invention; and the principle, once established, was readily taken up by other instrument makers of the time, and at their hands underwent various modifications and improvements.

The valves were at first made of square pieces of solid brass, about 1 inch in thickness, kept in their normal position by means of a spring, and having the wind passages bored parallel in the same horizontal plane. A trumpet thus constructed is described later in the work, and valves of this description were made by the German maker Schuster, as early as 1818. As, however, instruments constructed with such contrivances could not be compared with the key bugle, either in intonation or agility, Stölzel designed a tubular valve, much smaller and lighter, and which for some time held its own. These valves were made by the maker Charles Sax, of Brussels, and were generally applied to the two-valve cornets then coming gradually into use. The scale of instruments with two valves had necessarily certain gaps, and in order to render it truly chromatic, a third valve was added at a subsequent date. The bore of all these early valves was exceedingly small, averaging only some ·38 inch, the bottoms of the pumps* being utilised as wind-ways, thus causing many abrupt turns in the air column.

The various endeavours to improve upon these valves led to many different contrivances. One of the earliest of these was patented in 1824 by John Shaw, a farmer, residing at Glossop, Derbyshire, and called by him "transverse spring slides." Shaw's *slides*, or *staples*, were made either ascending or descending, and consisted of U-shaped pieces of tubing placed at right angles to the main tube of the instrument, and fitted with touch-pieces, by the depression of which the moveable tubing became either cut off from (if *ascending*), or added (if *descending*) to, the main wind-way of the instrument. This system of Shaw's was afterwards improved upon by the German maker Schott, and for a time was generally used in Germany and Austria; and, for the larger instruments, possessed the advantage of presenting a wind-way less constricted and of greater diameter than was possible with the Stölzel valves; and valves of somewhat similar construction, though much improved, are still employed for instruments used in the Belgian Army.

Until about 1846 the bottoms of valves were still utilised as wind-ways, to the detriment of the tone, and in the early three-valved cornets, or cornopæans, as they were called in England, the air-passage entered usually at the side of the first valve, and, passing through the pumps, left by the bottom of the third. About this time a larger bore came into general use, and has since been adopted generally; and a further improvement was made by which there were fewer angles in the wind-ways of the valves, the air-passages being built up within the pumps.

The well-known Belgian instrument maker Adolphe Sax, a son of the Charles Sax already mentioned, commencing business on his own account in Paris in 1842, applied himself particularly to improvements in brass instruments, and produced a valve of somewhat greater

* The pistons are technically termed *pumps*.

diameter, in which the passages in each piston were all disposed in one horizontal place. These valves, though still of clumsy form, presented advantages greatly in excess of any hitherto constructed, and were for a time in general use in brass instruments supplied to the French army.

The desire to ensure a wind passage absolutely free from abrupt turns, and yet of the same sectional area throughout, led the French maker Halary to patent a system of valves consisting of revolving plates, instead of pistons. The original idea, however, was due to John Shaw, of Glossop, who appears to have been then a brass worker, and to have abandoned his former profession of farmer. The idea was eventually patented by Shaw in 1835, and in his instrument as first made, the air-way passed through a loop of tubing fitted upon an **I**-shaped plate. There were two plates of this shape placed face to face, one fixed and one moveable, rotating upon a pivot placed in the centre of the **I**. Upon the moveable piece were two separate loops of tubing of different lengths, the windway passing through the shorter of the two when the plate was in its normal position. By slightly rotating the plate, the longer loop of tubing was brought into use. For these **I**-shaped plates, circular discs were shortly afterwards substituted, and the principle was applied to instruments of all sizes. Two trumpets of this construction, one with the **I**-shaped plates, and one with the circular discs, were in this Exhibition, and were the work of John Köhler, of Henrietta Street. The latter instrument is elsewhere described in detail (*see* No. 405), together with a further development of the same principle. These *patent lever* instruments, as they were called, had but a brief existence, although their construction offered, in theory, many advantages. At the opening of the Crystal Palace, 18 of them were supplied for the band of that institution, which then was under the direction of Mr. H. Schallehn, afterwards Director of Music at the Royal Military School of Music. The difficulty of keeping the plates properly wind-tight was found practically insurmountable, and the system was consequently discarded by the makers.

The principal improvements as regards a free air passage through the pumps are due to Dr. J. P. Oates, an English doctor of medicine and clever acoustician. Some of these improved pistons were exhibited by Dr. Oates in the 1851 International Exhibition, where they gained a prize medal. The improvements consisted, in the words of the inventor, chiefly in "*equitrilateral* valves, in which the apertures leading into the windways were placed upon the periphery of the piston, at the point of an equilateral triangle drawn upon the transverse sectional area of the piston." An improvement upon these pistons was made in 1852, and registered, becoming known as the "eclipse" piston. It was adopted by M. Antoine Courtois as the first piston in his celebrated cornets, the "equitrilateral" (slightly altered by placing the main windway too near the centre) being used as the second.

Dr. Oates invented also, about the same time, a piston which had four straight windways, and which was afterwards patented by Alphonse Sax, in Paris, and can be seen upon some of this maker's instruments. It is much to be regretted that none of Dr. Oates' inventions were patented by him in his own name; he appears to have disposed of his ideas, and they were produced by various instrument makers as their own inventions, and patented as such.

The rotary valve, or cylinder action, in which the pump is replaced by a brass cock, was of German origin, and was probably invented about 1820. It is certain that it was in general use some 55 years ago, and in Germany and Austria has retained its place to the present day.

The French maker Gustav Besson, in conjunction with Rödel, patented, in 1851, a system in which the main windway was carried straight through the centre of the valves, and was circular throughout; but the openings in the second valve being of larger section than the corresponding wind-way, caused an angularity that was found detrimental to the tone of the instrument. An improvement upon this construction, by which a direct wind passage was secured for the first and third valves, was effected by the same maker in July 1854, and patented in France. These improved pistons were fitted to the instrument, No. 404, described in detail elsewhere.

M. Besson, in 1855, produced a system of valves in which the same bore was preserved throughout all the windways, in every possible combination of the pistons; this was a very decided improvement upon any system previously constructed, and at the expiration of the patent the invention was adopted by instrument makers generally. A sectional model of these valves was exhibited in this collection, and a further explanation of them will be found upon another page.

Messrs. Besson found that these valves were better suited to the larger instruments, and they still employ them for their euphonions. In 1874 they succeeded, by a combination of their 1854 and 1855 patents, in producing a system of valves by which greater brilliancy was assured for instruments such as the cornet, etc., which require a brighter and more penetrating quality of tone. A detailed description of these valves is unnecessary here, since they are largely employed for the best instruments made by this firm.

The well-known action applied by M. Antoine Courtois to his beautiful cornets was, as has been remarked, an ingenious application of the invention of Dr. Oates. This action was considerably improved by M. Courtois, and was employed by the English maker Mr. Henry Distin for some considerable time. To reduce the weight of the pump, and thereby ensure a more rapid execution, Mr. Henry Distin patented, in 1864, what he called his *light valve*, in which the pump was made in a single tube, the air passages being secured with silver solder. A particular arrangement of spring action was also included in the patent. These light valves were adopted, at the expiration of the patent, by many makers, and are largely used by Messrs. Boosey and Co. (who added Mr. Distin's business to their own in 1868) for many of their instruments at the present time.

The use of the valves, as is well known, is to vary the length of the wind-column, by adding or cutting off certain lengths of tubing. As has been already remarked, in order to allow of a chromatic scale throughout the compass of a wind instrument of this class, there must be seven different lengths of wind column available, answering to the seven positions of the slide trombone. This, in the case of ordinary three-valved instruments, is accomplished in the following manner. The open tube and the pistons, when employed singly, allow of the production of the following harmonic series :—

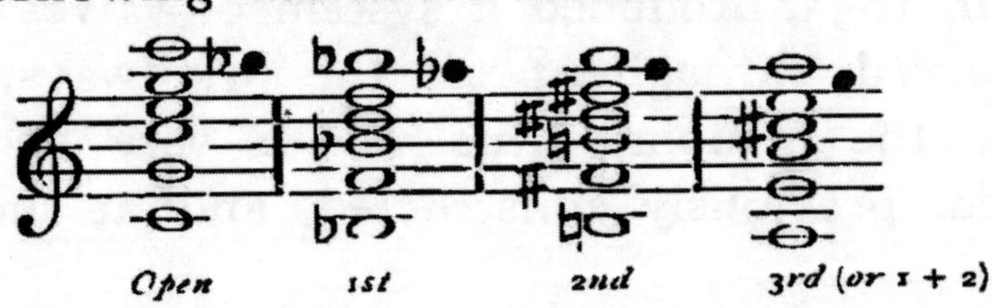

The seven positions are completed by the use of several valves together; these combinations produce—

2nd + 3rd *1st + 3rd* *1st + 2nd + 3rd*

The notes printed in black are not generally used, being either for acoustical reasons wanting in truth of intonation, or being more conveniently taken by other fingering. Since the union of any two pistons does not give the theoretical length of tubing required for the true production of these intervals, the performer is obliged to *humour* certain notes; and this want of truth of intonation is especially noticeable in the lower register, in which, as can be seen, certain notes cannot be produced by a single valve; so that, unless the player's *embouchure* is relaxed, these lower notes are invariably too sharp.

To correct this defect, inherent in all three-valved instruments, many ingenious contrivances have been made. A rough approximation is very generally attempted by making the third valve tubing somewhat longer than is required to produce a tone and a half difference in pitch. As this valve is seldom used singly, a slight lengthening of its tubing is a useful compromise when it is used in conjunction with the first or second valves, or with both together. The French maker Adolphe Sax, wishing to assimilate the valve trombone to the slide instrument, devised, about 1850, a six-valve system, by which a separate valve was employed for each position, and in which no two valves could be employed in combination. These valves were made *ascending*, instead of *descending*, the lowest note upon the instrument being that of the open tube. This system, theoretically perfect, was for a time in use, and was supported strenuously by Berlioz and other distinguished musicians of that day. But, unfortunately, it introduced practical difficulties so great that its use was ultimately abandoned. The construction of these six-valved instruments is described fully upon page 207. Various other devices had been tried by Sax; and an arrangement was introduced in 1853, by Gustav Besson, by which the slide of any piston could be lengthened by means of a

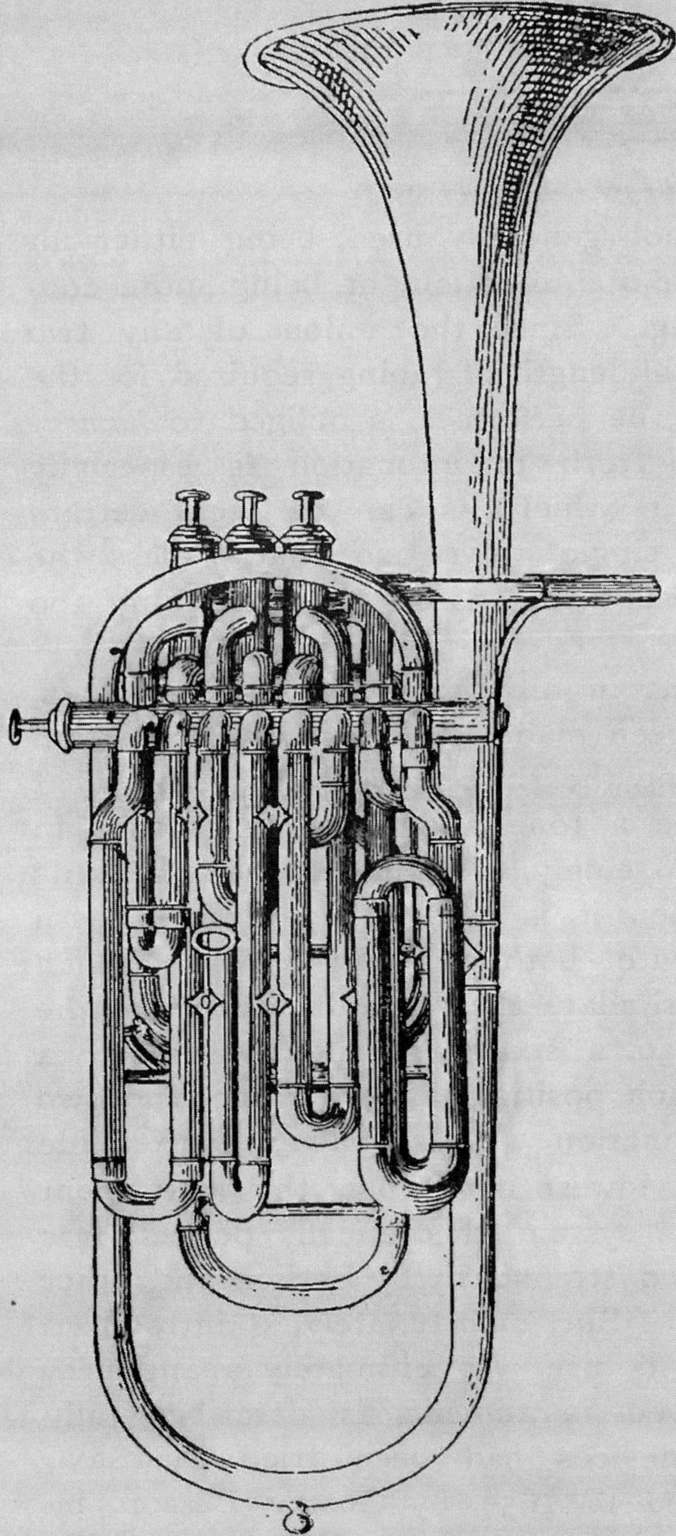

M. BESSON'S *Registre* OF 1857.

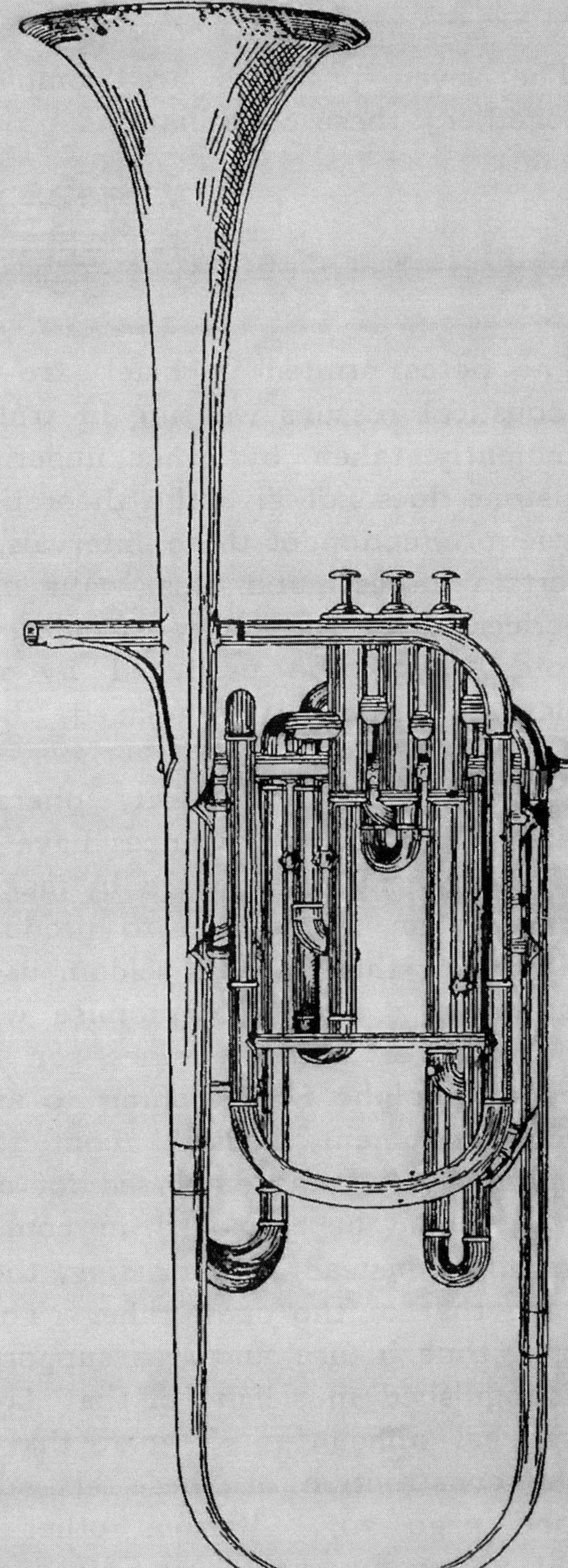

M. BESSON'S *Registre* OF 1856.

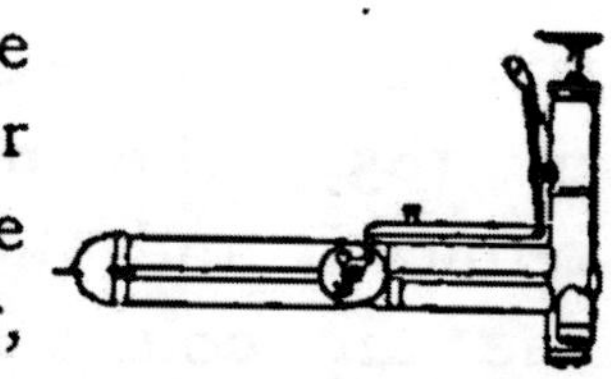

cylinder, connected with a touch-piece placed at the side of the piston itself, and could be employed either as a compensator, or to extend the compass of the valve notes. The arrangement, shown in the engraving, being found in practice too intricate, was discarded.

A method of correcting the intonation of the lower register, yet preserving the usual three-valve fingering, consists in substituting a duplicate set of tubings, of longer length, which are brought into use by the depression of a valve or lever. The invention of this arrangement has been attributed to Courtois, and the device was tried by Sax previous to his invention of the six-piston system. It is certain that the late M. Gustav Besson patented in 1856 a system having the same object. It consisted of a long horizontal valve, called a *registre*, which brought into use at the player's will other tubing, lowering the pitch of the instrument a semitone, and substituting at the same time a duplicate set of valve tubings of the necessary theoretical length. As applied to the ordinary three-piston instruments, the use of the registre enabled eight *dependent* positions to be produced. The following year M. Besson patented an improved *registre*, very similar in outward appearance, but which gave eight *independent* positions. The registre itself lowered the pitch two tones. Together with the three pistons and the open tube five independent positions were produced; the employment of the registre in conjunction with each of the three pistons separately, gave three others. The arrangement of the air passages is exceedingly ingenious, and is described at length in the French patent specification. The general appearance of the tubing of these instruments is shown in the engraving upon the opposite page.

In 1858 MM. Besson and Giradin designed a compensating system, which they patented. It consisted of an addition of two pistons, placed below the others; when these pistons were depressed, the slides of the three ordinary valves were automatically lengthened proportionately. The mechanism was complicated, and too delicate to be of practical use. Accordingly, in the following year, M. Besson designed a system by which the same result was differently secured. This device he called his *transpositeur*, and it was equally useful as a compensator. A registre, as before, lowered the pitch two tones, and in conjunction with three pistons constructed with a duplicate set of tubings, gave eight dependent positions; as compared with the patent of 1857, the number of openings in the pump were considerably reduced, and the disposition of the passages gave greater freedom for the air column. An illustration of a euphonion thus constructed will be found upon page 209. The *transpositeur* met with success, and was patented in England in 1859. Various infringements were made upon the system, and the idea was largely made use of by various makers.

In 1874 M. Léon Cousin patented in France a system somewhat similar to the six-piston arrangement of Sax, but in which the sixth piston is dispensed with. In M. Cousin's instrument the pistons are made *descending*, and produce the following scale:—

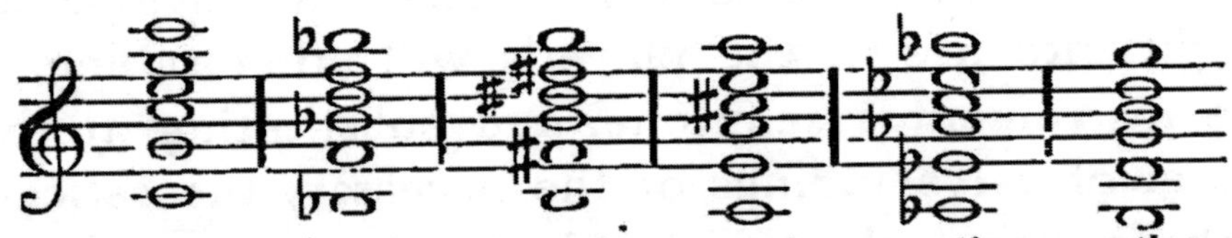

The pistons, however, are so constructed that they can be used in combination, hence the note *c'*♯, wanting in the above series, is produced by the combination of the second and fifth valves, and the compass of the instrument can be extended, by using combinations of valves, downwards chromatically to *c*♯; there is, of course, no compensation for valves used in combination.

Passing by a device, invented about 1874 by M. Thibouville-Lamy, of Paris, in which, by means of two keys placed upon the bell, the length of the wind column is adjusted to the theoretical length required for the production of the harmonic series produced by combinations of valves, we arrive at the first really *automatic* arrangement for ensuring this result.

This most ingenious device was invented in 1874 by Mr. D. J. Blaikley, and perfected and patented by him four years later. It consists in a peculiar construction of the valves, by which, when two or three pistons are employed in conjunction, the length of the air column is adjusted *automatically* to the exact theoretical length required to ensure absolutely correct intonation.

The improvements, by which this is effected, consist in passing the tubing connected with the third valve through the first and second valves in such a way that, when the third valve is pressed down, the vibrating column of air passes through passages in the first and second valves in addition to the two passages in the third valve, as used in the common arrangement; and for the purpose of bringing additional tubing into action in connection with the first and second valves, as required for correct intonation, when they are either or both used in combination with the third, Mr. Blaikley adds two air passages to each of these valves, and in connection with each pair of passages a loop, or circuit of tube, of the required length, which is added to the effective length of the instrument only when the third valve is used in connection with the others. Such additional tubing compensates for the lowering of the pitch of the instrument due to the pressing down of the third valve.

By help of the annexed Drawings, this will be more clearly understood. Figure 1 is a front elevation of the valves with the pistons up; and Figure 2 is a back elevation, showing all the pistons down. The same letters of reference indicate like parts in both Figures. The dotted line A, A, Figure. 1, shows the air passage

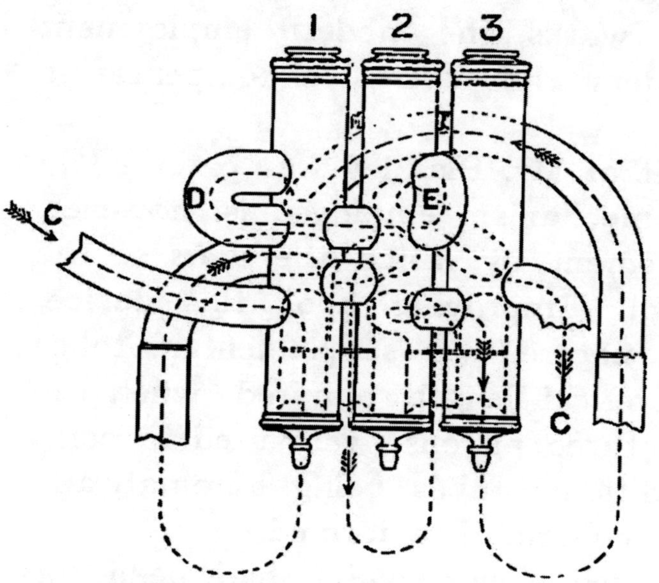

FIG. 2.

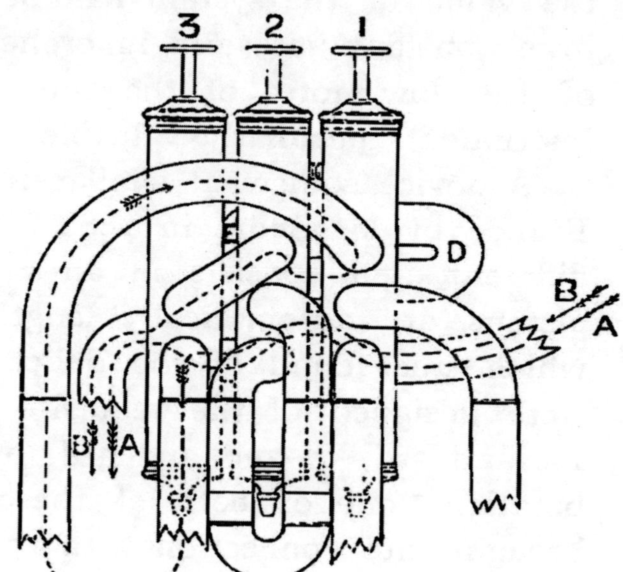

FIG. 1.

through the piston for "open" notes, that is to say, notes produced with the pistons up; the line B B in the same Figure indicates the air passage when the third piston only is pressed down. In Figure 2 the line C C represents the air passage when all the pistons are pressed down; D is the additional tubing connected with the first piston; and E the additional tubing connected with the second piston.

The action of the apparatus is as follows:—When either the first or second piston only is pressed down, the air passages are of the same length as in instruments of ordinary construction, but when either or both of those pistons is or are pressed down together with the third piston, then the air passage is lengthened by the additional length of tubing D or E, or both, thereby lengthening the air passage in inverse proportion to the number of vibrations of the required notes.

Since the fingering of the instrument remains unchanged, the value of this arrangement cannot be over rated; and when applied to the larger instruments, in which the size and looseness of the *embouchure* enhances the difficulty of correction by means of the lips, its utility is especially evident. Euphonions and tubas thus constructed have been adopted for some years at the Royal Military School of Music, where the value of the system has been proved by the experience derived from constant use; and in orchestral works, the modern employment of the low notes of the tuba renders the four-valve compensating instruments peculiarly valuable.

A device somewhat similar to that of Mr. Blaikley was patented in France by M. Sudre in 1881. The mechanism employed is, however, different, and consists in an arrangement by which the *slides* of the pistons are automatically lengthened. Improving upon this device, which was found of too delicate a nature, two supplementary tubes were designed of the requisite theoretical length required, when the 1st and 3rd, or 2nd and 3rd, or all three pistons, were used in combination; one or both of these additional tubes being automatically brought into connection with the air column thus formed.

M. Victor Mahillon, of the Brussels *Conservatoire*, had been for some time endeavouring to procure a like result, and in 1886 he produced his *piston regulateur*, by which the air column produced by the depression of the first and third, or all three, pistons at the same time, was made of the requisite length. The fingering of the instrument remained unaltered; but it was necessary to bring the additional tubing into use by the depression of a supplementary valve. Improving upon this, M. Mahillon succeeded in constructing an automatic arrangement, of which a diagram (an exact facsimile, reduced in scale, from that in the patent specification) is annexed, and which he designated his *automatic regulating pistons.*

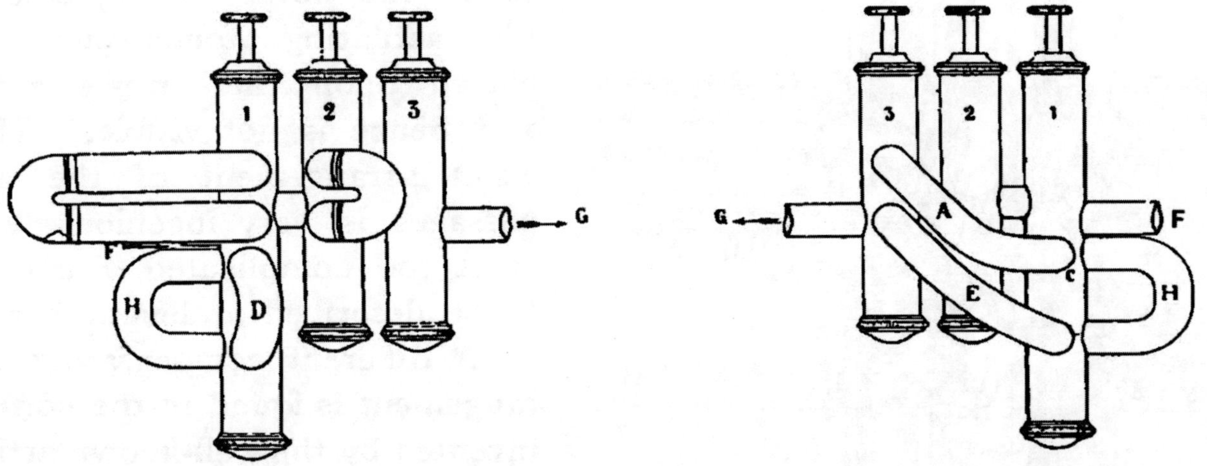

In the diagram it will be seen that when the third piston is employed alone, or in combination with the second, the air column passes through the branch A of the additional tubing attached to the third piston, enters the first valve at C, and, passing through the bend D into the branch E, rejoins the main tubing F G. The additional tube A D E is of the exact theoretical length required to produce a lowering in pitch of a tone and a half. Each time, however, that the first and third pistons are employed in combination, the air column passes through the branch A of the additional tubing, and enters the first valve at C, whence it passes into the bend H (which is longer than the bend D to a degree necessary to ensure the exact theoretical length required, when the two additional loops of tubing are employed simultaneously) to E, rejoining the main tubing F G.

An improvement upon the "registre" of Gustav Besson, already mentioned, has been patented in the last year by his successors (Patent No. 6649, A.D. 1890). In this arrangement the third valve itself acts as the registre, and, when used in conjunction with any of the other valves, causes the air column to pass into a duplicate set of valve tubings of the requisite theoretical length. Hence the combinational valve notes and their harmonics are perfectly true. The registre can be also applied as a transposer, when it becomes a fourth valve, and is placed horizontally at the side and moved by a lever. The annexed woodcut will explain this; the valve is in its normal position; the dotted lines show the position when the lever is depressed; the actuating touch-piece is placed upon the reverse side, and hence is not visible. The exact arrangement of the air passages is very ingenious, but is of too complicated a nature to be described at length here.

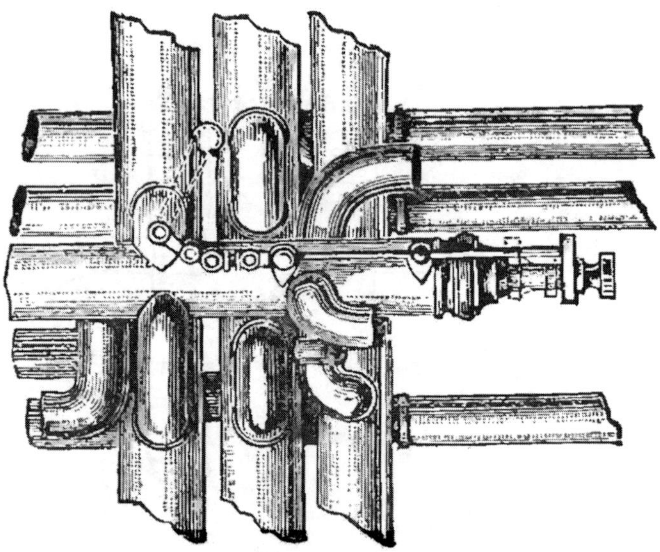

A different compensating arrangement is found in the cornet invented by the well-known artist M. Arban, and for some time adopted at the Paris *Conservatoire*. M. Arban's system is described more particularly in a subsequent page, and therefore needs only passing mention here.

Another compensating device consists in applying a set of valves to the slide trombone or trumpet. The instrument can thus be used either as a *slide* or *valve* instrument; in the latter case the slide can be employed as a compensator.

Whilst speaking of valved instruments this article would be incomplete if it failed to mention several applications of a single valve to a slide instrument. This single valve has, in the case of the trombone, been used variously; an arrangement by which the air column thus brought into use lowered the pitch one fourth, was constructed by M. Besson, with the object of lessening the distance required between the shifts. A trombone constructed with this extra valve gave 10 positions instead of seven, and the usual length of the slide was therefore unnecessary. Similar applications have been made both to the trumpet and cornet by M. Antoine Courtois, and shake valves, giving a tone or semitone difference in pitch, are frequently applied to the slide trombones used by American and French solo players.

The most recent application of such an arrangement was used at a recital at Trinity College, Cambridge, in February this year (1891). A work of Schütz was performed requiring

on the bass trombone, and intended for the *F* instrument (being impossible upon the *G*); an attached valve was made by Messrs. Boosey and Co. for the *G* instrument, with tubing to give the tone from the low *D* of the *G* trombone to the *C* required.

An endeavour to simplify the fingering of valved instruments was made in 1860 by Mr. Richard Carte, who, in conjunction with the cornet player Macfarlane, patented a device, by which all the sharps and flats could be produced by the depression of an extra valve (giving a semitone difference in pitch). This allowed the same fingering required for the natural notes, with the addition only of the extra valve, thus facilitating the use of certain keys usually difficult of execution. Rapid execution, however, was impossible, and, consequently, the device never became general.

The use of valves has led at different times to attempts to produce a double instrument, by means of two sets of tubings of different proportions, the air passing into either at the player's will by the depression of a valve. Distin endeavoured to combine the trumpet and bugle thus, and his example was followed by M. Mahillon. As, however, the proportion of the bore of the bugle is so entirely different from that of the trumpet, their attempts met with scant success, the true quality of both the trumpet and bugle being absent; and an attempt of the same kind was exhibited by M. Chediwa in the Paris Exhibition in 1889. A combined euphonion and baryton, or trombone, was made by C. G. Conn, of Elkhart, Indiana, U.S.A., three or four years ago. The instrument succeeded in America; the English makers, Boosey and Fontaine Besson, have made similar instruments for American players. In such a combination both instruments suffer, as it is impossible to preserve the true trombone tone, with pistons large enough in bore for the euphonion. This defect M. Fontaine Besson has endeavoured to correct in his *Doublophone*, in which the pistons are made with two distinct sets of passages and valve tubings, of proper proportions for the euphonion or trombone. The valve, by which either set is brought into connection, is placed almost immediately below the mouthpiece; hence, only the mouthpiece and a very short length of tubing are common to both instruments.

However ingeniously these double instruments are constructed, such devices appear suitable only for a display of virtuosity, and therefore can scarcely be considered of much account for any serious musical purpose.

Valved instruments, as used at the present day, may be said to consist of three groups, which are thus formed:—

1st Group.—Instruments which make use of all the harmonics up to the 16th, such as the valve-horn and valve-trumpet.*

2nd Group.—Instruments which make no use of the harmonics above the 8th, and which do not habitually employ the fundamental sounds, such as cornets, bugles (including all the saxhorns), and valve trombones.

3rd Group.—Instruments which make no use of the harmonics above the 8th, and which employ the fundamental sounds, such as euphonions, tubas, &c., and therefore possess in addition a compass of nearly an octave below that of instruments in Group 2.

The earlier valve instruments were the valve-horn, the valve-trumpet, and cornet. The latter appears to have been a gradual growth rather than an original invention, and can neither be considered as a trumpet nor yet as a bugle. Its tubing, almost cylindrical except near the bell, resembles that of the trumpet, and yet it makes use of the same harmonic sounds as the bugle. It has been said that the cornet is a development of the old *posthorn;* but if this be in reality the case, all trace of that instrument has vanished, for the proportions and tone-quality of the cornet are very different. The cornet has been for some time one of the most important instruments in military bands; and of late years there has been a growing tendency to replace by its use that of the trumpet in the orchestra. This is much to be regretted, for the majestic and penetrating quality of the trumpet is completely absent in the more common-place, and even vulgar, sound of the cornet, more agile though the instrument may be.

* The scale of the trumpet begins practically at the 3rd harmonic.

The application of the valve to the Kent bugle, or cor-à-clefs, about 1843, by Sax, was the origin of a complete family, virtually bugles, and called by the generic name of saxhorns. These instruments have since been known by various names. They consist principally of Flügel horns, or valve bugles, alt horns, tenor horns, or barytons, &c., and are too well known to need further description; their tubing is conical, and their compass, as has been said, lies between the 2nd and the 8th harmonics inclusive. They are chiefly employed in wind bands, and rarely if ever in the orchestra.

The instruments mentioned in Group 3, although in reality saxhorns, yet differ in that they are constructed with tubing of sufficiently large proportion to allow of the production of the fundamental sounds. And this peculiarity is turned to account, and thus considerably augments their compass, besides producing a full and rich quality of tone entirely wanting in instruments of smaller proportions. As the notes in the first octave, lower than can be produced upon three-valve instruments by the conjunction of several valves, are frequently required, a fourth valve, lowering the pitch two and a half tones, is very often added, and, for a solo instrument, the fourth valve is absolutely necessary. And so, as can be understood, these instruments possess the enormous compass of some three and a half octaves. This group of instruments are of more recent invention than the other valved instruments, and are used now to replace the ophicleides and bass horns once employed in military bands, where their introduction has proved of the highest value. Introduced of comparatively recent years into the orchestra, they are now of general use; and, indeed, a full orchestra that did not possess at least one euphonion and tuba, would not be considered complete. The fundamental of the euphonion is $B_{,}\flat$ or C; of the bass tuba $E_{,}\flat$ or $F_{,}$; and of the contra-bass tuba $B_{,,}\flat$ or $C_{,}$.

There are, besides those just mentioned, another family of valved instruments, whose proportions are a sort of compromise between those of the horn and of the bugle. They were first described by Sax, and called by him saxtrombas; the mouthpieces resembled those of the horn in shape, and were made of suitable sizes. The invention of these instruments has been claimed for the German musician Wieprecht, and instruments of a somewhat similar nature were certainly employed at a previous date in the German army. The saxtrombas formed a complete family, but only that in *E♭* or *F*, which was used to replace the horn in military bands, remained in practical use. Of a somewhat similar nature is the Koenig horn, constructed by Courtois in 1855, and still used in many military bands, and the more recent tenor cor, and cornophone.

Of very similar construction are the *tenor-tubas*, in *B♭*, for which Wagner has written in his "Nibelungen Tetralogie." Of a compass, lying between the 2nd and 12th harmonics inclusive, they were in proportion somewhat similar to the horn, and were intended to be played by a horn mouthpiece. They had four valves, and a vertical bell turned towards the right of the player. The valves gave *upon the tenor-tubas* (not the bass), a half tone, one tone, one and a half tones, and two tones. The description of them here given has been gathered from an article of the *Zeitschrift für Instrumentenbau* (published at Leipzig), of Nov. 1st, 1884.

380.

TRUMPET, in *C*. This curious looking instrument is one of the earliest valve trumpets in existence. The valves are in square boxes; the pistons consist of square blocks of solid brass, the wind passages being bored in them; there are two passages in the same horizontal plane. The extra tubing is calculated to lower the pitch of the instrument a semitone, and a tone, respectively, for each valve. Total length 1 foot 11½ inches. Plate X., fig. C.

Lent by the *Conservatoire Royal de Musique*, Brussels.

381.

CORNET, with two pistons, in *A*. The bore is exceedingly small, being only ·38 inches in diameter. The valves are of very early pattern, being of the construction attributed to Stölzel and Blümel. The first valve lowers the pitch of the instrument a semitone, the second valve lowers it a tone. The wind-way entering by the bottom of the first valve leaves by the bottom of the second, thus necessitating several right-angled turns. Engraved "C. Saxe, Bruxelles." Plate XI., fig. B.

Lent by the *Conservatoire Royal de Musique*, Brussels.

382.

TRUMPET, in *F*, with two pistons. The valves are constructed upon much the same system as those of the cornets just mentioned. They lower the pitch a semitone and a tone respectively. The pistons are placed parallel to the length of the instrument. There is an additional crook for *E*♭. Engraved "Potter." Length 1 foot 9½ inches.

Lent by Messrs. George Potter and Co.

383.

VALVE HORN, with three pistons. There are no crooks upon this instrument, but with a small crook of the present day the pitch note is *B*♭. The valve mechanism is of Austrian invention, and is formed of three pairs of parallel pistons. When all are in their normal position, there is a direct wind-way through all three pairs. There are three levers or keys, one of which is connected with each pair of pistons by a crank action. The depression of a key causes the corresponding pair of pistons to *rise*, and thereby opens an air passage, which passes, by a right-angled turn, along the length of one piston, through the extra tubing, and returns through the lower end of the other piston. This instrument is engraved "Mainz bei B. Schott's Söhnen," and probably dates from about 1830. Extreme width 1 foot 11 inches. Plate XI., fig. E.

Lent by the *Conservatoire Royal de Musique*, Brussels.

384.

VALVE HORN, with three pistons. The valve action can be removed altogether. The pitch note of the instrument, as it stands, is *F*. The valve action consists of pairs of pistons, placed very similarly to those noticed in No. 383; but in this case the pistons *descend* in order to bring the valve tubing into action. Engraved "J. G. Schmidt, in Leipzig," and probably made about 1830. Greatest width 22 inches.

Lent by Messrs. Besson and Co.

385.

BASS HORN, OR VALVE OPHICLEIDE, in *F*. This instrument is also called the clavicor. There are three pairs of pistons, and they are moved by a mechanism somewhat similar to that applied to the modern cylinder action. Each pair of pistons, in *rising*, opens air-ways, which throw the additional tubing into connection with the main wind-way of the instrument. The system is very similar to that of No. 383. The instrument is of German make, and of very indifferent intonation. It is, nevertheless, interesting as showing the transition stage between the ophicleide and the euphonion.

Lent by the *Conservatoire Royal de Musique*, Brussels.

386.

TRUMPET, with two horizontal valves. Marked "Improved and made by Chas. Pace, 49, King Street, Westminster."

There are three tuning bits, two straight and one bent, and four crooks. The instrument, when played, is held horizontally as a slide trumpet; it is intended to be used with the bent tuning bit with every crook. With the long straight tuning bit and the bent one, the trumpet stands in *F*. With the different crooks and bent tuning bit, it stands in *E*♮, *E*♭, *D*♮, and *C* respectively. The pitch is much flatter than the present regulation pitch, and is closely in agreement with the French Diapason Normal. This pitch is about that of the Philharmonic Society, under Sir Geo. Smart, about 1830.

The two valves are formed each by a single short inner tube, which slides inside the main tube of the instrument. As the centre of this inner tube is stopped, the air-way does not traverse the whole length of the valves; but it is diverted through a side-hole communicating with a short loop or bridge of tubing, by means of which it enters the valve again through another side-hole. A short arm projects from the valve through a slot in the main tube, by means of which the valve is connected with the actuating finger-piece, to which the spring is attached. When the valve is "down," the two side-holes, instead of being connected by the *short* loop or bridge-tube, are connected by means of a *second* loop, long enough to flatten the pitch a semitone or a tone, according to the valve employed. Probably made about 1840.

Lent by Colonel Shaw-Hellier.

387.

Cornet. Reproduction, with two pistons with screws. This shows a rather later development of the arrangement of the Stölzel valves. The wind-way here enters through the bottom of the second valve, and leaves by the bottom of the first. The second valve lowers the pitch a semitone, and the first a tone, as in the instruments of the present day. The bore, somewhat larger than that of the instrument No. 381, is similar to that employed at the present day.

Lent by Messrs. Besson and Co.

388.

Cornet, in *B♭*, with three pistons. The wind-way enters by the side of the first valve, and leaves by the bottom of the third. This model seems to have been universally adopted, and valves thus constructed were in general use up to about 1853. A similar action has, for the cheapest models of cornets, practically held its own even up to the present day.

Lent by Messrs. Ward and Sons.

389.

Cornet, in *B♭*. This cornet has valves invented by Adolphe Sax, and of very large diameter, all the passages in the pistons being disposed in one horizontal plane. The bell is detachable, and is attached by means of a ligature screw. Stamped "Ward, Maker, Liverpool, 1848."

Lent by Messrs. Ward and Sons.

390.

Cornet, or Cornopæan. Engraved "John Köhler, London." With embossed silver rim to bell, and Macfarlane's clapper shake key. Plate XI., fig. C. The valve system is that described under No. 388.

The first application of the clapper shake key upon the cornet is due to the cornet player, Macfarlane, who was employed in the orchestra at Drury Lane for many years. The clapper shake key appears to have been re-introduced by Distin in 1856, provisional protection being granted; the patent, however, was not proceeded with. The principle had been applied to the key bugle some years previously, and a beautiful instrument having three shake keys, made by "John Köhler," may be found described under No. 369.

Lent by Messrs. Köhler and Son.

391.

CORNET, or "CORNETTO." This instrument is practically a Flügel horn. The valve construction is very similar to that of No. 388, a form almost universally employed for the earlier valve instruments. There are no tuning slides to the valves in this instrument, consequently the intonation must have been very imperfect when the instrument became warm, after being played for a short time. Made by Butler, of Dublin, about 1830.

Lent by G. Butler, Esq.

392.

CORNET. Engraved "George Smith, Birmingham." A clapper shake key appears to have been added to this instrument at some subsequent period.

Lent by Colonel Shaw-Hellier.

393.

CORNET, in *B♭*, with clapper shake key.

Lent by Messrs. Ward and Sons.

394.

CORNET, in *C*, with clapper shake key.

Lent by Messrs. Ward and Sons.

395.

CORNET, in *B*♭, with shake key. Stamped "Macfarlane's Improved Cornopæan. Köhler, Henrietta Street, Covent Garden, London."

Lent by Messrs. Boosey and Co.

396.

CORNET, in *B*♭, with an extra *G* crook. With three narrow valves with outer screws. The construction of this cornet does not differ in any material point from that of No. 388, described on page 201. Instruments of this model were used by the Distins on their tours from 1839 to 1845.

Lent by Messrs. Besson and Co.

397.

TRUMPET, in *E*♭. This instrument is provided with three valves, giving the usual additional lengths of tubing. An interest attaches to this specimen, as it is a reproduction of the valve trumpet employed by Spontini, who first introduced it in the orchestra of the opera at Berlin for the production of his opera "La Vestale." Length 1 foot 5 inches.

Lent by Messrs. Besson and Co.

398.

CORNET, in *B*♭. Early French model. The valve construction of this cornet shows, compared with those previously mentioned, an advance in instrument making.

The wind-way enters at the side of the third valve, and leaves by the bottom of the first. Cornets made upon this model are still manufactured in France, in cases where cheapness is of more consideration than quality of tone.

Lent by Messrs. Boosey and Co.

399.

CORNET, in *B*♭. This instrument is, both as regards construction of the valves and disposition of the tubing, a great step in advance of any already described. The second valve is larger than in the Stölzel model, and affords room for one horizontal, and two sloping, wind-ways. The first and third valves differ little from the Stölzel model. There are still several right-angled turns, but the bottoms of the valves are not actually employed as wind-ways. Stamped "Lausedat. Clermont Ferrand." Probably about 1835.

Lent by Messrs. Besson and Co.

400.

CORNET, in *B♭*. With three wide valves (Perinet's patent), made about 1839. The three valves are constructed with built-up air passages, and add additional lengths of tubing equivalent to a semi-tone, a tone, and a tone and a half respectively. The construction of the bore, and the abrupt turns in the air passages, are very greatly modified, but the openings in the valves are larger than the corresponding wind passages; there is therefore an angularity when the valves are depressed, and hence the disposition of the air passages is not equalized, as is the case in instruments of the present day. Stamped "Besson, à Paris."

Lent by Messrs. Besson and Co.

401.

CORNET, in *B♭*. French model. This instrument is merely a slight modification of the Perinet model described previously.

Lent by Messrs. Boosey and Co.

402.

BASS, in *B♭*. Skeleton shape, and 6 feet high. By Adolphe Sax, 1850. There are three thick valves. All three passages through the valves are horizontal, the lower one being for the open notes; the other two, which are in use when the valve is depressed, are placed side by side, in the same horizontal plane as in the ordinary German cylinder action of the present day.

Lent by Messrs. Besson and Co.

403.

CORNET, in *B*♭. Rödel Besson, 1851. The passage for the open notes in this instrument goes straight through the centre of the valves, and is circular in section throughout. The passages for the valve notes are still considerably constricted, and are disposed at right angles to the main passage, the passages in the second valve being larger than the corresponding air column. Valves of this description were largely used by both French and English makers till within the last few years.

Lent by Messrs. Besson and Co.

404.

CORNET, in *B*♭. This beautiful instrument, formerly won as a prize at the Gymnase, Paris, by a cornet-player named Hulmet, of the 55me du Ligne, is of interest as being probably one of the most perfect cornets of the time when it was made. In construction the second valve somewhat resembles that of the Perinet, but the first and third valves contain holes pierced vertically above each other, and connected by a wind-passage having a short semi-circular course built up within the valve itself. This system of valves was patented by Gustav Besson in 1854; a direct passage was secured for the first and third valves, but the passages in the second valve were smaller than the corresponding air column. A valve, somewhat similar to the first and third valves of this cornet, was employed by Distin, and is found in the bass instrument No. 416. Stamped "G. Besson, à Paris." This instrument is probably about 1854.

Lent by Messrs. Besson and Co.

405.

A PAIR OF TRUMPETS, in *E*♭. With John Shaw's "Patent Lever" valves. By John Köhler. Plate X., fig. E. The peculiarity of these instruments consists in the unique construction of the valves, which were invented by Shaw and patented in 1838. These valves were also called "disc valves" by the inventor. They consist of a pair of discs or plates, one fixed and one moveable; the fixed disc has two, and the other four, perforations cut of the same diameter as the wind-ways of the instrument. These plates are formed with perfectly true faces, which move freely upon each other. The fixed disc carries upon it two lengths of tubing, one for the normal position of the valve, and one for the supplementary wind-way, which latter is thrown in in place of the former when the disc is rotated by means of the depression of a lever or touch-piece. This valve, however theoretically perfect, was found not to answer: the difficulty of keeping the plates air-tight was too great to be overcome.

Mr. Köhler made instruments constructed upon this principle for some years, and introduced a rather different disposition of the air-passages, thereby securing greater rapidity of execution. The valves employed were modifications of this. The difference consisted in the moveable discs having but two very short crescents of tubing fixed upon them, instead of the whole supplementary wind-way as before. The extra length of tubing was placed upon the fixed plate, which, in this case, was pierced with four openings. The outside appearance of the moveable valve plate was merely that of a flat plate, with two bulb-like excrescences. When the valve was rotated by means of a lever, the extra tubing was brought into use. The engraving, a facsimile of that in Mr. Köhler's original prospectus,

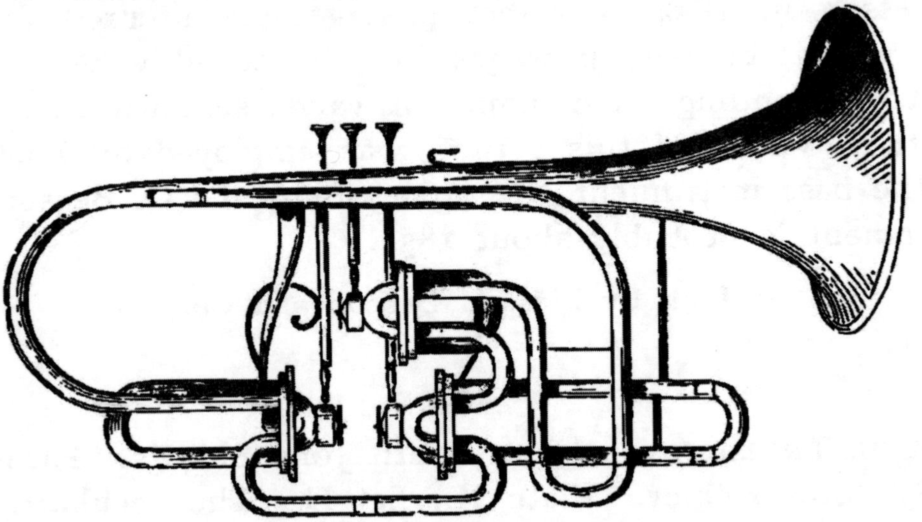

PATENT LEVER CORNET.

shows a cornet constructed with the improved patent lever valves; and these valves were applied to brass instruments of all sizes.

The jury of the Great Exhibition of 1851 apparently thought well of this principle, and remarked that "the ingenious contrivance for obtaining a free wind course to the valve instrument is highly successful." But notwithstanding this eulogium, the valves were found to leak eventually, and soon became useless, and the principle was therefore abandoned.

Lent by Messrs. Köhler and Son.

406.

Barytone, in *B*♭. With six pistons, and parabolic funnel-shaped bell, which can be turned so as to direct the sound where required. This instrument is constructed upon the celebrated six-piston system invented by Adolphe Sax. The piston action here is the reverse of the modern arrangement, the pistons cutting off successive lengths of tubing, in place of adding. The fundamental pitch of the instrument is *E* (written *f*♯), the nominal pitch of *b*♭ (written *c*) being obtained by the depression of the first valve, which shuts off the extra tubing. The depression of each successive valve cuts off tubing, raising the pitch a semitone. It will be seen, therefore, that instruments made in accordance with this system give seven independent positions, absolutely accurate in intonation, it not being possible to use any two valves together. Engraved "No. 30015, Nouveau Saxhorn Baryton en Si♭. Adolphe Saxe. Facteur. Breveté."

The harmonics employed are from the 2nd to the 8th inclusive. The open tube gives the following series:—

The pistons when depressed give the following successions:—

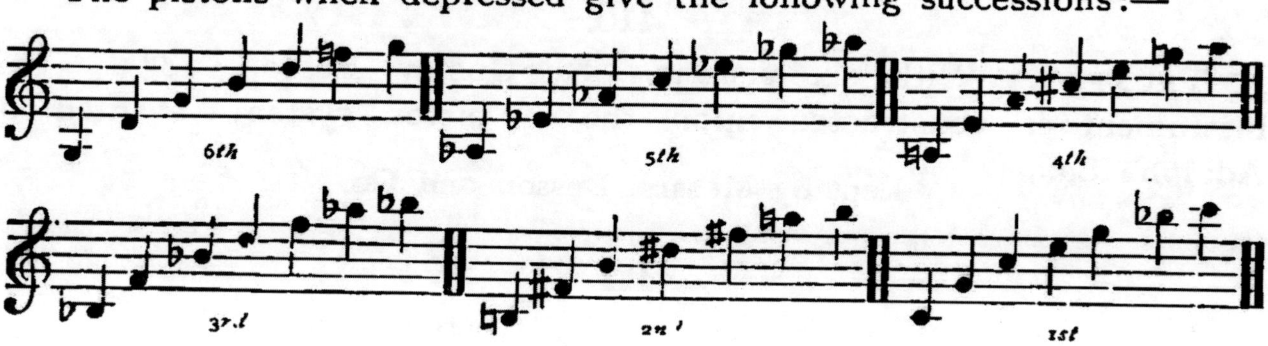

Lent by Messrs. Besson and Co.

407.

EUPHONION, in *B♭*. With seven pistons and moveable funnel-shaped bell. By A. Sax, 1854. The six pistons are independent, and produce the same successions as described for the barytone preceding. The seventh piston, worked by the thumb of the left hand, is, in its normal position, *down*, and when *raised* it lowers the pitch of the instrument by two tones and a half. It can be used in conjunction with any *one* of the others, and is intended to produce the same results as are obtained by means of the fourth valve upon modern instruments.

Lent by Messrs. Besson and Co.

408.

BOMBARDON, in *E♭*. With six pistons and moveable funnel-shaped bell. By A. Sax. 1854. The principle involved is as described above. The instrument is engraved "Nouveau Saxhorn Contrebass en *E♭*. Adolphe Saxe. Facteur. Breveté." Plate VIII., fig. C.

Lent by Messrs. Besson and Co.

409.

FLÜGEL HORN, in *B♭*. With three descending and one ascending valve. The ascending valve cuts off tubing equal to a rise in pitch of one tone; the other three valves descend by a tone, semitone, and tone and a half respectively. This was the old model used in the French infantry, and made by Adolphe Sax in 1854. Length 19 inches.

Lent by Messrs. Besson and Co.

410.

TRUMPET. With six pistons. By Gustav Besson, 1855. This instrument is constructed upon the six-piston system invented by Adolphe Sax.

Lent by Messrs. Besson and Co.

411.

EUPHONION. With six pistons. By Gustav Besson, 1855.

Lent by Messrs. Besson and Co.

412.

TROMBONE. With six pistons. By Gustav Besson, 1855. There is an alternative bell, which can be used to replace the ordinary one when it is desired to throw the sound behind the player.

Lent by Messrs. Besson and Co.

413.

TENOR FLÜGEL HORN. With five valves (two ascending and threc descending). By Adolphe Sax, 1856. The valvcs of this instrument could not be worked, and the pitch and system could not therefore be ascertained.

Lent by Messrs. Besson and Co.

414.

EUPHONION, in *B*♭. Called "Besson's Transpositeur," and made by Gustav Bcsson. This instrument is of interest as being one of the early attempts to rectify the lower register of brass instruments. It formed the subject of a patent in France in 1859, and provisional protection was granted in the same year for the invention in England. Each of the piston valves is furnished with twice the usual number of openings and air passages; one set communicates with a set of piston tubes of the ordinary length, the other with an additional set of rather longer piston tubes, which are calculated to produce sounds exactly a semitone lower in pitch than the former. The fourth valve, called the *registre*, or "transposing stop," is worked by the left hand. In the normal

No. 414.

O

position of the fourth valve the shorter set of tubings upon the first, second, and third valves are in use; upon the depression of the fourth valve the longer set of tubings are employed. The pistons are dependent, the fourth valve, when used alone, lowering the pitch of the instrument a semitone. The use of this arrangement rendered the following scales, usually difficult or impossible, easy of execution, viz.: those of *D*♭, *G*♭, *A*, and *B*, whilst the intonation of the harmonic series of *E* and of the lower register became perfectly true.

The system, compared with the same maker's patent of 1857, described upon page 189, and which was made with independent positions, is simpler; and the reduction of the number of air passages through the *registre*, or fourth valve, renders the instrument less liable to get out of order.

The same system was applied to all brass instruments, and in the case of the basses, the registre, or "transposing stop," instead of lowering the pitch a semitone, lowered it a perfect fourth, the duplicate valve tubings being constructed of the necessary additional length.

Lent by Messrs. Besson and Co.

No. 415.

415.

BARYTONE, in *B*♭, with five valves. Made by Gustav Besson about 1857. The first, second, and third valves lower the pitch of the instrument a tone, semitone, and tone and a half respectively. The fourth valve cuts off tubing, and so raises the pitch one tone. The fifth valve lowers the pitch of the instrument a semitone.

Instruments constructed upon this system were invented in 1857 by Gustav Besson and patented in France. They were known by the name "enharmonique," there being 32 different positions; their use presented many advantages, as regards both intonation and facilities for execution in all keys. This can be better understood by referring to the tablature below; the fingering of each series is placed above.

The intonation of the seventh harmonics, printed as crotchets, is, of course, not in accordance with any temperament employed in modern music. The notes printed as semibreves are produced with simple fingering; those printed as minims are produced by the aid of special fingering. The two additional valves, acting as transposers, simplify the fingering of certain keys, usually of very difficult, if not impossible, execution, besides allowing for the production of shakes of all kinds upon every note of the chromatic scale. The annexed engraving, a facsimile of that in M. Besson's specification of December 1, 1857, shows the position of the extra tubing and valves, as originally designed for a cornet thus constructed. This system was shortly afterwards applied to all brass instruments.

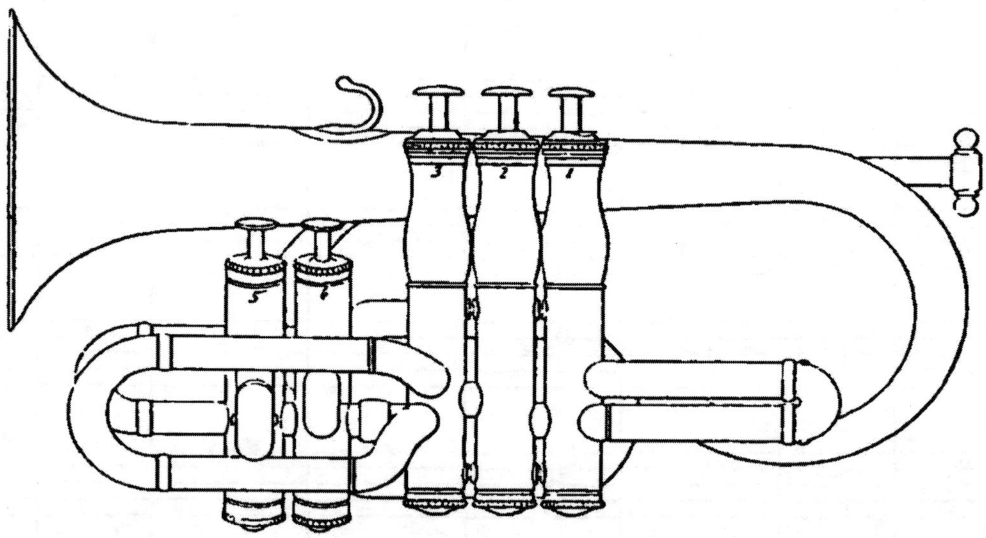

A rather different arrangement, but designed with much the same object, had been made by M. Gustav Besson in 1855. To reduce the mechanism a single rotary cylinder, constructed with two separate

Fig. 3.

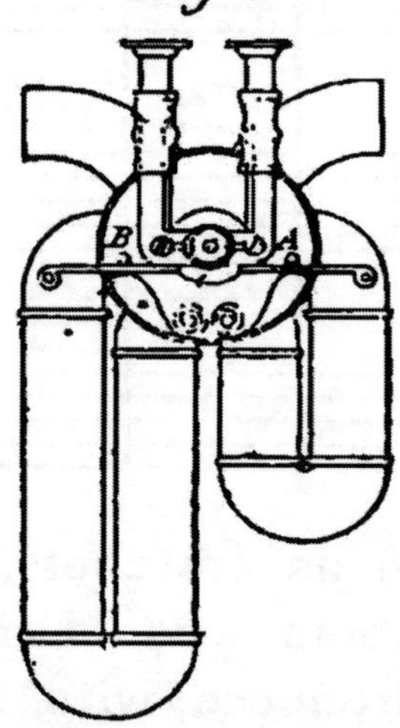

Fig. 4.

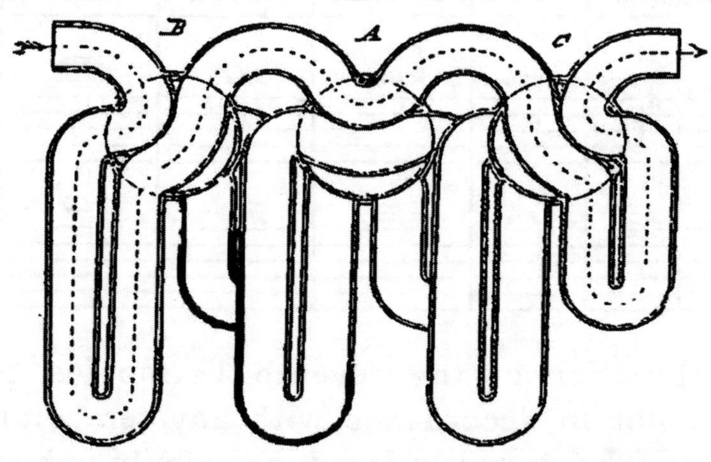

touch-pieces which could be moved either way, was employed. This enabled, by the use of each cylinder, three separate positions to be obtained. The diagram, a facsimile of that in the French specification of 1855, enables this to be more easily understood. Fig. 3 represents the exterior of one of the cylinders. Fig. 4 is a section; the extra tubing may be, of course, of any length required. A, B, and C (Fig. 4) show the different positions of the cylinder when at rest, and when depressed either way. This arrangement, as practically employed, allowed of twenty-six different positions, and the diameter of the wind passages through the cylinders not being constricted, the intonation of the instrument did not suffer.

Lent by Messrs. Besson and Co.

416.

B♭ Contra-Bass. A monster model, made by Henry Distin for use in the "Flügel Horn Union" in 1862. With three valves; there are two passages only in each valve. The four holes in each piston, being placed vertically above each other, are connected in pairs by semi-circular passages built up within the valves, so that there is no abrupt turn in any of the wind passages. The height of this instrument from the ground is nearly eight feet.

Lent by Messrs. Boosey and Co.

417.

Euphonion. With extra set of slides to tune "fourth valve notes." This instrument shows an early device to bring the notes produced by the fourth valve into tune. There are two distinct sets of passages through the valves, and corresponding lengths of tubings; the lower set of three passages in each valve is ordinarily in use; the upper set of three passages in each valve, and duplicate set of tubings, comes into use only when the fourth valve is down. The instrument as it stands is in *B♭*. With the fourth valve depressed the pitch is lowered to *F*, the duplicate valve tubings being tuned to agree with this note. This system was probably designed originally by Antoine Courtois, but discarded by him subsequently, and it somewhat resembles that employed by Gustav Besson in his "registre" of 1857, described previously.

Lent by Messrs. Higham and Co.

418.

EUPHONION, in *B♭*. With long fourth valve. The tubing in connection with the first, second, and third valves passes through the fourth valve. In the fourth valve there are extra passages, so placed that when the valve is down a duplicate set of tubing is brought into action with the first, second, and third valves. This duplicate set of tubings is tuned to agree with *F*, which becomes the pitch note of the instrument when the fourth valve is down. The extreme length of the fourth valve, and the fact that there are nine distinct passages through it, constitutes the weak point in this arrangement of pistons. This system was designed originally by Adolphe Sax. Stamped "Distin, London," and probably made about 1867.

Lent by Messrs. Boosey and Co.

419.

TROMBONE, in *B♭*. Large calibre, with four compensating pistons. Made by Boosey and Co. With the fourth valve down this instrument can be used as a bass trombone in *F;* as by the compensating arrangement, the valve slides, on the depression of the fourth valve, are automatically adjusted to the lengths required for an instrument in *F*.

This instrument was designed by Mr. D. J. Blaikley, and made as an experiment in 1874. The essential difference between the valve system employed, and any other previously designed on a "compensating" principle, lies in the reduction of the number of passages through the valves. The idea, as worked out for three-valve instruments, became the subject of the "Compensating Pistons" patent in 1878 (No. 4618), and described, in the introduction to this section, upon page 191.

Lent by Messrs. Boosey and Co.

420.

CORNET, in *B♭*. By Antoine Courtois, with removeable echo attachment. This instrument is one of the original cornets of this maker, made about the year preceding his death.

The echo attachment appears to have been either invented, or introduced into England, by the late Mr. John Köhler, instrument maker, of Henrietta Street. It consisted then, as in this instrument, merely of an extra bell with a contracted mouth, which could be brought into play by the depression of a piston. Whether the credit of the invention does not belong rightly to Sax is extremely doubtful, for these echo cornets appear to have been made by both Sax in Paris, and in England by Distin, much about the same time. The *Sunday Times*, however, of Sept. 11, 1859, ascribes the invention to Mr. Köhler. No patent would appear to have been taken out for it, and the idea was adopted universally by all instrument makers.

Lent by Colonel Shaw-Hellier.

421.

CORNET, in *B♭*. By Courtois. Koenig model. Shown as an example of a cornet largely used at the present day.

Lent by S. A. Chappell, Esq.

422.

CORNET, in *B♭*, with three light valves. By Boosey and Co. The valve is the "Patent Light Valve" of Mr. Hy. Distin slightly modified. The patent has expired.

Lent by Messrs. Boosey and Co.

423.

CORNET, with piston water-key. This appliance, outwardly resembling a supplementary piston, permits the moisture to be removed from the instrument without removing the mouthpiece from the lips.

Lent by Messrs. Rudall, Carte and Co.

424.

CORNET, in *B♭*. With Mahillon's regulating pistons. For an explanation of the "regulating" pistons, an ingenious device for securing correct intonation, see the introduction to this section, page 193.

Lent by Messrs. Mahillon and Co.

425.

CORNET, modern. By Butler, London, 1890.

Lent by G. Butler, Esq.

426.

CORNET-ARBAN. The system upon which this instrument is constructed was invented and patented in France in November 1883 by M. J. B. Arban. The instrument stands in *C*, thus playing the written sounds, and not as a transposing instrument. There are four valves, the first, second, and third being placed as ordinary pistons and lowering the pitch a tone, semitone, and tone and a half respectively; the fourth is a cylinder connected with a lever, and is worked by the middle finger of the left hand, lowering the pitch of the instrument a tone and a half. The slide of the third piston is fitted with a mechanism, worked by the index finger of the left hand, by which it can be lengthened instantly to produce a difference in pitch of two tones, instead of a tone and a half, its normal position. The pistons therefore lower the pitch a semitone successively, giving the harmonic series of *B*♮, *B*♭, *A*♮, and *A*♭. Hence, there are five positions upon the instrument, providing notes of perfectly accurate intonation. To render this system absolutely perfect, there must be two more positions. These are arranged for by an ingenious piece of mechanism, which connects the slides of the first and second pistons with the lever of the fourth, and therefore when the latter is depressed, the slides of the first and second pistons are automatically lengthened, closing again when the lever of the fourth valve is released.

The tablature of this instrument gives in all a choice of twenty-one different positions, instead of seven; and hence, it allows for the production of numerous enharmonic intervals, usually possible only upon the slide trombone, or stringed instruments, such as the violin. The system can, of course, be applied to all valved instruments, and with the larger varieties has much to recommend it. A complete method was written for this most ingenious instrument by the inventor, M. Arban, the celebrated cornet player, and late professor at the *Conservatoire*, Paris.

M. Arban finding that the additional weight of this cornet, combined with the complicated mechanism, was a serious obstacle to its being generally adopted by artists, produced the year following, in conjunction with M. Bouvet, an instrument of simpler construction.

M. Bouvet, a civil engineer, had already turned his attention to the construction of valved instruments, and had invented a system of unique design, and which had many advantages. It consisted in the employment of seven independent positions, for which six pistons were required. To simplify the fingering the *octave* and *super-octave* harmonics *only* were employed, the flats and sharps being produced by the depression of two touch-pieces, connected with two cylinders of peculiar construction, called *distributeurs mécaniques*. The system, although patented in France in 1884, does not seem to have been followed up by the inventor.

MM. Arban and Bouvet produced in conjunction in 1885 an instrument having the advantages of the Arban cornet of 1884, but without the complicated mechanism. In the Arban-Bouvet cornet there were the same 21 positions; but practically 14 only were employed. And the success of this instrument, the use of which M. Arban rendered obligatory for his pupils, was such that a further improvement was made, by which the system was applied to cornets with three pistons only. The Arban-Bouvet system was also applied generally to brass instruments of all kinds.

Lent by S. A. Chappell, Esq.

427.

FLÜGEL HORN, in *B*♭. With three patent compensating pistons. By Boosey and Co.

Lent by Messrs. Boosey and Co.

428.

HORN. With two pistons and four crooks. By Antoine Courtois. Shown as an example of an instrument much employed. The model is copied from that of Raoux, whose instruments are now scarce, and highly prized by horn players. Greatest width 22 inches.

Lent by S. A. Chappell, Esq.

429.

HORN. With three pistons and four crooks. By Antoine Courtois. Of a similar model to preceding instrument, but with the addition of the third valve. Greatest length 44 inches, greatest width 21½ inches.

Lent by S. A. Chappell, Esq.

430.

TENOR SAXHORN, in *E♭*. With three light valves. By Boosey and Co.

Lent by Messrs. Boosey and Co.

431.

TENOR COR, in *F*, with *E♭* crook. With three light valves. By Boosey and Co.

The tenor cor has a bell of the French horn type, though not quite so wide across the mouth. The mouth pipe of the instrument tapers down to fit a mouthpiece, the shank of which is, in size, between that of the French horn and tenor saxhorn. The cup of the mouth-piece is a deep cone, and this, combined with the taper of the instrument, results in producing a tone quality much resembling that of the French horn. Exact imitation is, of course, impossible, since the same notes upon the horn are related to a different fundamental, the eighth harmonic on the horn corresponding with the fourth upon this instrument.

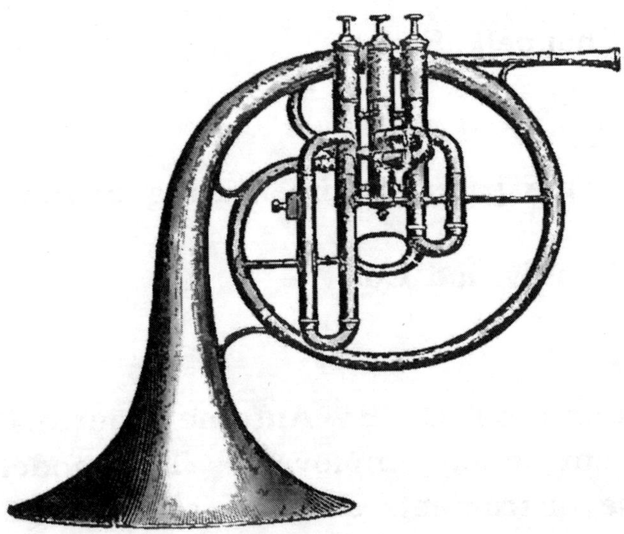

TENOR COR.

The tenor cor is an improvement upon the tenor saxhorn, which, being virtually a bugle, has too bold a tone to replace the horn. The Koenig horn, designed for the same purpose in 1855 by the player Koenig, and made by Antoine Courtois, was a saxhorn constructed in the shape of the horn and with a downward bell; it differed little in its proportions from the ordinary tenor saxhorn; a slight deepening of the cup of the mouth-piece and the position of the bell somewhat modified the tone. The Koenig horn and tenor cor are both used in military bands in which French horns do not exist.

Lent by Messrs. Boosey and Co.

432.

CORNOPHONE, in *F*, with alternative slide for *E*♭. By Besson and Co. The instrument is virtually an improved tenor saxhorn, but as the proportions of the bore are different, and the taper is much greater, the tone-quality more nearly resembles that of the French horn. The mouthpiece is a deep cone, almost exactly like that of the horn.

CORNOPHONE.

These instruments are constructed of various sizes, so as to form a complete family; and certain of them have been lately employed by M. Lamoureux, in his orchestra at Paris, in place of tubas, for the performance of portions of Wagner's "Walküre."

Lent by Messrs. Besson and Co.

433.

BARYTONE SAXHORN OR ALTHORN, in *B*♭. By Boosey and Co. With three compensating pistons.

Lent by Messrs. Boosey and Co.

434.

EUPHONION, in *C*. Four compensating pistons; engraved and electro-plated. The euphonion in *C* is commonly used in the orchestra, the *B*♭ instrument being the more suitable for military bands.

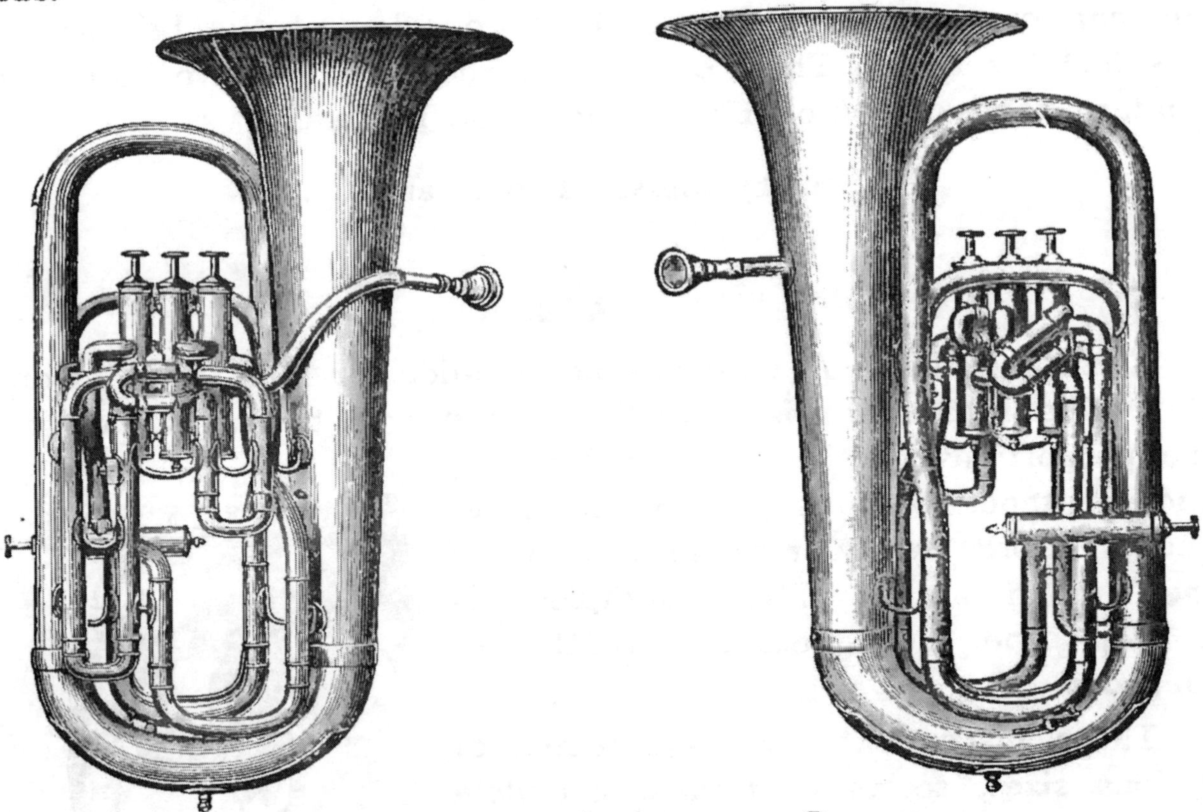

EUPHONION. WITH COMPENSATING PISTONS.

The false intonation below

inherent in the ordinary four-valve instrument, is by the compensating principle corrected, so that a true chromatic scale can be obtained down to the pedal *C*, without false fingering. And as can be seen from the engraving the extra weight of this arrangement is almost nothing.

Lent by Messrs. Boosey and Co.

435.

EUPHONION, with extra short action. The short action in this and the instruments numbered 439 and 442 is gained by constructing the air passages through the valves with a sectional area of oval shape. Hence, without diminishing the section of the wind-ways, it is possible to place the holes in the pumps at a greatly diminished vertical interval. This "oval bore" has been employed by different makers at various times, and is popular with some professional players on account of the rapidity of the shake it allows of, which is nearly as rapid as that obtained by a cylinder action.

Lent by Messrs. Rudall, Carte and Co.

436.

EUPHONION, in *B*♭. By Boosey & Co. With four compensating pistons. Used both for harmonies and as a solo instrument in military and brass bands.

Lent by Messrs. Boosey and Co.

437.

EUPHONION. With five valves. By Besson & Co. The valve system is that usually applied to four-valve instruments. The fifth valve lowers the pitch a semitone, and thus is useful as a transposer, transposing instantaneously a semitone lower. The use of this extra valve allows too of the production of certain notes, *i.e.* *B*♮ and *C*♯, that do not exist upon the ordinary four-valved instruments. By the help of the fifth valve certain scales, usually difficult or impossible, are of easy execution; while the intonation of the notes,

usually sharp, is corrected.

Lent by Messrs. Besson and Co.

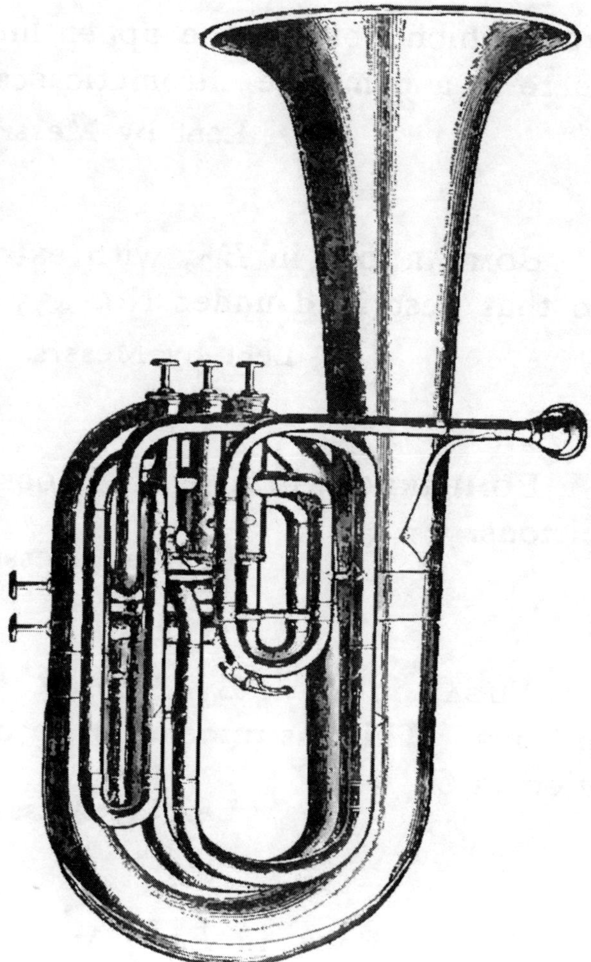

EUPHONION. WITH FIVE VALVES.

438.

Tuba, in *F*. With four compensating pistons. By Boosey and Co. The larger bass saxhorns, and modern varieties of them, are usually called *tubas* in the orchestra, and *bombardons* in military bands, the difference is merely in the name. The lowest open note of this instrument is

but effective valve notes can be produced down to

from which note to the upper limit of the compass of the instrument there is a complete chromatic scale of about 3½ octaves.

Lent by Messrs. Boosey and Co.

439.

Bombardon, in *E*♭, with extra short action. The action is similar to that described under No. 435.

Lent by Messrs. Rudall, Carte and Co.

440.

Bombardon, in *E*♭. By Boosey and Co. With three compensating pistons.

Lent by Messrs. Boosey and Co.

441.

Tuba, in *C*. By Boosey and Co. With three compensating pistons. This instrument is an octave lower in pitch than the euphonion in *C*.

Lent by Messrs. Boosey and Co.

442.

Contra-Bass, in *B*♭. An octave lower than the euphonion in *B*♭. This instrument has the short action described under No. 435.

Lent by Messrs. Rudall, Carte and Co.

443.

Contra-Bass, in *B♭*. With three compensating pistons. By Boosey and Co.

Lent by Messrs. Boosey and Co.

444.

Antoniophone, or Snail Model. By Adolphe Sax. This curious-looking instrument is merely an ordinary bombardon; the tubing is arranged so that the instrument may resemble a snail shell as much as is possible, the valves, three in number, being in the centre of the coils. The bell is detachable, and the instrument can be played either with the bell uppermost, or under the arm, as that of a French horn.

The shape was originally designed by the late Antoine Courtois, and was named after the inventor.

Lent by Messrs. Besson and Co.

445.

Euphonion, with three pistons. The bell can be turned so as to throw the sound in any direction required. Instruments thus constructed were made by Gustav Besson, from 1851 to 1855, and called by him Neoform. The moveable bells were, however, made both by Courtois and by Adolphe Sax about the same period. The tubing of this instrument is wound round itself in snail fashion, the valve mechanism being inside. The extreme width is 20½ inches.

Lent by Messrs. Besson and Co.

446.

Tenor Saxhorn, with seven distinct bells. Designed by the cornet player Distin, who used to play upon it at various places of entertainment. The instrument is said to have cost its designer in experiments and actual workmanship nearly £400! This extraordinary instrumental curiosity was made between 1860 and 1865. There are six (independent) ascending pistons, the system being that of Sax, described previously.

There is also an echo bell, which can be used with any one of the pistons, by the depression of a supplementary valve, at the player's will. An instrument somewhat similar to this, made by Sax, is now in the Museum of the *Conservatoire* at Brussels.

Lent by Messrs. Boosey and Co.

447.

HORN, with valve attachment. By Moritz. The valve attachment is placed just below the mouthpiece, and puts the instrument in *B*♭. The valves lower the pitch a semitone and a tone respectively. The total length of the tubing is 3 feet 11 inches, the instrument being shaped like a large U.

Lent by the *Grossherzogliches Museum* in Darmstadt.

448.

FLÜGEL HORN (SOPRANO), in *E*♭. Formerly used in French bands, but abandoned in 1850, as being too fatiguing to blow.

Lent by Messrs. Besson and Co.

449.

TRUMPET, in *E*♭. With removeable chromatic attachment. Exhibited in the 1851 Exhibition. Length 1 foot 6 inches.

Lent by Messrs. Besson and Co.

450.

TRUMPET, in *E*♭, three valves. Formerly used in French cavalry bands. The instrument is practically only an ordinary chromatic trumpet; the bell is placed upright, like that of a modern euphonion. Length 2 feet 1 inch.

Lent by Messrs. Besson and Co.

451.

QUARTETT OF FLÜGEL HORNS. Used formerly by the bands of the French Chasseurs à pied.

Lent by Messrs. Besson and Co.

452.

Horn, in *C*. By Moritz. This instrument is in shape very similar to No. 447, but has not the chromatic attachment described.

Lent by the *Grossherzogliches Museum* in Darmstadt.

453.

Valve French Horn. With upright bell, as formerly used in the Russian Army. By Gustav Besson. Length 25½ inches.

Lent by Messrs. Besson and Co.

454.

Barytone. French regulation pattern. Remarkable only for the poorness of its design.

Lent by Messrs. Besson and Co.

455.

Trumpet. Ovoid shape. By Hatsany, 1840. The tubing of this trumpet is wound in a flat convolute of oval plan, in order to shorten the length of the instrument. An additional length of tubing, brought into use by the depression of a valve, lowers the pitch a tone. Length 1 foot 2½ inches.

Lent by Messrs. Besson and Co.

456.

Slide Trombone (Alto), in *F*. With one piston, lowering the instrument a fourth, in order to facilitate the production of the notes usually gained by the employment of the seventh position. By Gustav Besson. Length 1 foot 11 inches.

Lent by Messrs. Besson and Co.

457.

In order to show in detail the construction of some of the most important valve actions that have been used from time to time upon brass instruments, the following models were exhibited :—

1. A model of the action generally attributed to Stölzel, and consisting of two pistons only, both being of an exceedingly small bore.

This action is in every way similar to that employed in the cornet made by Ch. Sax, of Brussels, and previously described (No. 381).

2. A model of an action frequently employed in the early days of valve instruments; there are three pistons, the arrangement of the air-passages and extra tubing being similar to that described under No. 388.

3. A model of the early French action described under No. 398.

4. A model of an action designed by Adolphe Sax. The pistons are unusually thick, and, for the size of the bore, very heavy. The diameter of the bore is only ·38 inch. The passages for the open notes run *straight* through the centre of the valves. When the valve is depressed, the passages bringing the extra tubing into connection are disposed at right angles to the main windway.

5. A model of the system called "Besson's Clear Bore." This action was patented in France in 1855 by Gustav Besson, and it was virtually an improvement upon that of Perinet. Previous to this the passage of the second valve presented an angularity, and consequently the notes produced by the combination of 1 + 2, or 2 + 3, or 1 + 2 + 3 valves were of bad quality. The pistons in this action preserved the same sectional area of the wind column throughout, and allowed a bullet, fitting the bore exactly, to pass through, in whatever position the valves might be. Eight pistons of different kinds were included in the patent, and they could be assembled in 512 different ways! And M. Besson's second valve could be used with first and third pistons of the Perinet or Rödel design.

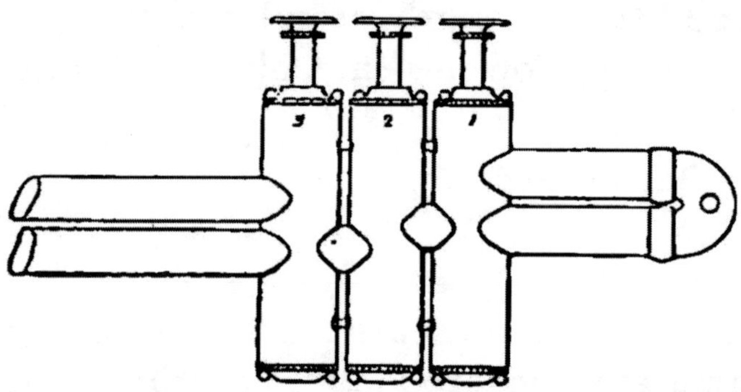

The engraving, a facsimile of that in the French specification, represents the usual form of the action as first made, the springs being placed below the pumps. The specification itself should be consulted for further detail.

6. A sectional model of the "Courtois" action, made by Henry Distin.

7. A sectional model of the "Patent Light Valve" invented by Henry Distin. This "light" valve is largely used now by various

instrument makers, the patent having expired long since. The piston, or *pump*, is made of a *single* tube of metal only; the air-passages are fastened into it with silver solder. The spindle and spring were also included in the patent. Previous to this valves had been made of *two* tubes, one placed inside the other, the inner tube being previously fitted with the air-passages. The extra weight of this latter arrangement, and its consequent influence upon rapid execution, is of course evident.

8. A sectional model of the "Compensating Pistons" invented by Mr. D. J. Blaikley, and made by Messrs. Boosey and Co. The compensating pistons are described at length in the introduction to this section.

9. Two models of the "Cylinder" action. This arrangement is largely used in Germany and Austria. The *pump* is replaced by a four-way cock of brass, turned perfectly true, and moved by a series of cranks connected with a key. The action is extremely delicate, but for solo playing has many advantages, not the least being the very rapid and singularly clear shake of which it is capable. Indeed, the rapidity of a shake produced thus can be equalled only by that upon the flute.

NOTE.—As it has been found almost impracticable to adopt a uniform scheme of comparative pitch notation for instruments of all families, described in this work, without danger of misconceptions arising in certain important cases, the following may be useful. The notation shows in real sounds the 4th harmonics produced: the 4th harmonic being the usual tuning note upon most brass instruments.

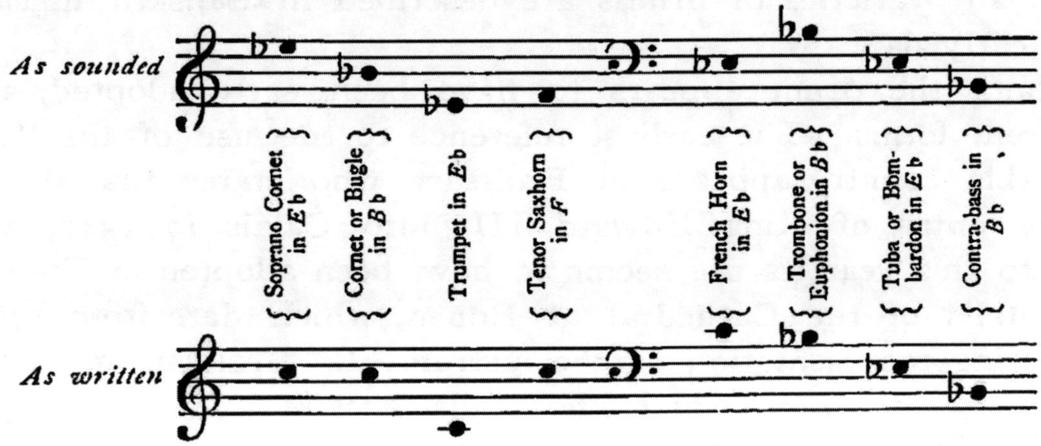

XII.

CLASS—INSTRUMENTS OF PERCUSSION.

THE employment of instruments of percussion appears to date from very remote times. Instruments of this kind are now usually classified as follows:—

(1) Those of definite sonorousness, such as harmonica and kettledrums.

(2) Those of indefinite sonorousness, such as the large drum (*grosse caisse*) and the side drum (*caisse claire*) used in the orchestra, or in military bands; also cymbals, triangles, sistra, &c.

The introduction of the drum to Europe has frequently been attributed to the Moors, who are said to have brought it from the East with other musical instruments. Whether this idea can be accepted as correct is extremely doubtful. It is, nevertheless, certain that the drum was used in Germany from very early times, and it seems more than probable that the use of this instrument was first adopted by the Romans, from the East, and carried by their conquests into different countries of Europe, whence it became generally adopted. That we must look to the East for the real origin of the drum appears absolutely certain; for the earliest civilization was of course Eastern, and the old sculptures — Assyrian, Egyptian, and Indian—prove beyond doubt the ancient popularity of the instrument, and many varieties of drums are described in Sanskrit musical treatises of early date.

In England the drum appears to have been early adopted, and it had different forms. The earliest reference to the use of the "big drum" in this country appears in Froissart, who states that it was used at the entry of King Edward III. into Calais in 1347, and subsequent to this year its use seems to have been adopted in France. Upon the stalls of the Cathedral at Rouen, which date from 1467, is an interesting representation of the instrument. Froissart mentions another variety of drum which he calls *nacaire*. Now *naqqarch* is the word still employed in Arabia, Persia, and India for drums, and it is applied generally to kettledrums. Whether *kettledrums* were meant by Froissart, or not, is a point of great interest; for, unless this is so, the use of the kettledrum in England would not appear to have been adopted until a very much later date, about 1606. Kettledrums, however, were in use in Germany at a period more remote, and Prætorius (*Syntagma*, 1618), gives an illustration of a pair of kettledrums, tuned by means of screws, and which differ little in appearance from those of modern times. In Nicholls' well-known *Progression of James 1st* mention is made of the entertainment of Christian IV. of Denmark, and H. Roberts, quoted by Nicholls, describes particularly the kettledrums then used. As this is apparently the first mention of the use of the instrument in England, it is better to quote the passage; he says, "the King of Denmark's drume, riding upon a horse, with two drumes, one on each side of the horse's necke, whereon hee strooke two little mallets of wood, a thing verie admirable to the common sorte, and much admired."

The side-drums of two centuries ago, and earlier periods, were of much larger size than the small modern instruments. It has sometimes been said that the popularity of the drum dates from the time of Richard I., who had become accustomed to their use during the Crusades, and it is certain that from that period the drum became recognised in this country as an essentially military instrument. It was frequently carried upon the back of a man, who walked immediately in front of the drummer, and this practice was continued till the latter half of the last century. There are many old prints still to be met with that show this. A method somewhat similar was applied to kettledrums, and many of the works upon pageantry, which contain illustrations, show kettledrums carried in this manner. The side-drums, up till the reign of Queen Elizabeth, were, as has been said, of very large size. They were carried almost horizontally at the left side of the player, and were of course beaten upon one head only. In point of size they were rather larger than the *tenor* drum of the present day, and which is occasionally used in military bands. Thoinot Arbeau (*Orchesographie*, 1589) gives an illustration of the side drummer of that date, and from contemporary works it seems that this method of using the instrument was universal. Prætorius and Père Mersenne, too, describe the use of the drum; and it is interesting to note that the employment of the *snare* is noticed by all three writers. These side-drums were generally played in bands, associated with fifes of various kinds, and in the 16th century the use of these bands had become almost as universal as at the present day.

Of the introduction of the drum into the orchestra it is more easy to speak with certainty. Left previously to military use exclusively, they were first introduced in the orchestra of the Grande Écurie by Lully, and since that time have been considered a necessary adjunct. At first a single pair of kettledrums were employed; Berlioz, however, introduced the use of three, and this number is now to be found in most large orchestras in Europe. According to M. Lavoix (*Histoire de l'Instrumentation*), the side-drum—caisse claire—was made use of by Marais, a composer now almost forgotten, who lived from 1636 to 1728; and it was employed with effect in the tempest scene in his opera of "Alcione." Gluck afterwards made use of it in "Iphigénie en Tauride," and the example thus set was followed generally by other composers. The tambourine, or tambour de basque, was once used in military bands, but, except for special effects, its use has long since been discontinued.

Of other percussion instruments it is only necessary to state that, of Eastern origin, they are used merely as rhythmical accompaniments. Cymbals and triangles are found in all military bands, and an occasional use is made of castanets.

The collection of percussion instruments in the Exhibition was very large; but to avoid needless repetition, it is thought more advisable to give a general view of this section, than to describe each instrument under a separate heading.

The kettledrums and trumpets used on State occasions, and graciously lent by Her Majesty the Queen, were placed in a case by themselves, and attracted much attention. The banners were of silk beautifully embroidered and fringed with gold lace. The drums were principally of interest as having been made by Cornelius Ward, and being an early example of a mode of tuning invented and patented by him in 1837. This tuning arrangement, now so commonly employed, consists of a right and left handed screw, acting in conjunction with a series of pulleys, and so arranged that, by a single turn of the hand, all the braces become tightened simultaneously. The drums measure in diameter 1 foot 4 inches, and 1 foot 5 inches, respectively; and are 9 inches in depth.

In another case could be seen the celebrated pair of silver kettle-drums belonging to the Royal Horse Guards. These beautiful drums are engraved with the following inscription:—

Given by King George the Third,
April the 23rd, 1805,
To his Royal Regiment of Horse Guards
as a Testimonial of its Honourable and Military Conduct
on all Occasions.

The drums are 14 inches in depth, and measure in diameter 1 foot 11 inches, and 1 foot 9 inches respectively. They are represented in the frontispiece.

A side-drum of the reign of Queen Elizabeth, measuring 1 foot 10¾ inches by 1 foot 10½ inches, lent by Messrs. Henry Potter and Co., was of interest. This drum belonged originally to the armoury at the Tower of London, and was sold as "condemned stores" some fifty years ago to the late Mr. Potter. There were also a set of old drums belonging to the "Royal Revenue Corps," and a set belonging to the "Law Association," all of which were of interest. Messrs. Ward and Co. lent a curious bass drum built in staves in the same way that a cask is made; this drum measured 2 feet by 2 feet 6 inches wide, and in construction is probably unique.

There was also a side-drum which formerly belonged to a regiment of Prince Charles Stuart's army, and was left by a straggler, during the retreat in 1745, in the village of Arkholme, Lancashire. This drum remained as an heirloom in the same cottage family in which it was then left, until it was bought, in 1880, by the Rev. W. B. Grenside, of Melling, its present possessor. It measures 1 foot 5 inches by 1 foot 4¾ inches, and it still bears the marks of bullet holes.

A side-drum of almost the same date and shape, lent by Colonel Shaw-Hellier, measured 1 foot 7 inches by 1 foot 6 inches.

From the collection of Messrs. Henry Potter and Co., were lent interesting old kettledrums of the early part of this century, and once used in the Honourable East India Company's service. An old bass drum of the same period measured 2 feet 6 inches in length by 1 foot 10 inches in width. Messrs. J. and R. Glen, of Edinburgh, lent a drum dating from 1794, of almost identically the same size; an old brass side-drum, once belonging to the 25th Regiment, and parted with by them in 1796, was 1 foot 4¾ inches long by 1 foot 3½ inches wide. Three side-drums, made about 1850, were lent by Mr. Butler, and differ little in shape.

A bass drum of great interest was lent by Messrs. Mahillon and Co. This drum is painted with the Royal Arms, and with an inscription "VII. or Queen's Own Hussars." Its history is curious and deserves to be recorded. After the battle of Waterloo it was found by a Belgian gentleman living at Brain l'Allend, and was taken away by him, as a memento of the day. After his death this drum was given by his son to the local band at Boondael, from whose possession it passed into the hands of its present owners.

A collection of curious old drums, and portions of the shells of drums, belonging to Messrs. George Potter and Co., the well-known drum makers, of Aldershot, was disposed in artistically designed trophies round the walls of the gallery. The collection embraced a drum 30 by 24 inches, said to have been used at the battle of Blenheim; also one 30 by 28 inches used at Waterloo. There were portions of the shells of drums once belonging to the 2nd Battalion of the 17th Regiment; the 56th; the 2nd Battalion 6th Royal Warwick; the 1st Life Guards; the 1st Battalion 12th Regiment; the 53rd Light Infantry; the 2nd Battalion 8th King's. Some models of modern drums, made by Messrs. Potter, served to show more the recent construction of these instruments.

A pair of kettledrums taken from the French at the battle of Dettingen by the 7th Dragoon Guards, then Ligonier's Horse, were not the least interesting of these military relics, and attracted the attention of many. These drums were, after the action, presented to the regiment, in recognition of the fact that, as stated in the official accounts, "Ligonier's Horse here gained great reputation." Of great interest, too, were an odd looking little pair of Afghan kettledrums, belonging to the officers of the XXth Regiment, and taken at Kandahar on September 1st, 1880.

Of the old tambourines formerly used in military bands there were several examples; the two which attracted the most attention being an instrument 1 foot 8 inches in diameter, dating from 1750, now in the possession of Colonel Shaw-Hellier; and one, of rather later date, belonging to Messrs. Henry Potter and Co.

There were specimens of the old Turkish Crescent (*chapeau chinois*), once a favourite adjunct to military bands, and known in former years by the familiar nick-name of "Jingling Johnny." They consisted of brass hoops, hung with little bells tuned more or less musically, and ornamented with gilded crescents and long streaming tails of horse-hair. They were carried upon poles some six feet high, and, within the memory of some living, negroes were specially enlisted for this duty, and sometimes also to beat the tambourines. Two specimens of "Jingling Johnnies" belonging to the Edinburgh University represented probably the most imposing examples of this noisy implement. Of late years a place, as regards outward appearance, somewhat similar to that once occupied by the Turkish Crescent would appear to have been taken by the Glockenspiel, which, though more musical in quality of tone, yet does not combine well with brass and reed instruments; except for special effect the Glockenspiel is better laid aside. This instrument, now constructed of vibrating bars of steel beaten with metal striker, takes its origin from the wooden Strofiedel, which of late years has appeared occasionally in the orchestra, and has been used with such effect by M. Saint-Saëns in his well-known *Danse macabre*.

APPENDIX.

AN ESSAY ON MUSICAL PITCH.

BY D. J. BLAIKLEY.

THE examination and comparison of a number of instruments made at different times and in different countries, and designed with reference to different scale systems, bring into prominence the question of musical pitch. Indeed, some consideration of it cannot be neglected or ignored if a confusion of ideas is to be avoided as regards the objects aimed at by the makers of, and performers upon, the instruments described in this Catalogue.

The "pitch" of a note is its position, high or low, in the whole range of sound, and can only be definitely determined by measuring the frequency of the vibrations causing that note; in this country it is reckoned according to the number of double or complete vibrations, or swings to and fro, per second. Although it is only of recent years that accurate means have been devised for measuring vibrational values, it must be remembered that the sense and perception of pitch, both relative and absolute, may, and does, exist in a high degree, without any conscious knowledge of vibrations; it still remains, however, that the difference of vibrational values, as manifested by beats, is the readiest and most accurate means of determining slight departures from consonance, even to the highly-trained ear.

The pitch of a note as determined by the measurement of its vibrational frequency is, for the sake of distinction, called its "absolute pitch"; its relationship to a given standard, or to other notes in its own scale, is its "relative pitch." We may with propriety speak of a sound as being low or high, apart from any idea of a standard pitch, accordingly as our ears tell us that it lies towards one extreme or the other, either of our total range of hearing, or of the total range of some particular instrument; but when we say that it is flat or sharp, some standard is either expressly or impliedly referred to. For instance, *G* on the first line of the bass clef  may properly be called a low note, absolutely considered, and would probably be so described by every one in popular language; but if a certain precise vibrational value, say, of 100 vibrations, were given to the note, it would be sharp relatively to the French Diapason Normal standard, and flat relatively to our Philharmonic standard. Again, the note *e'*,  considered absolutely, could not be described either as a low or a high note, for it lies at about the middle of the range of hearing, but it is high with respect to the compass of a man's voice, and low with respect to that of a woman. Whether in any particular case it is flat or sharp, can only be determined by reference to a standard.

For many years previous to 1880 it had been generally recognized that considerable changes had from time to time been accepted in the numerical vibrational value of a note bearing a certain name, as *a'* or *c''*; in other words, the *a'* or *c''* had been at times higher, and at times lower, than at others. The true character and extent of these changes had, however, never been fully investigated or tabulated until the late Mr. Alex. J. Ellis took up the examination of these points, and our present exact knowledge of this branch of the subject dates from March 1880, when he published in the *Journal of the Society of Arts* his paper "On the History of Musical Pitch." So far as the following notes are concerned with the history of the matter, the facts have been drawn chiefly from Mr. Ellis's work.

Standards of Pitch.—Before entering in any detail upon the various pitches that have been and are in use, it will be convenient to note that a standard may be either theoretical or actual. Now a theoretical standard can be brought into practical use only through a tuning-fork or other such instrument, and if such an instrument is officially sealed or in any way certified, it, in itself, becomes an actual standard, although it may not agree with the theoretical value it is intended to represent. As an example of a purely theoretical pitch, the customary scientific pitch of 512 vibs. for *c''* may be taken; this is based upon the number 2—512 being equal to 2 raised to the ninth power (2^9). On the other hand, the standard forks made for the Society of Arts in 1860, which were intended to represent *a′* 444 and *c″* 528, are really *a′* 445·7 and *c″* 534·5, so that the actual standard, as represented by the fork, was in the case of the *c″* about one-fifth of a semi-tone higher than its theoretical value of *c″* 528.* As an instance of close agreement between theoretical and actual values the French Diapason Normal should be named. This fork, intended to give 435 vibs., is by the best measurements found to give 435·4. This exceedingly small difference, although distinctly and easily measurable, is of no practical consequence in music.

At the present day the tuning-fork is universally accepted as the most generally convenient instrument for use, both as a standard and as a carrier or measurer of pitch, but it cannot be too clearly understood that in the sense in which we speak of "the standard yard"† or "the standard pound"‡ there is no standard of pitch in this country. The case is different in France, where the Diapason Normal, referred to above, exists, not merely as a theoretical standard, but as an actual fork carefully preserved in the Museum of the *Conservatoire* at Paris. The superiority of the tuning-fork over the old pitch-pipe blown by the mouth lies in the small degree of its variation; as the slight variation which is due to changes of temperature is known, it can always be allowed for when accurate observations are required. The objections to the tuning-fork, when used to give the pitch for a band, are its comparatively weak tone and evanescent sound. Metal reeds, such as those used in harmoniums, are, *if sounded under a constantly equal pressure of wind*, in some ways preferable to tuning-forks, for their tone is strong, and they can be kept sounding for any

* This value (528) for *c″* was advocated by the Society of Arts Committee, because on this basis the intervals of the major diatonic scale can be represented by whole numbers. This is true, however, only of the scale of *c* in just intonation, which gives for *a′* 440; the *a′* 444 (nominal) of the Society of Arts is in equal temperament to *c″* 528.

† The British Standard Yard is the distance, at the temperature of 62° Fahrenheit, between two marks on a certain bar which is kept in the office of the Exchequer at Westminster.—(*Rankine.*)

‡ The Standard Pound Avoirdupois is the weight, at the temperature of 62° Fahrenheit, and under the atmospheric pressure of 30 inches of mercury, in the latitude of London, and at or near the level of the sea, of a certain piece of platinum which is kept in the Exchequer Office at Westminster.—(*Rankine.*)

length of time. In the reed-tonometer, constructed by Herr Appunn, with which Mr. Ellis made his first series of measurements, there were, unfortunately, no means of maintaining equality of pressure; the pressure was not constant even while one reed was sounding, and when two reeds were speaking instead of one, further change of pressure ensued, hence Mr. Ellis's first results obtained by this apparatus were vitiated, but with proper precautions a reed-tonometer can be made a very valuable instrument, deserving more attention than it has hitherto received.

Division of the Octave or Scale Systems.—As all instruments are not tuned from the same pitch-note—*a'* and *c''* being those chiefly used—it is necessary, when accurate comparisons are required, to know the scale system to which any instrument whose pitch is noted conforms. The major diatonic scale in just intonation, that is, when its different notes as used in harmony are the most satisfying to the ear, has its intervals in the following order:—

c		*d*		*e*		*f*		*g*		*a*		*b*		*c*
8	major tone	9	minor tone	10	semi-tone	$10\frac{2}{3}$	major tone	12	minor tone	$13\frac{1}{3}$	major tone	15	semi-tone	16
4	major third			5	minor third			6	-	perfect fourth			-	8
3	-	perfect fourth				4	-	-	perfect fifth		-		-	6
2	-	-	perfect fifth		-		-	3	-	perfect fourth			-	4
1	-	-	-		octave		-		-		-		-	2

In this scale system it will be noticed that a perfect fifth, as from *c* to *g*, comprises a major and a minor third, or two major tones, a minor tone, and a semi-tone. The fifth, from *d* to *a*, however, comprises two minor tones, a major tone, and a semi-tone; the difference between the two forms of fifths is, therefore, that between a major and a minor tone, or the comma of Didymus, ratio, 80:81. In other words, the *a*, which is correct in either the scale of *c* or that of *f*, is too flat for the scale of *d*. Other similar difficulties arise in passing from scale to scale, the root of them all being simply the arithmetical fact that the fraction $\frac{1}{2}$ (the ratio of the octave), raised to the seventh power $(\frac{1}{2})^7$, is not identical with the fraction $\frac{2}{3}$ (the ratio of the fifth) raised to the twelfth power $(\frac{2}{3})^{12}$. The first of these values represents an interval of seven octaves, the second an interval of twelve perfect fifths, and the working out may be written down thus:—

Octaves $\begin{cases} c\text{———}c\text{———}c\text{———}c\text{———}c\text{———}c\text{———}c\text{———}c \\ \quad\tfrac{1}{2} \times \tfrac{1}{2} \times \tfrac{1}{2} \times \tfrac{1}{2} \times \tfrac{1}{2} \times \tfrac{1}{2} \times \tfrac{1}{2} = \tfrac{1}{128} \end{cases}$

Fifths $\begin{cases} c - g - d - a - e - b - f\sharp - c\sharp - g\sharp - d\sharp - a\sharp - e\sharp - b\sharp \\ \tfrac{2}{3} \times \tfrac{2}{3} \times \tfrac{2}{3} \times \tfrac{2}{3} \times \tfrac{2}{3} \times \tfrac{2}{3} \times \tfrac{2}{3} \times \tfrac{2}{3} \times \tfrac{2}{3} \times \tfrac{2}{3} \times \tfrac{2}{3} \times \tfrac{2}{3} = \end{cases}$

$$= \tfrac{4096}{531441} = \tfrac{1}{129 \cdot 746}$$

The difference between the two results, *i.e.*, between $\frac{1}{128}$ and $\frac{1}{129 \cdot 746}$, is known as the Pythagorean comma, the Pythagorean or theoretical Greek scale having been based upon such a succession of perfect fifths. A similar difference would evidently show itself on working through perfect fifths downwards, *c*—*f*—*b*♭, &c., to *d*♭♭; therefore, the notes *d*♭♭ and *b*♯, when derived from *c* through perfect fifths, are respectively flatter and sharper than *c*; the amount will be best appreciated by comparing the numbers of vibrations, *c* being taken as 512. We would then have *d*♭♭ = 505·1, *c* = 512, and *b*♯ = 519. As key-board instruments have had almost universally only twelve keys to the octave, the key or digital used for *c* has had to do duty also for *d*♭♭ and *b*♯, and the necessity for some compromise led to the introduction of temperament. In the modern or equal temperament the accumulated error is distributed over the twelve fifths, so that each fifth is tuned the twelfth part of a Pythagorean comma flat. This mis-tuning of the fifths is barely appreciable in practical music, but the error of the thirds, major and minor, is considerable, and is very perceptible on fixed toned instruments, such as the organ and harmonium. Equal temperament has come into general use only during the last fifty years; it was preceded by the mean-tone temperament, which prevailed throughout Europe for centuries.

This temperament—the mean-tone—was based upon maintaining the true ratio of the major third 4 : 5, and neglecting the sub-division of the same into two unequal tones, the major and the minor, as required in just intonation: substituting for these, two equal or "mean" tones. The error of flatness in the fifths with this temperament is more than twice as great as in the "equal," but the most serious objection to it, and the cause of its practical disappearance, was that when used in the customary way with only twelve keys to the octave, it was necessary to throw the accumulated errors into the less used keys, with such bad effect that the free modulation required in modern music was practically impossible.

The practical importance of noting instrumental temperament in connection with any record of pitch is that the proper conversion may be made between the *a′* and *c″*, or the *c″* and *a′*, according to the pitch-note taken. The ratios are given below for just intonation, and for equal and mean-tone temperaments:

a′ being the pitch-note, multiply by 1·200 for *c″* (just)
,, ,, ,, ,, 1·189 ,, (equal)
,, ,, ,, ,, 1·196 ,, (mean)
c″ ,, ,, ,, ·833̇ for *a′* (just)
,, ,, ,, ,, ·841 ,, (equal)
,, ,, ,, ,, ·836 ,, (mean).

As an example of using these figures we may take the French Diapason Normal of nominally 435 vibs.:

435 × 1·200 gives *c″* = 522 (just)
435 × 1·189 ,, *c″* = 517·2 (equal)
435 × 1·196 ,, *c″* = 520·3 (mean).

Supposing the *a′* to have been taken from an organ, or other such instrument, it is therefore evident that the value of *c″* could not be properly entered on any record of pitches until the temperament was known.

Historical Outline.—The oldest instrument referred to by Mr. Ellis was the great organ of the cathedral of Halberstadt, in Prussian Saxony. This organ was finished in 1361, and restored in 1495. According to the dimensions given by Prætorius in 1619, its *a′* would be 505·8; this, in all probability, represented its pitch when restored, and possibly its original pitch. At about the same date another organ pitch was also in use, according to the measurements given by Arnold Schlick in 1511. These two pitches stand at about a fourth, or five semi-tones, apart, and are representatives of the highest and lowest church pitches. In the same way, and as late as the time of Mersenne (1636–1648), both a low and a high chamber pitch were used, with even a greater difference between them than existed between the church pitches, for his low chamber pitch *a'* was 403, and his high *a'* 563, about three tones higher than the former, and about one tone higher than the high church pitch, as given by himself.

It is evident that these great differences could not arise from mere errors of workmanship; neither could they arise from a gradual change of pitch, such as has gone on in this country—and in a less degree on the Continent—since the beginning of the present century, for both the extremely high and the extremely low pitches were in use at the same time. They were, doubtless, deliberately adopted to meet certain requirements of the time, which it is difficult now to trace.

Early in the 17th century, the consideration of the advantages to be obtained from uniformity in pitch appears to have made some way. Prætorius, in 1619, gave a drawing with dimensions for the half-foot *c'''* pipe, with the express object of leading organ builders in the direction of uniformity, and Mr. Ellis, having had a pipe made to these dimensions, found the corresponding *a'* in mean-tone temperament to be 424·2. Whatever was the chief constraining influence, the fact is well established that during the 17th, 18th, and the early part of the 19th century, the mean European pitch varied very little from that suggested by Prætorius, and was rather more than a semi-tone lower than our present "concert pitch." For this low pitch the works of Handel, Mozart, and the other great classical musicians, were undoubtedly written, and it was used by the Philharmonic Society when founded in 1813, the *a'* of their piano being then tuned to 423·7.

The examination of all the instruments exhibited in the Loan Collection of the Royal Military Exhibition showed that those made before the present century were practically in accordance with the mean European pitch above referred to. In some cases the original pitch had been altered, and in other cases, owing to uncertainty about moveable parts—such as mouthpieces—being original, or from general want of repair, it was difficult to judge of the original pitch with certainty. Sufficient examination, however, was made for it to be evident that a number of instruments made at various times and in various countries during the 17th and 18th centuries, were more closely together in pitch than a similar collection of instruments of modern manufacture would be, brought together from different countries in Europe, including Great Britain.

This notable difference is due to the rise of pitch during this century, which has been checked in some countries, and has remained practically unchecked in others. The chief cause of this change is thus summarized by Mr. Ellis:—"The rise in pitch began at the great Congress of Vienna, 1814, when the Emperor of Russia presented new and sharper wind instruments to an Austrian regiment of which he was Colonel. The band of this regiment became noted for the brilliancy of its tones. In 1820 another Austrian regiment received even sharper instruments, and as the theatres were greatly dependent upon the bands of the home regiments, they were obliged to adopt their pitch. Gradually at Vienna pitch rose from *a'* 421·6 (Mozart's pitch) to *a'* 456·1, that is, 136 cents (or hundredths of an equal-tempered semi-tone), or nearly three-quarters of a tone. The mania spread throughout Europe, but at very different rates. The pitch reached *a'* 448 at the Paris Opera in 1858, and the musical world took fright."

The commission appointed by the Emperor of the French determined on *a'* 435, and this theoretical standard was very closely obtained, for the mean of the best measurements of the Diapason Normal, as actually made in 1859, is 435·4 at 15° C. or 59° F. This pitch, although about a quarter of a tone flatter than the Paris opera pitch of 448, was not a novelty, but was fairly in agreement with many pitches in use in Europe at the time. It was a compromise between the old mean European pitch and modern developments, and as a compromise it had been anticipated by Sir Geo. Smart in England, as will presently be shown.

In this country the rise from the Philharmonic pitch of 423·7, as adopted by Sir Geo. Smart in 1813, to the present pitch of 452·5, is marked by a second fixing by Sir Geo. Smart about the year 1828, when *c''* 518 was agreed upon as a standard, giving in mean-tone temperament (the temperament used at the time) *a'* 433, or in equal temperament *a'* 435·4, exactly French pitch; this *c''* 518 fork is now in the possession of Mr. A. J. Hipkins. Sir Geo. Smart's own fork of this period is an *a'* 433·2. A second re-fixing of the Philharmonic pitch took place under Sir Michael Costa; the mean pitch of the band from 1846 to 1854 having been *a'* 452·5, as recorded by Mr. Hipkins. It has so remained to the present time, so that, although sometimes slightly exceeded, it has been practically the same for about forty-four years—possibly longer, for it is probable that the pitch under Sir Michael Costa was due not to the deliberate introduction of a higher standard, but merely to the recognition of a gradual advance from the time of Sir Geo. Smart. Mr. R. S. Rockstro has in his possession a fork *a'* 447·1 tuned in the orchestra of the Philharmonic Society in 1845, and this seems to point to a gradual rise.

The importance of the Philharmonic pitch in connection with wind instruments generally, arises from the fact that, according to the Queen's Regulations, it is the pitch to be observed in army bands. The wording of the regulation is: "In order to ensure uniformity throughout the regimental bands of the service, the instruments are to be of the same pitch as that adopted by the Philharmonic Society." This pitch has, therefore, a quasi-official character, and the Queen's Regulation respecting it is the nearest approach to anything like an official or Government recognition or declaration of a standard of pitch in this country. With a view to keeping this standard, and checking further rise of pitch, Colonel Shaw-Hellier, the commandant of the Royal Military School of Music, early in last year (1890) requested Mr. Hipkins to verify the standard *b'*♭ fork at Kneller Hall, and in this examination the writer assisted Mr. Hipkins. To keep to a whole number for *c''*, this note was taken as 538, giving in equal temperament *b'*♭ 479·3 and *a'* 452·4 at the medium temperature of 60° Fah. This is about two-thirds of a semi-tone higher than the French Diapason Normal. The old drum and fife band pitch, which is still in use in a few army drum and fife bands, agrees, however, very closely with the Diapason Normal; it is probably a survival of Sir Geo. Smart's Philharmonic pitch of 1828. As this pitch was very largely in use throughout the army, the fact is worth noting, especially as it appears to have escaped the notice of Mr. Ellis in his valuable "History."

It is the opinion of some authorities that inasmuch as a practically constant pitch has been preserved by the Philharmonic Society for between forty and fifty years, there is now little room to fear a further rise. But it should be remembered that the causes which led to the gradual rise, which Sir Geo. Smart attempted to restrain in 1828 by the introduction of his compromise pitch, are still in operation, and both this attempt and Sir Michael Costa's decision in favour of *a'* 452·5 indicate rather the acceptation of existing facts than an opinion unfettered by surrounding circumstances. Sir Michael Costa's Philharmonic pitch, which in his time was looked upon as high, and was distinctly higher than that of pianos and other instruments in general private use, is now no longer so, for it is not unusual to find pianos sharper than this pitch, and many military bands and orchestras customarily play sharper. In short, that which may be called the customary or popular pitch has fully come up to, and in some cases has overpassed, the highest recognised standard. Action based upon a recognition of the causes can alone prevent the process continuing.

Among these causes the chief are probably the liability to error in copying tuning forks through the heating caused by filing, and the desire of every wind-instrument player to be assured that his instrument is fully sharp; for although every such instrument can be tuned down by the player, it is impossible for him to raise its pitch. If there is any doubt about the pitch of a new instrument in a band, a player will always give "the benefit of the doubt" in favour of a slight sharpening, and however slight this may be in each individual case, the ultimate result must be a gradual average sharpening of the band as old instruments fall out of use, unless the band is strictly kept down in pitch to a fork or some other reliable standard.

Temperature plays an important part in the variation of the pitch of wind instruments; its influence, therefore, will now be entered upon in some detail, and for the sake of comparison its effect upon tuning forks and metal reeds is also noted.

TUNING FORKS.—Tuning forks flatten with increase of temperature; the amount of this flattening is about 1 vibration in 16,000 for every degree Fahrenheit, equal to three-tenths of a vibration in 10° on the Kneller Hall *b'*♭ fork of 479·3 at 60°.

The fork is therefore

at 40°	Fahrenheit	479·9
" 50°	"	479·6
" 60°	"	479·3
" 70°	"	479·0
" 80°	"	478·7

The difference here noted is, of course, too small to be of any consequence in practical music; it is sufficient, however, for it to be a matter of importance that the temperature at which a standard fork has a given rate of vibration should always be stated, and this difference has also to be borne in mind when forks are adjusted or tuned to a standard fork by filing. A fork is heated by handling, and especially by filing; consequently a fork which immediately after filing appears to be in agreement with a standard will be found after a few hours to be appreciably sharper.

METAL REEDS.—These also flatten with increase of temperature, but the amount of total fluctuation depends somewhat upon the resonating chamber associated with the reed, and no exact rate of variation can be given. It may be generally taken as rather greater than that of tuning forks.

WIND INSTRUMENTS.—We have now to consider the effect of temperature upon the instruments in a wind band. The result of increase of the heat of the air as from a winter to a summer temperature is equal to a rise of pitch of a quarter of a tone between 47° and 73°, a very ordinary range of temperature. The full effect of this variation is seen in the flue pipes of organs, but the variation of the reed pipes is less uniform. In wind instruments also the full effects can be observed if the comparison is made directly a large instrument, say a euphonion, is blown into at two different temperatures; for instance out of doors at 47°, and then indoors at 73°, after the instrument has been in the warm room long enough to have risen to the higher temperature. The difference of a quarter-tone between 47° and 73° is equal to slightly more than 1 per cent. in the number of vibrations for every 10 degrees Fah., so that a cornet giving *b'*♭ 479·3 at 60° would give 479·3 + 4·8 or 484·1 at 70°, nearly 5 beats sharp, if the pitch were taken in each case before the instrument is appreciably warmed by the breath. In practice, however, this condition of things is soon modified; the effect of the breath is, in this country at least, always to sharpen the instrument by raising its temperature, but as this warming is proportionately greater at low temperatures than at high, the general result is that the variation is not so great as the temperatures of the air outside the instrument would indicate. Whatever the outside temperature, the air inside an instrument at the mouth-piece end will soon be raised to about 90°, so that if we assume a range of temperature outside the instrument of from 50° to 70°, and assume also that the air about the bell-mouth has a similar range, it is evident that the mean range of temperature *in* the instrument will not be so great as 20°, nor will the variation of pitch be so great as 20° would indicate. For in the one case, the mean temperature in the instrument is something between 90° at the mouth-piece and 50° at the bell-mouth, or say $\frac{90^\circ + 50^\circ}{2} = 70^\circ$ and in the other case something between 90° and 70°, or say $\frac{90^\circ + 70^\circ}{2} = 80^\circ$, so that the range of temperature *in* the instrument may be only that between 70° and 80°, or 10°, while the range in the surrounding air is from 50° to 70°, or 20°.

The exact amount of variation varies in different instruments, for even the air in the bell-mouth is in small instruments soon somewhat warmed. As a rule, the smaller the instrument, it is proportionately the more highly warmed by the breath in cold weather; so that the range of variation of pitch in instruments when fairly warmed with playing, is less for flutes and clarionets than for large brass basses, the temperature of which at the bell-end rises very little above that of the surrounding air, however long they are played upon. In cold weather, therefore, the basses will be more below pitch than the clarionets, and in hot weather they will be more above.

From all this, it will be seen that the pitch of a band should be taken when the instruments are fairly warmed with playing, and when the general temperature of the air is about 60°. Neglect of these precautions has doubtless been one of the chief causes of the extravagantly high pitch of some military and brass bands. When it is remembered that if a cornet is made so sharp as to give the Kneller Hall *b′♭* directly it is blown upon at 60°, it will be four or five beats sharp by the time it is warm; and further, will rise another four or five beats in a hot concert-room, say at 80°; it will be seen how important it is, if Philharmonic pitch is to be observed, that the precaution should be taken of comparing instruments with the standard in the way suggested above.

For some years past the writer has taken observations of the comparative pitches of different wind instruments, when warm with actual use, and at various external temperatures ranging from 40° to 80°; the results are summarised in the following table, in which *b′♭* has been selected as the pitch note, as it is the most convenient one for military band instruments:—

VARIATION OF PITCH IN WIND INSTRUMENTS.

A rise of 10° Fah. in external temperature increases the pitch of	Per cent. of number of Vibrations.	Vibrations on *b′♭* 479·3.
Flute and Oboe - - - - -	·31	1·50
Clarinet - - - - - -	·43	2·06
Cornet and Trumpet - - -	·51	2·45
French Horn and Trombone - -	·60	2·88
Euphonion - - - - - -	·66	3·16
Bombardon - - - - - -	·73	3·50
Mean of Full Wind Band - - -	·54	2·60
Organ Flue Pipes - - - - -	1·05	5·04

The mean here given for *b′♭*, 2·60 beats for 10°, is equal to 2·91 on *c″*; but as the larger wind instruments which alter most are seldom used in the orchestra, an allowance of 2·5 beats on *c″* for every 10° is sufficient for orchestral variation. As concert-rooms are usually warmer than 60°, the standard temperature, "concert pitch" pianos are usually tuned to c'' 540; the difference between the standard c'' 538 and c'' 540 allows for the room being as warm as 68° without disturbance to the wind band, for the instruments rising 2·5 vibrations in 10° on c'', would rise exactly from 538 to 540 in the range of 8°, from 60° to 68°.

It will be evident, from the foregoing data and remarks, that as instruments vary in different degrees with temperature, it is impossible that all the instruments in a band can rise and fall exactly together. The manufacturer may be expected to make them so that they stand well together at a medium temperature; but the adjustment necessary to ensure a good *ensemble* at extreme temperatures must be left to the judgment and experience of the players.

A SUGGESTED NEW STANDARD.

THE following considerations, although forming no part of a review of the actual position of the musical pitch question in this country, are added to the foregoing short sketch as an expression only of the personal opinion of the writer, and in the belief that the standard suggested has never hitherto been proposed.

Of the four standards to which reference has been made, two, viz., c'' 512 and c'' 528, are purely theoretical, each resting upon an easily understood arithmetical basis, but being unrepresented in actual music in this country, unless by mere coincidences. The two most in use, viz., a' 435·4 and a' 452·4, rest upon no arithmetical basis of whole numbers whatever, for although the pitch a' 452·4 agrees with c'' 538, the lower octaves of this c'' require fractions to express their vibrational values.

For the purposes of demonstration and experiments in acoustics, in which it is convenient to have whole numbers for the vibrations of the notes of the common chord in just intonation, there is an advantage in either of the two first named standards, but in the practical construction of modern instruments, which are in equal temperament and not in just intonation, the advantage of this particular form of numerical simplicity vanishes.

The ratios of the intervals of the equal temperament scale are shown in Table I., and the vibrational value or frequency of any note taken as a pitch note being given, that of any other related note in this temperament can be found by use of the multiplier corresponding to the difference in semitones between the two notes.

Example: $c' = 269$; find e'. e' being four semitones above c', multiply 269 by 1·2599,

$$269 \times 1{\cdot}2599 = 338{\cdot}91 \text{ value of } c'.$$

EQUAL TEMPERAMENT.

TABLE I.			TABLE II.					
Difference in semitones.	Note.	Ratio, or relative frequency.	Note.	Absolute vibrations.	Note.	Absolute vibrations.	Note.	Absolute vibrations.
12	*c*	2·00000	*g*	200·00	*g'*	400·00	*g''*	800·00
11	*b*	1·88775	*f*♯	188·78	*f'*♯	377·55	*f''*♯	755·10
10	*a*♯	1·78180	*f*	178·18	*f'*	356·36	*f''*	712·72
9	*a*	1·68179	*e*	168·18	*e'*	336·36	*e''*	672·72
8	*g*♯	1·58740	*d*♯	158·74	*d'*♯	317·48	*d''*♯	634·96
7	*g*	1·49831	*d*	149·83	*d'*	299·66	*d''*	599·32
6	*f*♯	1·41421	*c*♯	141·42	*c'*♯	282·84	*c''*♯	565·68
5	*f*	1·33484	*c*	133·48	*c'*	266·97	*c''*	533·94
4	*e*	1·25992	*B*	128·49	*b*	256·98	*b'*	503·97
3	*d*♯	1·18921	*A*♯	118·92	*a*♯	237·84	*a'*♯	475·68
2	*d*	1·12246	*A*	112·25	*a*	224·49	*a'*	448·98
1	*c*♯	1·05946	*G*♯	105·95	*g*♯	211·89	*g'*♯	423·78
0	*c*	1·00000	*G*	100·00	*g*	200·00	*g'*	400·00

In Table I. *c* is taken as the basis, but it is immaterial what note of the scale is represented by unity, so long as the figures given are taken to set forth ratios only and not frequencies. If, however, the scale of ratios or multipliers could be used to represent actual vibrational as well as proportional values, we would have a standard for the musical scale of a similar character to those usually adopted for other scientific work involving measurements. In such standards, either unity, or some power of ten, is taken as a datum to which variations can be referred for comparison, and from which proportions can be calculated. In the given table of ratios, the removal of the decimal point two places gives 100·00 as the basis of the scale in place of 1·0000, and this number happens to agree closely with the vibrational value of *G*,  which in Philharmonic pitch is 100·67, and in French pitch is 96·97. There is a suitability in the note on the lowest line of the customary musical staff being taken as a datum, and if it can be shown upon examination that the value $G = 100$ is one that in the event of any general standard being adopted in this country would create the least disturbance, the strongest practical reason would be added to the arithmetical advantage of a simple and easily remembered numerical basis.

Table II. shows the scale fully written out for three octaves on the proposed basis of $G = 100$; in this scale $a' = 448·98$ and $c'' = 533·94$, or in whole numbers 449 and 534 respectively.

The Society of Arts' *c''* fork as actually made in 1860 gave 534·46, equal to *G* 100·1; so that, although intended to give *c''* 528, it was quite unintentionally exceedingly close to the standard now proposed.

Table III., annexed, shows how widely spread throughout Europe at the time of the French Commission in 1858–9, and also at the time of the Society of Arts' investigations in 1859 and again in 1869, were different pitches varying but a very few vibrations from the proposed *a'* 449, based upon *G* 100. The tendency towards a gradual rise in pitch, already noticed in the body of this Appendix, as illustrated by Mr. R. S. Rockstro's Philharmonic fork *a'* 447·1 of the year 1845 as compared with *a'* 452·5 between 1846 and 1854, is to be seen also in the Milan pitch of 446·6 as given by Marloye's fork in 1845, compared with the pitch in 1856, 450·3 as sent to the French Commission.

The total range of pitch covered in Table III. from *a'* 435·0 to *a'* 457·9 is equal to $\frac{89}{100}$ of a semitone.

TABLE III.

TABLE OF MODERN MUSICAL PITCH.

The range of pitch comprised in this Table is one equal-tempered semitone, divided into tenths, as indicated by the thick horizontal lines.
The vibrations are given for a' and c'' in equal temperament.
The variation in decimals of a semitone, above or below the proposed a' 449, of each pitch noted is shewn in the third column.

a'	c''	VARIATION.	——			DATE.
441·0	524·5	·31	Organs	Lewis's church organ standard	London ...	1879
			Operas	Dresden, 1859	Paris	1836–9
440·0	523·2	·35	Fork	Scheibler's or Stuttgart standard	Stuttgart ...	1834
			Organs	Gray and Davison's standard pipe	London ...	1878
438·9	522·0	·40	Fork	Theatre Orchestra	Dresden ...	1869
437·4	520·2	·46	Forks	Opera, according to Delezenne	Paris	1854 *ante*
436·0	518·5	·51	Organs	Bishop's church organ standard, 1878 ...	Broadwood's vocal, London ...	1859
435·4	517·8	·53	Fork	Diapason Normal, as made	Paris	1859
435·0	517·3	·55	Fork	Do. do. as intended	Paris	1859

[*To face page 250.*]

It is probably beyond controversy that as a mean between the pitches, for which the classical writers of the last century and the chief operatic composers of the present century wrote, the French Diapason Normal is the best, but the fact that a pitch of from 445 to 450 for *a'* was used for many years in all the leading opera houses of Europe, shows that the practical danger lies in passing this limit, or in going more than a quarter of a tone above French pitch. The possibility of the general introduction of French pitch into this country was examined by the Society of Arts' Committee in 1859, and again by a Committee appointed at a public meeting in St. James's Hall, London, in 1885, convened by the Royal Academy of Music in consequence of a communication from the Foreign Office; but the recommendation in favour of its introduction, proceeding from the 1885 Committee, was without results, in consequence of the expense which such a change would have entailed. It should also be noticed that although in 1885 instrument makers professed their readiness to make instruments to whatever pitch was decided upon, the real difficulty in the way of any great change is the pitch of existing instruments, and especially of the great organs, and this can only be removed by the owners or custodians of these instruments being willing to meet the necessary expense.

The general introduction of French pitch as a national standard appears to be impracticable on the score of expense. Brass instruments could be altered to it without either great cost or damage, but so great an alteration of wood wind instruments is not only generally impracticable, but in some cases impossible. Even if all military and orchestral wind instruments were thus altered, the difficulty of using them with unaltered organs would be as great as at present, for many of the most important of these are above French pitch. To this reason must be added the opinion of many, which although not perhaps preponderating, is doubtless wide-spread, that a lowering to the Diapason Normal is greater than an all-round consideration of circumstances and artistic interests requires.

The amount of flattening which wood wind instruments can bear without serious injury to intonation is about one-fifth, or at the most one-fourth, of a semitone. Instruments at the present military pitch of nominally *a'* 452·4, but practically of about *a'* 455 to *a'* 457, as nearly all bands play sharp, cannot, therefore, be used with the large church organs, which are about half a semitone, or rather more, below this; but if band instruments were re-tuned to the proposed standard *a'* 449, there would be no serious difficulty in using them with church organs on special occasions, for the amount of flattening required would not exceed the limits named above.

Many wind instruments exist and are in use which were made when the pitch was somewhat lower than it is at present. Such of these as have been cut to agree with the present high pitch, and have suffered in consequence, would be improved rather than deteriorated by being re-tuned to *a'* 449.

The substance of the considerations given in some detail above, is summarised in the following notes:—

The present Philharmonic and Kneller Hall pitch is practically in universal use in this country, in India, and in the colonies for all wind-band music. Such deviations from it as are to be found are usually and unfortunately in the direction of a still higher pitch. The most important exceptions are Her Majesty's private band and the band of the Royal Italian Opera, Covent Garden, which are tuned to French pitch.

A lowering to the Diapason Normal, which is about two-thirds of a semitone lower than the Kneller Hall standard fork, and very nearly a semitone lower than the highest wind-band pitch in actual use, has been suggested, but has been found impracticable on account of the expense that would be incurred.

In the event of any renewed attempt to adopt a general standard of pitch in this country other than the present Philharmonic, it is submitted that a standard based upon $G = 100$ presents the advantage that in computations the ratios of the equal temperament scale give at once the frequency of each note without further calculation.

This proposed pitch is closely in agreement with that used in all the chief European opera houses for many years during this century, and with the Society of Arts' standard *c''* fork as made and widely copied. It is a quarter of a semitone higher than French pitch.

Existing instruments, with perhaps a few exceptions, could be adjusted to this pitch with accuracy and at comparatively small cost. Many that are now in use would be distinctly improved by the alteration.

If so altered, wind instruments could be used with the most important cathedral and church organs, the difference not being more than could be regulated by the usual means. The present difference is too great to be overcome by means of the tuning slides.

The suggested standard, being a mean between the highest and the lowest pitches in actual use in this country, would probably cause less confusion and expense in connection with its adoption than any other.

Those singers who find the present Philharmonic pitch too high, would find a distinct advantage in that now proposed. At the same time, the change would not be so great as to call forth opposition from those who consider the French pitch too low.

DESCRIPTION OF PLATES.

No. of Plate.	Subject.	Maker and Date.	Owner.	Description.
Frontispiece	Silver Kettle Drums ...	1805. Given by King George III.	Royal Horse Guards ...	page 231
Plate I. (*facing p.* 1)				
A ...	Cylinder Flute (*facsimile*)	Original; 17th cent.	Brussels Conservatoire	29
B ...	,, ,,	,, ,, ...	,, ,,	28
C ...	,, ,,	,, ,, ...	,, ,,	28
D ...	,, ...	C. Rafi; 15th or early 16th cent.	,, ,,	28
E ...	,, ...	16th cent.	,, ,,	28
F ...	Fife	,, ...	,, ,,	27
G ...	Cone Flute (Quantz) ...	F. Boie; early 18th cent. ...	Mrs. Zoeller	30
H ...	,, (8 keyed) ...	R. Potter; late 18th cent. ...	Rev. F. W. Galpin ...	32
I ...	Cylinder Flute	T. Boehm; 1850 *circa* ...	A. Hays, Esq. ...	45
K ...	Bass Flute	Wigley and McGregor; 1811–16	Brussels Conservatoire	35
Plate II. (*facing p.* 23)				
A ...	Oliphant	Portuguese; 15th cent. ...	G. Donaldson, Esq. ...	142
B ...	Flute Douce	Villars; 18th cent.	,, ,, ...	9
C ...	Cone Flute	Laurent; 1806 *circa*	,, ,, ...	34
D ...	Tabor Pipe	French; late 18th cent. ...	,, ,, ...	15
E ...	Cone Flute	Wood; 1815 *circa*	,, ,, ...	36
F ...	Flute Douce	Denner; late 17th cent. ...	,, ,, ...	7
G ...	Cornetto Curvo	16th or 17th cent.	,, ,, ...	158
Plate III. (*facing p.* 53)				
A ...	Tenor Pommer (*facsimile*)	Original; 16th cent.	Brussels Conservatoire	71
B ...	Discant Schalmey ...	16th cent.	,, ,,	71
C ...	Alto Pommer (*facsimile*)	Original; 16th cent.	,, ,,	71
D ...	Bass Pommer	Strehl; 16th cent.	,, ,,	72
E ...	Flute Douce, Bass ...	16th or 17th cent.	,, ,,	13
F ...	,, in *g* ...	,, ...	,, ,,	11
G ...	,, in *a* ...	,, ...	,, ,,	10
H ...	,, in *c'* ...	,, ...	,, ,,	10
I ...	Sourdine Bass (*facsimile*)	Original; 16th cent.	,, ,,	98
K ...	Sourdine Contra-Bass (*facsimile*)	,, ,, ...	,, ,,	99
L ...	Musette Bass (*facsimile*)	,, ,, ...	,, ,,	73
M ...	Bass Galoubet	16th cent.	,, ,,	15
Plate IV. (*facing p.* 64)				
A ...	Chalumeau in *g'* ...	16th or 17th cent.	M. Césare Snoeck ...	110
B ...	,, in *c'* (*facsimile*)	Original by Denner; late 17th cent.	Brussels Conservatoire	*See Errata*
C ...	Tibia (*facsimile*) ...	Original; Greek or Roman ...	,, ,,	109
D ...	Clarinet in *a*	Denner; late 17th or early 18th cent. ...	,, ,,	111
E ...	Cromorne (*facsimile*) ...	Original; 16th or early 17th cent.	,, ,,	99
F ...	Flûte à Colonne ...	16th or early 17th cent. ...	,, ,,	9
G ...	Clarinet in *c'*	Willems; 1750 *circa* ...	M. Césare Snoeck ...	112
H ...	Double Flageolet ...	18th cent.	Darmstadt Museum ...	18

No. of Plate.	Subject.	Maker and Date.	Owner.	Description.
Plate V. *(facing p. 96)*				PAGE
A ...	Bass Clarinet	German; 18th cent.	Brussels Conservatoire	123
B ...	"	Papolini; 18th cent.	" "	123
C ...	Fagottino in *G*	17th cent.	" "	74
D ...	Basset Horn in *f* ...	Grenser; late 18th cent. ...	Rev. F. W. Galpin ...	128
Plate VI. *(facing p. 101)*				
A ...	Schalmey	Haka; 17th cent.	M. César Snoeck ...	73
B ...	Oboe	Power; 1800 *circa*	Messrs. Rudall, Carte & Co.	88
C ...	Cornettino recto in *d'* ...	16th or 17th cent.	Rev. F. W. Galpin ...	156
D ...	" curvo in *d'* ...	16th cent.	Brussels Conservatoire	156
E ...	Cornetto curvo in *a* ...	16th or 17th cent.	Rev. F. W. Galpin ...	157
F ...	" muto in *f* ...	17th cent.	" ...	159
G ...	Oboe	Küsder; 18th cent.	Mrs. C. Zoeller ...	86
H ...	Dulcian in *c*	Wood; late 18th cent. ...	Messrs. J. & R. Glen	77
Plate VII. *(facing p. 131)*				
A ...	Serpent	Early 18th cent.	Colonel Shaw-Hellier	160
B ...	Cornetto torto (*facsimile*)	Original; 17th cent.	Brussels Conservatoire	159
C ...	Bass Horn	Late 18th cent.	Mr. Q. Cecconi ...	165
D ...	Serpent	1840 *circa*	W. Bateson, Esq. ...	164
Plate VIII. *(facing p. 136)*				
A ...	Ophicleide	Ward; 1848	Messrs. Ward & Sons...	167
B ...	Contra-Bassoon	Haseneier; late 19th cent. ...	Cyril Spottiswoode, Esq.	82
C ...	Bombardon	A. Sax; 1854...	Messrs. Besson & Co...	208
Plate IX. *(facing p. 152)*				
A ...	Highland Bagpipe ...	Celtic; 1409	Messrs. J. & R. Glen ...	57
B ...	Racket (*facsimile*) ...	Original; 16th cent.	Brussels Conservatoire	100
C ...	Border Bagpipe	English; late 18th cent. ...	Rev. F. W. Galpin ...	62
D ...	Irish Bagpipe	Kernia; late 18th cent. ...	G. Butler, Esq. ...	62
E ...	Cornemuse	French; 17th cent.	C. Van Raalte, Esq. ...	60
F ...	Musette	" late 17th cent. ...	Brussels Conservatoire	58
Plate X. *(facing p. 174)*				
A ...	Trumpet	Haas; 1694	Brussels Conservatoire	143
B ...	"	Bull; late 17th cent. ...	T. Harper, Esq. ...	144
C ...	" (with 2 pistons)	Early 19th cent.	Brussels Conservatoire	198
D ...	"	Haas; 17th cent.	" "	143
E ...	" (with 2 discs) ...	Köhler; 1838 *circa*	Messrs. Köhler & Sons	205
Plate XI. *(facing p. 182)*				
A ...	Slide Trombone... ...	Hainee; 1668	Brussels Conservatoire	177
B ...	Cornet (with 2 pistons) ...	C. Saxe; early 19th cent. ...	" "	198
C ...	" (with shake key)...	Köhler; 1850 *circa*	Messrs. Köhler & Sons	201
D ...	Key Bugle (Halliday's)...	Turton; 1810 *circa*	Colonel Shaw-Hellier	168
E ...	Valve Horn	Schott; 1830 *circa*	Brussels Conservatoire	199

INDEX.

A

B

C

D

E

F

M

N

O

P

Q

R

S

T

U

V

W

Z